PERGAMON INSTITUTE OF ENGLISH (OXFORD)

Materials for Language Practice

The Language of Literature

*A stylistic introduction to
the study of literature*

OTHER TITLES IN THIS SERIES INCLUDE:

BINHAM, P. et al.
Hotel English
   Communicating with the international traveller

Restaurant English
   Communicating with the international traveller

BLAKEY, T.
English for Maritime Studies

DUNLOP, L. and H. Schrand
Communication for Business
   Materials for reading comprehension and discussion

GILLIBRAND, P. and V. Maddock
The Manager and His Words
   An introduction to the vocabulary of business English

*Includes audio cassettes

The Language of Literature

A stylistic introduction to the study of literature

by

MICHAEL CUMMINGS

and

ROBERT SIMMONS
York University, Ontario, Canada

PERGAMON PRESS

OXFORD · NEW YORK · TORONTO · SYDNEY · PARIS · FRANKFURT

U.K.	Pergamon Press Ltd., Headington Hill Hall, Oxford OX3 0BW, England
U.S.A.	Pergamon Press Inc., Maxwell House, Fairview Park, Elmsford, New York 10523, U.S.A.
CANADA	Pergamon Press Canada Ltd., Suite 104, 150 Consumers Road, Willowdale, Ontario M2J 1P9, Canada
AUSTRALIA	Pergamon Press (Aust.) Pty. Ltd., P.O. Box 544, Potts Point, N.S.W. 2011, Australia
FRANCE	Pergamon Press SARL, 24 rue des Ecoles, 75240 Paris, Cedex 05, France
FEDERAL REPUBLIC OF GERMANY	Pergamon Press GmbH, Hammerweg 6, D-6242 Kronberg-Taunus, Federal Republic of Germany

First edition 1983

Library of Congress Cataloging in Publication Data

Cummings, Michael (Michael Joseph)
The language of literature.
(Language teaching methodology series)
(Materials for language practice)
Bibliography: p –
Includes index.
1. English language—Style. 2. Style, Literary. I. Simmons, Robert
(Robert E.) II. Title. III. Series. IV. Series: Materials for language
practice.
PE1421.C8   1982   801'.95   82-12210

British Library Cataloguing in Publication Data

Cummings, Michael
The language of literature—(Materials for language practice)
1. Style, Literary
I. Title   II. Simmons, Robert   III. Series 808'.02   PN203
ISBN 0-08-028629-1

Printed in Great Britain by A. Wheaton & Co. Ltd., Exeter

for

Elinor M. Cummings
and
Doreen Uren Simmons

Foreword

This is how the authors describe their purpose in writing the book: it is "to make the student a stylistician, someone who can comprehend literary texts through a comprehension of their language structures. Someone who can say not only 'I know what I like' but also 'I know why I like it, because I know how it works'."

Perhaps the first step towards becoming a stylistician, as the authors envisage the task, will be to recognize that literature is made of language. Not, of course, in the sense that architecture is made out of steel and concrete; steel and concrete are formless until some pattern is imposed on them by the builder. Language on the contrary is not formless, and this suggests that a closer analogy to the way literature is made of language would be the way that dancing is made out of movement of the body. Dancing starts from everyday actions like leaping and balancing and reaching, and these too are not formless; they are already highly orchestrated, "meaningful" patterns of bodily movement. But out of these patterns, further patterns can be created; and it is when we become aware of second-order patterns of this kind that we come to recognize something we call dancing, or bodily art.

To say that literature is made of language, therefore, is in no way to deny that it has a special status as verbal art. We may readily accept that there is some distinctive quality about certain texts which, however difficult it may be to define (as are many of the experiences we find most real), nevertheless stands out: there is a remarkable consensus on the question of what is literature and what is not. It is simply to point out that, whatever the special patterns and properties may be that lead us to refer to something as a literary text, they are there, so to speak, by courtesy; their existence depends on the patterning that already subsists in the (far from raw) material out of which all texts are made. It is also, we should add, to leave quite open the question whether, and in what sense, such special patterns are there at all; whether the property of "being literature" is an attribute of the text itself, or of some aspect of its environment — the context of the situation, perhaps, or the mental set of a particular listener or reader.

Language is meaningful activity. It is often taken to be the paradigm form of the act of meaning — the core of human semiotic, and a model (a descriptive norm) for all other forms of meaningful behaviour. Simply in order to understand the nature of language, whether we have any concept of literature or not, we have to be sensitive to patterns of meaning on all levels: the arrangement of phonic or graphic symbols, and the lexicogrammatical and semantic organization, present in every kind of text. Categories like rhythm, structural balance, metaphor, even depth of vision, that typically occur in the language of stylistic analysis, are not the monopoly of literature; they are part of the conceptual apparatus that has to be constructed to account for language in any guise. There are few, possibly no, linguistic categories that will appear in the description of literary texts which may not also be found in the analysis of texts of other, non-literary orders.

Students of literature sometimes feel that when linguists maintain that this strongly patterned quality, instead of being distinctive of verbal art, is in fact inherent in all use of language, they are somehow downgrading literature to an uninspired, and uninspiring, level of their own. But this is not so. Rather the contrary: by showing that language is intrinsically patterned in ways which are often thought of as being the prerogative of literature, we are really upgrading language, revealing something of its amazing complexity and depth, and so shedding some light on the otherwise unanswerable question of how it acquires its miraculous powers — including the power of creating literature.

By analysing a literary text as a verbal artefact, we are asserting its status as literature. There is no need for a stylistician to apologize for approaching it in this way. Not so long ago, "stylistics" was often seen as rather threatening; the linguistic analysis of a literary work would be denounced almost as if it was an indecent act, an uncouth violation of its integrity. To study the grammar of a poem was to destroy its vitality and inhibit the natural appreciation of its poetic qualities. Yet the experience of those who learnt to analyse a text proved to be quite the opposite. Far from damaging the object, or one's perception of it, the act of close and thoughtful linguistic analysis turns out to enhance one's awareness and enjoyment. What seemed flat becomes rounded, what was rounded has still further dimensions added to it. We might use this observation to supplement the triad of text, context of situation and reader: a fourth component of "literariness" would be the act of careful analysis. A text becomes literature in part because it is attended to, held up as an object of scrutiny; and since it is made of language, the most creative form of scrutiny is an analysis in linguistic terms, an analysis whereby the sounds and the forms and the meanings of the text are interpreted by reference to the phonology, the lexicogrammar and the semantics of the language of which it is an instance.

To return to our earlier analogy: if we choose to attend to an act of walking, at any comparable level — the physiological processes of a human being in motion, the grammar of troops on parade, the semantics of a religious procession — then by dint of our attention the walking becomes a piece of bodily art. In the same way language that is under attention becomes a piece of verbal art. And this has important consequences for the stylistician. To analyse any text is, potentially, to treat it as a literary artefact (I say "potentially" because there are also special purpose kinds of text analysis which do not come within this generalization); hence if we take a passage of casual conversation, or an interview, a commercial, a science lesson — a spoken or written text of whatever kind, and give a linguistic interpretation of it, then by treating it like literature we make it comparable to literature, and so we can ask what it is that leads us to deny it the status of literature and what processes would have to take place, what changes in the text and in its environment (including ourselves, in our attitude to it), in order for it to achieve that status. These explorations then serve in their turn as further sources of insight when we shift our attention on to other texts of a recognized literary genre.

Obviously the process of linguistic analysis is not going to change the text. Putting a text under attention will make it stand out, will make it glow, as it were, by a kind of Hawthorn effect; but it cannot transform it into something that it is not. The act of interpreting a text means treating it with respect, and hence bringing out all that there is within it; I have suggested that this is, in effect, turning it into literature, but it does not turn it into good literature, still less into literature that is lasting or "great". You may after come to feel, about a text that you have analysed, that it is beautiful — patterned like crystal, or like a complex piece of ballet. But beauty that lies solely in the eye of the beholder is strictly private beauty; it is not communicable. What a stylistician is engaged in, on the other hand, is first and foremost a public act. She is saying not only "I know why this text makes an impact on me" but, just as importantly, "I can make this understanding clear to you, and to anyone else who is prepared to follow and check out my reasoning."

Does this mean that the analysis of a text become a purely mechanical operation, or at least purely electronic — one that is fully programmable? I think not. In saying this I am not underestimating the potential of computational systems for carrying out operations of this kind. A great deal of text analysis is already computable; such "parsing" takes an enormous amount of memory and processing capacity, well beyond what was available twenty or even ten years ago, but no longer out of reach — becoming commonplace, in fact — in the eighties. Much work remains to be done before we have adequate parsers for texts of every kind; but we shall certainly get them. This, however, will not change my answer to the question. There are crucial elements in the stylistician's task that lie beyond the domain of parsing.

The analysis of a text *as a piece of literature* — stylistic analysis — always involves acts of interpretation. This does not mean that we lose contact with the text; each hermeneutic step can be ultimately related to what is there on the page. But even for the analytic phase, the operation of "parsing", one is selecting, out of the thousands of possible linguistic variables, just those features that will repay being studied; and this is far from being an automatic process. Still less automatic is the interpretative phase, when the stylistician is weighing and weighting different parts of the evidence, bringing together diverse features to show how they form a coherent, integrated pattern, and making judgements about the significance of such patterns in relation to the context of the work as a whole. It is not being suggested that analysis and interpretation are two separate portions of the task, to be performed in sequence with one starting only when the other has ended. They may be interleaved one with the other, or they may not even be distinguished operationally at all. In some problems they overlap — where there is more than one possible analysis, and it is necessary to adopt one or the other, or perhaps both. But conceptually they are distinct. An analysis may be wrong; an interpretation is not right or wrong, but more or less convincing, more or less penetrating and deep.

Let me return, then, to the goals of stylistic inquiry. The more immediate goal, as I see it, and one that is unquestionably attainable, is to show why and how the text means what it does. Note that this already requires both analysis and interpretation; and in the process you may, especially with a literary text, find that you have done more than simply show why it means what you knew it meant already. You may have discovered new meanings you had not previously been aware of — at least not consciously aware of, though you might have been reacting to them unconsciously. (In text analysis one is constantly being reminded of the unconscious character of linguistic processes and of the system that underlies them.) To attain this more immediate goal is to be able to say ''I can demonstrate why this text means all that I say it means.''

Beyond this, if we are treating the text as literature, lies a further goal that is much more difficult to attain: that of showing why the text is valued as it is. This might be taken as an aim that is characteristic of stylistics, as distinct from text analysis in general. Why do you like this poem better that that one? Why has this one been received into the canon of major literary works? Linguists have traditionally pleaded shy of this more daunting goal; but a stylistician will at least affirm that the patterns of language carry value, even while perhaps protesting that we still know very little about how value inheres in the text.

It helps, I think, to remember that value in a text is not to be equated with artistic value. When we analyse classroom discourse, for example, we are usually not just trying to find out how it works. We are interested in the extent to which it succeeds or fails: whether the students have been able to use language successfully as an instrument for learning with, and whether the teacher's verbal strategies have been conducive to their achievement of such success. In both the two major areas of the application of linguistics, educational and clinical, there is bound to be an evaluative element in almost any analysis of a text. Where stylistic analysis differs it is in the nature and the criteria of evaluation.

In the analytic phase, there is no difference between the treatment of a literary text and the treatment of any other kind of text: the categories and the methods are the same. Indeed it is essential for the stylistician's purposes that they should be. We started with the observation that literature is made of language; to this we could add, more specifically, that English literature (i.e. literature in English) is made of the English language, French literature is made of the French language and so on. The most important fact about any English literary text is that it is a text in English. Its meanings are derived from the system of the English language; and this remains true whatever innovations may be brought about by a creative writer — or a creative reader. Innovation, in fact, is only possible because there is something to innovate on; new meanings cannot evolve except by reference to old ones — that is, to the language in which they are created. Just as you can not understand a piece of English literature if you do not know English, so you will not be able to explain "how it works" if you do not relate it to the system of the English language.

Thus it is not from deviation but from conformity that a text derives its meaning; and this is as true of a literary text, however linguistically innovative, as it is of one in any other register. If a text is "deviant", then given that the deviation is meaningful only with respect to some norm shared by writer and reader alike, it will certainly be of interest to record and explain it. But the vast majority of literary works, whether prose or verse, do not bend the grammar of English in any way at all; and conversely texts in which "rules" are "broken" are generally not what we would think of as literary ones. The sensational headlines of mass circulation newspapers have more deviant grammar than will be found in a typical selection of modern poetry. Very few literary texts depend for their impact on a departure from the norms of the language in which they are composed.

If I want to know why I like a particular English poem, the first reason must be because I understand English. Appreciating a literary work requires an understanding of the language in which it is written — or languages, if it happens to be a multilingual work. This does not mean that we can have no appreciation of all of something that is written in a language we do not know: many people can enjoy listening to poetry in a language of which they understand nothing at all, reacting purely to the rhythms and the melodies and to the patterns of vowels and consonants. But this kind of appreciation is limited; it is not something from which one could derive a satisfactory interpretation of the work as a whole — except in the special case of poetry that consists purely of patterns of sounds or of written symbols, and even here one cannot appreciate the phonological or graphological patterning if one does not know the systems from which they are derived.

So the analysis of an English text will be in terms of the categories of the English language — English grammar, semantics, phonology and graphology — for a literary text just as for a child's composition, a weather report or a recipe. The task in each case is to show how the text is a product of the linguistic system, an instantiation of the semiotic processes that constitute the "meaning potential" of English. We cannot, however, analyse in respect of all possible features up to the limits of possible delicacy; it is here that the analytic strategies will begin to be differentiated, according to the register of the discourse and the purposes of the analytic enterprise. In analysing any text we try to ascertain what features will most repay analysis. In the language of advertising, for example, we are likely to be interested in the tactics of persuasion as these relate to the ideology and value systems of the potential customers. In a technical report our attention will probably be on the content, as represented in the grammar through logical structures and transitivity patterns. What makes the analysis of literature different, from this point on, is that we do not know in advance what features are the ones on which to focus attention. We cannot say "because this is a literary text, the interest will lie mainly in this feature or that". The distinctive qualities of the text may lie anywhere, in any areas of the linguistic system; very probably in the combination of features from different areas, and in their grouping into unique patterns of arrangement.

And this leads us to a second consideration which sets stylistic analysis apart from text analysis in general: in stylistics, we are likely to be concerned with the uniqueness of the text we are studying. With most types of discourse what is of interest is how the text under scrutiny is *not* unique; it has been selected because it is typical of its kind, and what we are trying to characterize is the register, using this particular text as a representative specimen. For example, there have been various studies of the verbal interaction between doctors and patients, studies that are undertaken as a way of helping to make clinical practice more effective or to improve the quality of medical education. In such instances the aim of the linguistic analysis is to characterize the register of doctor–patient communication in general. The investigator is not trying to establish the uniqueness of one dialogue between a particular doctor and one of his patients.

In literature too, where there are generalized registers or genres, broad categories such as "the novel" with perhaps a taxonomy of more specific types, the stylistician may be interested in the characteristics of a whole genre, and to that extent will treat a particular text as specimen rather than as object. A few genres — most notably certain forms of narrative — have been studied fairly extensively from a linguistic viewpoint; but we are far from having any general picture of the language of English literary forms: like other registers, literary genres are likely to be describable in terms of probabilities, for example lyric poetry as having an orientation to certain combinations of transitivity and mood; but in order to study these we have to go one step further and treat the text as a *sample*, make systematic quantitative comparisons between one bank of texts and another.

A third component of literary analysis is tracking the relation of a text to other texts that form part of its environment. Every text has some context of situation; but it has been pointed out that a literary text, unlike most other texts, largely creates a context for itself: it determines its environment, rather than being determined by it. This gives a degree of self-sufficiency to literature that is not shared by other forms of discourse. In one respect, on the other hand, a literary text is anything but self-sufficient: this is in respect of what is sometimes called "intertextuality" — the way it resonates with other texts that make up its own genre, or even with other texts outside its genre, including giant texts from the past like the Bible and Shakespeare in English. The latter are, in some way or other, part of the context for many registers of modern English, both literary and non-literary; their looming presence is often felt, but is for that very reason usually rather obvious. Less obvious are the various intertextual experiences that a writer brings, and that a writer expects a reader to bring, to the construing of a text on the basis of a shared awareness of what each has read before (otherwise they would probably not be meeting each other as writer and reader in the present instance). The recognition of intertextual resonance is a major factor in the critical tradition; but it imposes a different requirement on the stylistician, since the relationship of one text to another needs to be interpreted in linguistic terms, and this is by no means easy.

There is one other special feature of a literary text which affects the stylistician's task. In many instances a literary text has accumulated a number of satellite texts over time: critical commentaries, reviews, exegeses of various kinds; and these affect the nature of the text as an object, since if we are explaining how it means what it does, and how it comes to be valued as it is, we need to encompass in our explanations what other people have thought it meant and what values other people have said they found in it. What can a grammatical analysis suggest, we might ask, about a particular actor's interpretation of a part? How does our linguistic approach throw light on the text as used by a historian or judged by a literary critic? Every text except perhaps the most formulaic ones is a highly complex object; but a literary text is very often one that has had time to grow, with new dimensions of complexity added to it as it has become a host to further texts which would not have existed without it.

In case all this seems to make the task of stylistician too formidable ever to be attempted, let me finish with two kinds of reassurance. One is that, although the ultimate goals are high, the rewards begin coming in early; even the first stages are likely to be found challenging and revealing. The other is that not all the special features of literary texts are ones that are additionally problematic. For example, unlike many other texts, a literary artefact usually has clear boundaries: it has a beginning and an end, and we know what is part of it and what is not, which is not at all the case with a conversation or even with an interview or a diary. Furthermore, just because a work of literature is largely constitutive of its own environment, the text itself must occupy the central place in our attention. With a text of a pragmatic kind, we may have to describe a significant slice of the context of culture before we begin to focus on the words; whereas in the analysis of a literary work we can get straight down to business, confident that the meaning is there in front of us in the text. There is undoubtedly a world of meaning that lies beyond the wording on the page; but it is a world that is defined by the text, not a prefabricated construct into which the text must fit. This does not mean that the text is treated as an isolated thing, unrelated to the cultural, historical or other circumstances surrounding it; on the contrary, the interpretation attempts always to bring it into relation with its sociocultural environment. But a literary text enters in as an independent creation; it is not something that will ever become predictable, in the way that texts in other registers become partially predictable once we have given a detailed account of what these circumstances are.

What has been lacking up to now has been a book that will guide students systematically through the principles and methods of stylistic analysis. *The Language of Literature* has been written to meet this need.

M. A. K. HALLIDAY

Preface

The Language of Literature is an introduction to literature. The aim of any introduction to literature is to develop in a student an intuitive sense for what is important in a work, and to teach him to find and describe the sources of his intuition in the text. The object of this book is to develop the student's intuition of what is significant in the language of literature, and to teach him how to describe literary language stylistically. Since the means given to the student to describe literary language is the technique of linguistic description, this introduction to literature is also an introduction to the basic tools and basic concerns of linguistic analysis. However, linguistic principles are introduced here under what we feel are the most favourable conditions: as an adjunct to the study of literature. At the end of the course employing this textbook, the student should be able to do a thorough stylistic analysis of a literary text with a fair degree of technical sophistication. More important, he should know, in a much fuller sense of the word, what that text "means".

A textbook in stylistics runs the risk of making a dynamic field of research seem definable. In fact, contemporary approaches to stylistics are extremely varied because of the extraordinarily rapid growth of interest in the field over the last 25 years. Consequently, in this book we have tried to avoid giving the student and the general reader the impression that stylistics is simply a set of procedures. Certainly *The Language of Literature* attempts to impart a basic knowledge of stylistics, but it also tries to develop an appreciation of stylistics' openness to literary insight through the abundant use of student-oriented exercises in practical stylistics. Our hope is that the student will come to appreciate literature more, as, through stylistics, he learns to talk about it more articulately.

Even if it were possible to do stylistics without reference to modern linguistics, it would not be possible to do stylistics without reference to language. Because linguistic procedures remain such an important part of stylistics we have designed this textbook for use at the third- and fourth-year college and graduate levels, where a certain amount of basic linguistic information will be seen as an asset, not an additional burden. Nevertheless our interest in literature is primary. Therefore we have chosen to approach the English language within the framework of the "systemic" school of modern linguistics. Systemic linguistics affords the advantages of a grammar which is less complex than some of the alternatives, and an approach to lexis which we have found intriguing to students and useful in the analysis of texts. In addition systemic linguistics has always been very text-oriented and empirical in its approach, and this pays off in stylistic applications.

Our aim in designing this book was to produce a workable textbook with a lively and entertaining style. The tenor of our writing therefore tends to the informal, and we hope to have been able to gain the confidence as well as the interest of the student and the general reader. As a workable textbook, *The Language of Literature* has a well-defined plan of execution. The book progresses through the systemicists' "levels of language": that is, we begin with the role of phonology and graphology in literary texts, proceed to consider literary play with the formal structures of grammar and lexis, and end with analysis of literary context. Chapter divisions in the book reflect this orientation to the levels of language. However, each chapter contains one or more "Unit" divisions. It is the Unit which represents each successive self-contained lesson in the book. Our text is therefore a set of eleven Units also, each one building on the knowledge gained so far, each one introducing a new step in the stylistic understanding of literary texts.

Each Unit has the same format. Our basic aims are to show the student how stylistics is done, to give him the linguistic principles that allow him to do stylistics himself, to set him to work doing stylistics, and to review with him his knowledge of the material. Each Unit carries out these jobs in four separate parts. The "Analysis" part contains a short stylistic essay on a significant literary text. The "Framework" part is an exposition of the linguistic principles which were employed in the stylistic analysis. The "Application" part asks the student to read another significant literary text, and to complete a stylistic analysis of it which has already been begun for him. The "Questions for Review" part takes him back to the material of the Analysis and the Framework, and offers the student another opportunity to write a stylistic essay of his own.

This textbook could be used as a parallel workbook for some other introduction to literature, linguistics or stylistics, because it is full of practical exercises. But we intended it primarily as a classroom teaching textbook, and that is how we have used it ourselves. Each Unit is intended to provide the focus for several seminars. The content of the Unit is designed to serve various functions. First, it presents the student with a body of material which can be studied before the seminar. Second, it provides texts which the student can analyze as a preparation for the seminar. Third, it presents questions and exercises by which the student can test his own grasp of the material. Fourth, the topics presented in the material can serve as points of departure for in-class discussion or lecture. Fifth, some or all of the texts can be used for in-class analysis and discussion. Sixth, some or all of the questions and exercises can be reserved for controlled in-class testing. We have tested the eleven separate Units in a 3-hour per week course covering 26 weeks, in which the textbook material was integrated with other work, such as additional literary texts for written analysis, periodic tests, and the like.

Perhaps we should reaffirm that the aim of literature is still enjoyment. Stylistics is not intended to replace the enjoyment of literature with mere comprehension. Rather it is an avenue leading to increased enjoyment through the understanding of the ways in which texts have been put together.

Acknowledgments

In the course of writing and revising this book we have become indebted to a number of colleagues around the world who take an interest in stylistics and in systemic linguistics. The published work of David Abercrombie, Margaret Berry, M. A. K. Halliday, R. A. Hudson, J. McH. Sinclair and other systemicists has of course influenced every part of the book. For their helpful criticism we would especially like to thank Professor Richard Bailey of the University of Michigan, Professor Richard Handscombe of York University, and Professor James Martin of the University of Sydney. We are also grateful to Professors James Benson and Wm. Greaves of York University, and the many others who have in some way encouraged us to bring the work to completion. Not to be forgotten are those patient students of a 300-level course in stylistics at Glendon College, York University, who for two years coped with this text in its draft form. Perhaps our greatest debt is to Professor Michael Gregory of Glendon College, York University, not only for his published and unpublished work in systemics, but also for his creation of a Department of English Language and Literature which fosters and encourages a linguistic approach to literary studies.

We would like to thank the following authors and publishers for permission to reproduce copyright material:

Apollinaire, Guillaume, "La Colombe poignardée et le jet d'eau", from *Caligrammes*, Editions Gallimard.

Atmospheric Environment Services, Environment Canada, Environment Canada Forecast.

Beowulf, ll. 258–261, 2428–2450, from Fr. Klaeber, ed., *Beowulf and the Fight at Finnsburg*, 3rd edition, D. C. Heath and Company.

Birney, Earle, "Anglosaxon Street", from *The Collected Poems of Earle Birney*, reprinted by permission of the Canadian Publishers, McClelland and Stewart Limited, Toronto.

The British Library, photographic reproduction of fol. 184a from the Beowulf Manuscript.

Cummings, E. E., "love is more thicker than forget", "dying is fine but Death", from *Complete Poems 1913–1962*, Harcourt Brace Jovanovich, Inc.; and from *Poems 1923–1954*, Granada Publishing Limited.

Dickinson, Emily, "There's a Certain Slant of Light", Harvard University Press.

Durrell, Lawrence, from *Clea* by Lawrence Durrell. Copyright © 1960 by Lawrence Durrell. Reprinted by permission of the publisher, E. P. Dutton, Inc. Also reprinted by permission of Faber and Faber Ltd. from *Clea* by Lawrence Durrell.

Faulkner, William, from pages 330–331 of *The Sound and the Fury*, Random House, Inc. Alfred A. Knopf, Inc.; also reprinted by permission of Curtis Brown Ltd., London.

Ferlinghetti, Lawrence, "The pennycandystore beyond the El", from *A Coney Island of the Mind*. Copyright © 1958 by Lawrence Ferlinghetti. Reprinted by permission of New Directions Publishing Corporation.

Finlay, Ian Hamilton, "au pair girl", reprinted by permission of Wild Hawthorn Press.

Fitzgerald, F. Scott, from *Tender is the Night*. Copyright 1933, 1934 by Charles Scribner's Sons; copyright renewed. Reprinted with the permission of Charles Scribner's Sons. Reprinted with permission of The Bodley Head from *The Bodley Head Scott Fitzgerald, Vol. 2*. From "Winter Dreams" (copyright 1922 by Frances Scott Fitzgerald Lanaham; copyright renewed) in *All the Sad Young Men*. Copyright 1926 by Charles Scribner's Sons; copyright renewed. Reprinted with the permission of Charles Scribner's Sons. Reprinted with permission of the Bodley Head from *The Bodley Head Scott Fitzgerald, Vol. 5*.

Frost, Robert, "Acquainted with the Night", from *The Poetry of Robert Frost* edited by Edward Connery Lathem. Copyright 1928, © 1969 by Holt, Rinehart and Winston. Copyright © 1956 by Robert Frost. Reprinted by permission of Holt, Rinehart and Winston, publishers; and of the Estate of Robert Frost; Edward Connery Lathem; and Jonathan Cape Ltd.

Hemingway, Ernest, from *A Farewell to Arms*. Copyright 1929 by Charles Scribner's Sons; copyright renewed 1957 by Ernest Hemingway. Reprinted with the permission of Charles Scribner's Sons; and the Executors of the Ernest Hemingway Estate; and Jonathan Cape Ltd.

Hopkins, Gerard Manley, "Spring and Fall" and "God's Grandeur", from the fourth edition (1967) of *The Poems of Gerard Manley Hopkins*, edited by W. H. Gardner and N. H. MacKenzie, published by Oxford University Press for the Society of Jesus.

Investors Syndicate Limited. Reproduction of the Investors Syndicate Limited advertisement is by permission of the Winnepeg-based financial services company.

Kerouac, Jack, from *Doctor Sax*. Reprinted by permission of Grove Press, Inc.; and the Sterling Lord Agency, Inc.

MacLeish, Archibald, "Vicissitudes of the Creator", from *New and Collected Poems 1917–1976* by Archibald MacLeish. Copyright © 1976 by

Archibald MacLeish. Reprinted by permission of Houghton Mifflin Company.

Plath, Sylvia, "Tulips" (on pp. 206–207), from *Ariel*, published by Faber and Faber, London, copyright Ted Hughes, 1965. Also from *The Collected Poems* by Sylvia Plath, edited by Ted Hughes. Copyright © 1962 by Ted Hughes. Reprinted by permission of Harper & Row, Publishers, Inc.

Reed, Henry, "Naming of Parts", from *A Map of Verona*, Jonathan Cape Ltd.

Stein, Gertrude, from *The Making of Americans*, Harcourt Brace Jovanovich, Inc.

Strunk, William Jr. and E. B. White, from Chapter V, "An Approach to Style", in *The Elements of Style*, 3rd edition. Copyright © 1979, Macmillan Publishing Co. Inc.

Thomas, Dylan, "Fern Hill", "Do not go gentle into that good night", "A refusal to mourn the death, by fire, of a child in London", from *Collected Poems*, published by J. M. Dent; from *Under Milk Wood*, published by J. M. Dent.

United Stationery Co., Ltd., from "Assignment of Mortgage" form, reprinted by permission of United Stationery Co., Ltd., Scarborough, Ontario.

Updike, John, from page 9 of *The Centaur*, Random House, Inc., Alfred A. Knopf, Inc.; and Andre Deutsch Limited.

Williams, Emmett, "she loves me", reprinted from *concrete poetry britain canada united states* (Stuttgart, Edition Hansjörg Mayer, 1966). Copyright © 1966, 1974 by Emmett Williams.

Williams, William Carlos, "Nantucket" and "This is just to say", from *Collected Earlier Poems*. Copyright 1938 by New Directions Publishing Corporation. Reprinted by permission of New Directions.

Wolfe, Tom, from "Black Shiny FBI Shoes", in *The Electric Kool-Aid Acid Test*. Reprinted by permission of Farrar, Straus and Giroux, Inc. Copyright © 1968 by Tom Wolfe. Also by permission of International Creative Management.

Contents

Introduction

Reading Literature

What happens to us when we read literature? We take flight into another existence, into a secondary world of the imagination. We see and hear through language and respond to its stimuli rather than seeing and hearing our actual surroundings or responding to them. It is as though we are hypnotized, released from our own limited bodies and given the freedom to become anything, see anything, feel anything. Anything, that is, that has been conjured up for us by these curious black marks on white pages. These marks connect with two enormous storehouses in us—our knowedge of language and our experience of sensations and feelings. What our imaginations construct for us depends on those personal warehouses.

A literary work can be used like anything else, from ink blots to feelings, simply as a device for imaginative stimulation, a way to find out what we're thinking or feeling or who we are. Or it can be read as the precise record of a unique and specific experience—an experience we can share more fully the more fully we share its context and its language. This book is about such full readings. It seeks to show you how to use the text of a literary work to tap your own storehouses, and how to add to them.

The Text

What do we mean by literature? The texts in this book are called literature because the culture from which they sprang considers them so. When we investigate such literary artifacts we usually find that there is something extraordinary about the language in which they are framed. And when we ask members of that culture about their experience of the artifact we frequently find that they are interested in and moved by it. We may say then, that a work of literature is a text that is valued by its culture, that uses a special language, and that affects people with emotions that are valued for their own sake.

A literary text occupies a certain position in literary history. It is part of a tradition and has historical relationships with other texts that came before it and after it. Such a text is also a piece of language, and all language has design. Ordinary language makes an ordinary use of the possibilities of language design. Literary language makes an extraordinary use of these possibilities, and this helps to make literary texts memorable. Literary texts, besides having a certain reputation and a certain skilfulness of linguistic patterning, also affect their readers according to the way those readers perceive them. The perception of a literary text is affected by language design, and by the relationship of the text to the literary tradition. The value of the special use of language in literary texts is the creation of a special or interesting perception, which brings with it a feeling of pleasure.

In reading a text we create a perception of that text. We may well read a text fully and accurately, but unreflectively. Or we may reflect on our perception and attempt to record it. Such reflection may not be necessary in order to attain a perception of the given text. On the other hand, such reflection does assist in a reciprocal way with the creation of our perception. The difference between reflective and unreflective reading may lie in the way we deal with our intuitions about the text.

The Intuition of Literary Language

Intuition, or the recognition of meaningful patterns, is a mysterious process because it occurs initially below the level of consciousness. Yet we all intuit knowledge of all sorts daily. When we drive a car or hit a tennis ball or read a poem we are making patterns out of many minute bits of information, selecting some concrete action out of many possibilities. In language especially we perceive and create all kinds of complicated structures almost unthinkingly.

Ordinary language is made up of many kinds of normative structures. Literary language, however, frequently extends and modifies these structures in unusual ways. Our intuition of a literary text comes from the perception, however subconscious, of these patterns. Consequently, the way to make our intuition more conscious is to make the linguistic structure of the text more conscious. If you have ever argued for any length of time with a friend about the merit of some literary work you will have noticed how the discussion begins with general statements and proceeds to particulars as each disputant attempts to back up his opinion. In the process of discussion a new *conscious* understanding of the text begins to emerge. False intuitions about its nature fall by the wayside and a more coherent description emerges, a description based on actual features of the text that one can point to and demonstrate. The more useful and flexible the descriptive theory used, the more effective this procedure is in elucidating literary texts.

To describe a language process or event—for language, whether spoken or derived from a text, we know instinctively is an activity, an experience— to describe such an event is to fix it or freeze it in time, like pinning down a butterfly for minute examination. We end with a much better sense of the butterfly afterwards, but we should not confuse such analytical activity with the experience of watching the butterfly "flutter by". The experience of the poem is enriched by such a procedure, as "inside" knowledge enriches our experience of a horse race or an opera. But the gathering of that knowledge is a different experience. Students sometimes say "Analysis kills the poem". Yes, for analysis must immobilize what is really an action in order to operate. The poem comes to life again in performance. The butterfly is released. The butterfly watcher sees with new understanding and new enjoyment.

Of course analysis itself is also active. It is really a process of many separate intuitions leading to still further intuitions, as patterns are recognized, and then patterns among patterns. Criticism is the description of those patterns and their relationship to successively more general statements about the text, until in the end the general statement of a "theme" for a literary text has been enriched by a host of supporting and more specific statements. It is no longer an "opinion". Intuition has been transformed into reflective knowledge.

Linguistics, the Science of Language

To make precise descriptive statements about a stretch of language requires itself a special language: a theory of description with precisely defined terminology. Such a descriptive theory is the basis of any science. The science of language is called *linguistics*. Since language is a social process the study of it requires taking it out of time by means of recording it, or making a text, and turning it instead into an object. The components of the language process are: speaker/formation of text, auditor/decoding of text. As language object, these same components are subjected to meticulous analysis.

Language is a social phenomenon because of its highly conventionalized nature. We learn language from others and take with them a mutual part in creating it. The description of social processes in modern times is often based on a "structuralist" approach, which means describing a thing in terms of its parts and how they are related. Modern linguistics seeks to describe the language event as a complex of related parts.

Linguistics as a science has been developed to be capable of describing all languages and all language events. The reading of literary texts is just one kind of language event within the scope of linguistics. Consequently linguistics can describe literary texts by relating them to the various kinds of non-literary language that they are extensions of. The categories of linguistics, unlike the traditional categories of literary criticism, are applicable to the whole of language, not just to a part of it. As we have said, reflection on an intuition develops and deepens that intuition. Linguistic description is a very precise form of reflection on the intuition of meaning in language texts of all kinds. The more precise the description is, the more precisely the intuition of meaning may be stated.

Systemic Linguistics

In this book we are using a tradition within linguistics called "systemic" description. In systemic linguistics the factors that create meaning in language are grouped into three "levels". The first is the level of "phonology/ graphology"—the organization of physical substance as noises or marks which we use to transmit language. The second is the level of "form"—the conventions of lexical meaning and grammatical patterning. The third is the level of "context"—the relationship of certain kinds of language to certain kinds of situation.

The human throat can make a startling variety of noises, as anthropologists, singing instructors and nursery school teachers can testify. All such noises are at least suggestive of meaning. However, only some of the sounds are used in repeatable, conventionalized ways in a given language. These particular noises are used to build up codes which carry meaning. The study of these meaningful sounds occurs at the first level and is called *phonology*.

Graphology is the study of meaningful marks, the other substantial method of providing symbols with which to build up codes. Visual space can be organized in many different ways, but each language uses only a part of this potential. In English, the graphological codes are only partly related to the phonological codes, but even this need not be so.

The formal level is divided into the study of lexis and grammar. Recurring words with the same meaning regardless of grammar form the patterns of lexis. Lexical items can sometimes, as in the case of "jack-of-all-trades", contain more than one word. Lexis can have both denotative meaning (the dictionary definition) and connotative meaning (associations and nuances).

Grammar is the study of recurring patterns in the sequence of language, and of formal relationships between the bits of code. For example, the tendency for the group of words at the beginning of a sentence to form the "topic" is formalized in the concept of "subject". Grammar is thus an abstraction of a general idea from many individual events.

Despite the relatively fixed nature of lexical and grammatical form, the conventional meaning of a piece of language can change depending on its surroundings. The "fixed" element of formal meaning, then, actually refers to a "normal" context and beyond that to a "normal" situation. Putting an item of grammar or lexis into an unusual context can alter its meaning radically.

All these levels, are, of course, completely inter-related. The intermediate formal level depends on the substance-related level to carry its symbols and on the contextual level to control their meaning.

It is the perception that language is a *social activity* that informs systemic linguistics. The approach began with social anthropologists like Malinowski and was pioneered by British linguists like J. R. Firth and M. A. K. Halliday. It is a relatively uncomplicated theory of description which emphasizes the empirical perception of texts and the description of meaningful contrasts in language. The attention systemic linguistics gives texts makes it very suitable for literary analysis.

The kind of language-oriented analysis taught through this textbook is that branch of linguistics called *Stylistics*. Stylistics is a rapidly growing field in both critical writing and pedagogy. The aim of this book is to make the student a *stylistician*, someone who can comprehend literary texts through a comprehension of their language structures. Someone who can say not only "I know what I like", but also, "I know *why* I like it, because I know *how* it works".

The Levels of Language

SITUATION		
LEVELS OF LANGUAGE	Context	
	Form	grammar/ lexis
	Phonology/ Graphology	
SUBSTANCE		

In this arrangement of categories, "language", with its "levels", is placed between "situation", which refers to the reality that language pertains to, and "substance", which refers to the medium in which language is realized. Language organizes substance in imitation of reality, and so lies between. Language relates to situation through "context", the correlation of particular features in situation to particular features in the "form" of language. Language relates to substance through "phonology" *or* "graphology", procedures for encoding language form into either the spoken or the written medium. Form describes the recurrence of particular stretches of text, or particular relations, that have the same meaning (in the given context). Such stretches or relations may be either "lexis", referring to dictionary-type meanings, or "grammar", referring to the more general roles depicted in utterances.

Chapter One **Phonology and Phonetics**

OUR perception of language is first of all a sensory perception. We hear it or we see it. However, we seldom reflect on what we actually hear or what we actually see. Usually we are too busy interpreting the meaning of what we hear and what we see to think about the actual sounds or the actual shapes we are perceiving. Usually, it is only when we hear or see language in a foreign, unknown tongue, or alphabet that we become conscious of individual sounds or shapes that compose the language text. In such a situation we cannot understand the meaning, and the brain can give its undivided attention to the pure experience of sound as symbol.

One of the distinguishing characteristics of literary texts is the way in which they manipulate their sounds or letters. In ordinary texts we expect sound and symbol to be transparent to meaning. But in literature it often happens that the sounds or symbols of the medium become important in themselves. They are not there just to encode a meaning—their peculiar arrangement constitutes part of the meaning of the text. In losing their transparency, they become objects of attention. We are forced to reflect on the features of the medium of language, not just on the meaning which the medium conveys.

In this chapter, we are considering only the sounds of language. These sounds are divided into two groups. In Units 1 and 2, we consider only the sounds of language which occupy discrete places in the stream of speech. These sounds are already familiar to you as "consonants" and "vowels". Taken together we call these the "segmental" sounds, because each consonant and vowel constitutes one small segment of the whole spoken text. In Unit 3 we consider sounds which are not as localized as the consonants and vowels, which instead extend over longer stretches of spoken text, co-existing with the segmentals that occupy those stretches. These extended features of the stream of speech are called "supra-segmentals". The study of the segmentals will tell you something about the use of audible patterns and repetitions in literary texts.

We begin this study then on the lowest, most concrete level of language phenomena. The term "phonology" refers to the way in which language is encoded in its medium as sound. The term "phonetics" refers to the way in which individual sounds are formed by the apparatus of speech, or detected by the apparatus of hearing.

7

UNIT 1

Consonants: Articulation and Function

I. ANALYSIS: the Texture of Sound in Poetry

GOD'S GRANDEUR

The world is charged with the grandeur of God.   1
   It will flame out, like shining from shook foil;
   It gathers to a greatness, like the ooze of oil
Crushed. Why do men then now not reck his rod?
Generations have trod, have trod, have trod;   5
   And all is seared with trade; bleared, smeared with toil;
   And wears man's smudge and shares man's smell: the soil
Is bare now, nor can foot feel, being shod.

And for all this, nature is never spent;
   There lives the dearest freshness deep down things;   10
And though the last lights off the black West went
   Oh, morning, at the brown brink eastward, springs—
Because the Holy Ghost over the bent
   World broods with warm breast and with ah! bright wings.   14

—G. M. Hopkins

Gerard Manley Hopkins was a Jesuit priest and poet who lived late in the 19th century. He was a man of profound inner tensions that would "flame out" in his poetry. His inner conflict lay between a dedication to the life of the spirit through the virtue of absolute obedience to religious superiors and an opposing sensitivity to experience which sought an outlet in originality of language. In his poetry there is nearly always the suggestion of opposing tensions, frequently expressed by a syncopated rhythm that has had a great influence on modern poetry. He is famous for nature poems which succeed in filling the natural world with divine life; but he is equally famous for poems of despair. He was a scholar who derived his theory of poetry and nature from a medieval philosopher, Scotus; and he was a theologian who worshipped a Christian God who is both transcendent of and immanent to nature. Nature for him could reveal the divine, but it is not equal to the divine; rather, it is a veil drawn across the face of divinity.

This is the theme of "God's Grandeur". Here Hopkins' sense of inner tension finds appropriate expression in the idea of nature as "charged" with divinity which—no matter how "bleared", how "smeared with toil"—will continue to "flame out". There can be no more important theme for our age than this sense of the divinity in nature. At last we have begun to acknowledge the extraordinary beauty and fertility of our world and to condemn the "trade" and "toil" that obscure it.

The poem expresses above all a positive vision. Despite the generations, the wearing down of grass, the smell of man, there exists scarcely beneath the surface the eternal vitality and freshness of God. This energy leaps forth at every slightest opportunity, at every dawn, from within everything. Hopkins' powerful optimism easily raises us above the routine of toil, as a flash of true feeling can illuminate our profoundest depressions.

At the end of the poem is the image of the Holy Ghost, the third part of the Christian Trinity, who represents divine love. Hopkins' use of this image here implies that creation itself is an extension of the inner life of the Trinity, of the divine being. Life flows endlessly out of God through His spirit. How then can there be an end to it? The world is an egg brooded over by the divine spirit. And that egg will crack and the spirit of God again flash out. "There lives the dearest freshness deep down things" and "morning, at the brown brink eastward, springs" *because* of the Holy Ghost, the inexhaustible source of the universe. It is this kind of optimism, of wider vision, of faith in something beyond the smear and blear of a man-worn world, that our age needs to re-ignite our spirits. And, says Hopkins, it *will* flame out, in spite of everything we do, in spite of ourselves. This is God's grandeur.

In form the poem is a "Petrarchan" sonnet. The Petrarchan rhyme scheme (abbaabba, cdcdcd) is reinforced by the indented left margins, while the octet (8-line group) sets out a problem and the sestet (6-line group) resolves it. The sonnet is a traditional form and sets up certain expectations of serious subject matter and an argument structure. Your first impression may also include a sense of the suggestive power of the words, and of the density of sound patterning in the poem.

A good essay about a literary work begins with a good literary insight, and a student's exclamation after studying this poem—"But the line *itself* is charged!"—provides us with our starting point. Let us see how Hopkins' lines are charged with sound, as God, according to Hopkins, charged the world with grandeur. Our key point of examination will be that smallest part of language, the consonant. To explore it we will adapt for our own purposes two familiar terms from literary analysis, alliteration and onomatopeia; and we will trace Hopkins' use of consonants back to his studies in medieval poetry.

Alliteration

Alliteration—the repetition of an initial sound in different words, usually a consonant—is a common technique. It depends on our recognition of the similarity of certain sounds—sounds which on close inspection may not be very similar at all, but which we, as speakers of English, have agreed will be classed alike, for example, the initial "t" of "toil" and the "t" after "s" of "West". Test this difference by holding your hand before your mouth when you say these two words. Because we have agreed to use the single symbol "t" for these two sounds, we indicate that we are not aware of the difference of sound. To us, they are *functionally* similar, even though the correspondence between written symbol and spoken sound is frequently unreliable. In reality, sounds that we think of as identical sounds are only a class of similar sounds. Within the similarity of sounds arranged as alliterative pairs here by Hopkins, there is a great deal more variety than we may first suspect. The initial sound in "trade" actually resembles "ch" in many speakers, because of the following "r". Contrast this with the clear "t" of "toil".

Since rhyme and metre are traditional elements of the sonnet form, the extensive use of alliteration in this poem is its most unusual formal feature. In only one line (5) is there no alliteration, and there are numerous instances of double sets of alliteration, and also of multiple alliteration:

The world is charged with the grandeur of God.   1

It will flame out, like shining from shook foil;

It gathers to a greatness, like the ooze of oil

Crushed. Why do men then now not reck his rod?

Generations have trod, have trod, have trod;   5

And all is seared with trade; bleared, smeared with toil;

And wears man's smudge and shares man's smell: the soil

Is bare now, nor can foot feel, being shod.

And for all this, nature is never spent;

There lives the dearest freshness deep down things;   10

And though the last lights off the black West went

Oh, morning, at the brown brink eastward, springs —

Because the Holy Ghost over the bent

World broods with warm breast and with ah! bright wings.   14

The result of this unusual amount of alliteration is to sensitize us to all sorts of sound qualities in the poem. We become sensitive not only to the expected sonnet rhyme, but also to interior rhymes: "men"/"then", "seared"/"bleared"/"smeared", "wears"/"shares". In addition, we find some entire words are repeated: "man's"/"man's", "have trod"/"have trod"/"have trod". This density of repeated sounds is particularly notice-able in the lines (5, 6, 7) where the blearing of the world through man's activities is described. It is also strikingly effective in the climactic last line where two sets of triple alliteration occur, and virtually every syllable, stressed or unstressed, alliterates. (The question of assonance will be dealt with in the next unit.) This extra intensity of sound effects in the poem, added to the traditional effect of sonnet rhyming, results in our first impression of the poem as "charged".

When we begin to examine the particular instances of alliteration, we discover that alliteration can draw attention to meaning. If two words that are already commonly related in meaning are also related by sound the effect is striking. The title "God's Grandeur" provides a first example, one that is repeated in the first line. Other examples are "ooze"/"oil", "trade/"toil", "smudge"/"smell", "broods"/"breast", "deep"/"down". In other cases two words that would not normally be seen as related in meaning are given a relationship in the context of the poem; and then this relationship is underlined by alliteration: "foot"/"feel" (a feeling foot as opposed to a shod foot), "world"/"warm" (a warm world thanks to the Holy Ghost's brooding). Such relationships of meaning as well as sound shade into other examples of alliteration that seem simply to reinforce the general pattern of sound repetition. In three cases alliteration is used to reinforce a negative word that appears as the second alliterated item: "nature"/"never", "now"/"not", "now"/"nor". In some cases other words alliterate with two alliterated words linked in meaning, although they themselves do not relate directly in meaning: "world"/"warm"/"*wings*", "*dearest*"/"deep"/"down", "broods"/"breast"/"*bright*". In these cases there seems to be a tendency for us to attempt to associate the meaning of the third item with the established pair. The images of world, warmth, and wings unite in a conception of the world as an egg. "Deep"/"down" is seen as the place of the dearest feelings. The brooding breast shines brightly with love.

Alliteration is also an important factor in the *rhythm* of this poem. A poem has many rhythms. There is the rhythm set up by the stresses, which in English appear at regular intervals. (We will talk about this in the second unit following.) There is the rhythm set up by the line units, especially when, as here, the line endings are marked by rhyme. There is the rhythm set up by the pauses between grammatical units, or marked in different ways by punctuation and layout. And there is also the rhythm set up by various interior sound repetitions, including alliteration.

It is when these various units coincide that we find the strongest rhythmic effects. Rhyme and stress coincide with the end of each line here. In addition, in all but four lines (8, 9, 10, 12) the last syllable is also emphasized by alliteration or repetition. Most line endings are also marked by strong pauses (all but 3, 7, 11, 13). This coincidence of rhythmic effects makes the line the effective unit in the poem. What Hopkins does, having established the line as the unit, is to produce varied rhythmic effects *within* the line by manipulating stresses, pauses, and repeated sounds, particularly alliteration. The consonant, in alliteration, becomes the key organizing device of the rhythm of the individual line.

Hopkins and Old English Poetry

To explore the rhythmic features of the poem further, as expressed by its alliteration, we must turn to Hopkins' interest in the ancient forms of poetry. He had studied medieval language and poetry, and his interest in a continuity of language forms and poetic technique led him to parallel some of its features in his own work. The result is not an overt imitation but an echo, the most prominent feature being a high density of alliteration with a consequent effect on regular metre. The roots of this technique in English are found in poetry from the Old English period, A.D. 650 to A.D. 1100:

> Him se yldesta   andswarode,
>
> werodes wīsa,   wordhord onlēac:
>
> 'Wē synt gumcynnes   Gēata lēode
>
> ond Higelāces   heorthgenēatas.

The above is lines 258–261 from *Beowulf*, an Old English heroic poem which tells of the hero Beowulf's journey to Denmark from Sweden to defend King Hrothgar's hall against a ghost. Here, Beowulf is formally identifying himself to the Danish king's coastwatch.

> Him the leader ("eldest") answered,
> (the) guide of the troop, (his) word-hoard unlocked:
> 'We are, of the race of the Geats, people
> and Hygelac's hearth-retainers.

The language of the original is tenth-century English. The enormous differences between Old and Modern English are obvious and one reason for this is the intervening Norman Conquest. There are numbers of obsolete words: *werodes* ("troop's"), *gumcynnes* ("race's"), *leode* ("people"); but there are also some more recognizable forms: *him* ("him"), *yldesta* ("eldest"), *answarode* ("answered"), *heorth* ("hearth").

However, our interest in this text lies with its sound.

him suh i̲óol-duhss-tuh   áhnd-swáh-ruh-duh

wéh-ruh-duhss wée-zuh   wo̲hrd-hohrd awn-léy-uhk

wey sioont g̲uhm-kióon-nuhss   yéh-uh-tuh léh-uh-duh

awnd hée-yuh-lóck-uhss   heh-uhrth-yuh-néy-uh-tuhss

Old English poetry was probably intended to be chanted, with strong stresses and a marked caesura (pause in the line). From the above transliteration you should be able to reproduce the Old English rhythms and perhaps make an initial attempt to associate them with Hopkins' poem.

Determining the place of alliteration in this rhythmic structure requires a little more background. Old English poetry is built on a structure of four beats a line, distributed in two half-lines. Alliteration occurs in every line (and sometimes the alliteration of two different sounds, although this is rare). In the standard pattern the third stressed syllable is always alliterated with one, and often both, of the first two stressed syllables. The fourth stressed syllable is rarely alliterated.

The alliterated syllables have been italicized in the transliteration above, and this in turn requires some explanation. As we have seen in Hopkins with "trade" and "toil", very different sounds may be treated as *functionally* similar for alliterative purposes. This is true for Old English, too: *gumcynnes* was perceived as alliterating with *Gēata* (guhm-kióon-nuss, yéh-uh-tuh). Although we perceive the "g" sound and the "y" sound as different, Old English speakers did not.

The point is that the alliteration is a major factor in constructing and specifying the rhythm of the poetry, and it is this relationship between alliteration and rhythm that comes down through the history of poetry to Hopkins and beyond him to such modern poets as Dylan Thomas. The formal features of Old English poetry outlined above were general to Germanic verse of the heroic period, but were dropped in English after the Norman Conquest except in the west of England where the feature of dense alliteration was retained in such poems as *Sir Gawain*. The tendency for a mid-line caesura, and for some alliterative effects, however, remained.

A parallel to Old English technique in "God's Grandeur" is most easily seen in the first part of the poem. Lines 1, 2, 3, 5, 8, 9 all have essentially a four-beat Old English rhythm, organized by sound patterning as we see in the following chart. The slant and the star indicate stressed syllables which carry alliterations; the dash indicates stressed syllables which do not.

```
1  –  –  /  /
2  /  *  *  /
3  /  /  *  *
5  –  /  /  /    (repetition)
8  –  /  /  –
9  –  /  /  –
```

However, in the other lines also, the poem uses alliteration and other sound repetitions to organize the rhythm, most strikingly in the last line. Thus alliteration breaks out of the four-beat line, accumulates with other sound repetitions and intensifies our perception of all forms of sound in the poem, making its language more "charged".

If we look over the effects of alliteration in the poem as a whole we can perceive more general patterns. Alliteration is heavier than usual throughout this poem. The other forms of sound repetition which reinforce it tend to cluster in lines 4, 5, 6, 7 where man's smudge on the world lies heaviest. Relatively less alliteration occurs in the sestet than the octet, as if in the octet the "grandeur" was "gathering" in coagulated sound; in the sestet it is released. However, the last line remains a *tour de force* of alliteration where all the themes of the poem are gathered into two mighty sets of triple alliteration: God again "charging" the "world" with his "grandeur".

Onomatopoeia

It is obvious by now that the exploration of alliteration has taken us into the question of how the sound of a line may reflect its sense. A careful definition of the traditional term *onomatopoeia* will help us here. There are two opposed misconceptions about onomatopoeia, or the use of words which "imitate" natural sounds. One misconception is that it does not exist because it is not possible to imitate in words a "buzz" or a "chickadee". The other is that the words really *do* imitate the sounds successfully.

Onomatopoeia is actually the *mutual* reinforcement of sense by sound and sound by sense. One critic's ingenious variation on Tennyson's "murmuring of innumerable bees"—"murdering of innumerable beeves"—suggests that there is no natural connection between sound and sense. However, the real point is that in the Tennyson line sound and sense reinforce each other, while in the satirical version they do not. In other words, appropriate sound may attain significance because of a suggested meaning; hence the meaning is lent a force by emphasis.

Onomatopoeic effects are often consonantal, and there are many of these effects in "God's Grandeur". An important characteristic of the sounds in lines 1 and 2 is their "voicing". All vowels and many consonants are "voiced". Place your fingers on your Adam's apple and say "ah", "zzz", "bub" to perceive the source of voicing, which is vibration in the vocal cords. The consonants predominating in line 1 are voiced: Th– w–rld –s —rg–d w— th– gr–nd—r –f G–d. In this line also the consonants *cluster* to an unusual degree: —rld –s/ch–rg(–)d/w–th/th– gr– –f/G. (This list includes the clusters formed by consonants at the ends of words followed by consonants at the beginning of the next word since in pronunciation these are run together.) This density of clustering, together with the amount of consonantal voicing involved, combine to "charge" the line.

In line 2, by contrast, there is a high density of "unvoiced" consonants: –t f– –t –k –sh f– sh—k f–. Part of the sensual impression rendered is gained by the type of consonants involved; but part is also the effect of the contrast with the previous line's consonants, both in type, and in the absence of clustering. In fact, the voiced/unvoiced contrast is the *only* difference between some of these consonants: "t" and "d", "s" and "z", "f" and "v". Again, the sense of line 2—the rapid release of energy—is reinforced by the quality of consonantal sound. Both lines gain by having their contrasted meanings reinforced by contrasted sounds.

Consonants are also divided into "stops" and "fricatives". Stops—"t", "d", "k", "g", "p", "b"—are formed by stopping up the breath, and then releasing it. Place your hand before your mouth to detect the "puff" as these stops are "released" in the course of their articulation.

Fricatives—"f", "v", "s", "z", "sh", "zh" ("azure")—are formed by a constant rush of breath. Unlike stops, they can be prolonged as long as your breath holds out. (Affricates—"ch", "j" ("judge") are half-stop, half-fricative.) The onomatopoeia of lines 1 and 2 is again helped by this contrast, especially since the contrastive fricatives of line 2 also alliterate: "f", "sh". The sense of "charging" and "release" that the sound patterning of the octet and sestet gives us is echoed in lines 1 and 2 by the selection of consonants that first "charge" (voiced, stops) then "release" (unvoiced, fricatives) our articulatory energies.

To a poet the smallest part of language is significant. We have seen here just how significant the consonant can be. Everywhere we have looked in this poem we have seen Hopkins' theme reinforced by sound. Although we have focused particularly on consonants here, yet we might have chosen vowels, or even aspects of language such as syntax, lexis or context. Each focusing on an aspect of language would have illuminated Hopkins' poem in yet another way. It is this integration of theme and all aspects of language that is the mark of literature.

II. FRAMEWORK: Articulating the Consonants

Production of Sound

Sound is the basis of language. We learned to speak long before we learned to write, and the most prolific writer among us speaks many more words and sentences than he will ever put on paper. Similarly, language is the basis of literature. To learn something about language in order to read literature is as elementary as learning about the body when studying the dance. This book begins with sound because sound is the most basic element of language; it tries to teach something about language because language is the most basic element in literature.

Sound originates in the body as the movement of air in response to a muscular activity. The compression of the chest cavity by the raising of the diaphragm increases the air pressure in the lungs. This air escapes up the bronchial tubes, through the trachea (wind pipe) to the larynx. The vocal cords, which are cartilage membranes in the larynx, may vibrate, causing the air column to vibrate in turn. This vibration is called "voicing", but whether the vibration occurs or not, sound can still ensue. (See the diagram of the lower vocal tract.)

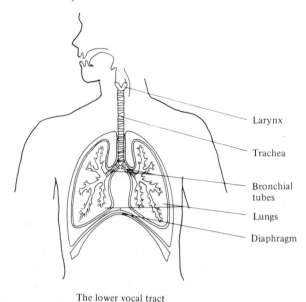

Larynx

Trachea

Bronchial tubes

Lungs

Diaphragm

The lower vocal tract

The column of air thus formed is modulated in the upper vocal tract in various ways before being released to the outside through the mouth and nose, thus transmitting sound. It is the deployment of lips, teeth, tongue and velum (the farthest-back part of the roof of the mouth) that produces the modulation of the air to create different sounds. (See the diagram of the upper vocal tract.)

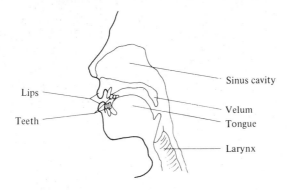

Sinus cavity

Lips

Velum

Teeth

Tongue

Larynx

The upper vocal tract

Nasalization of the sound occurs when the velum is lowered, opening the way of the escaping air to the sinuses. This is known in popular speech as "talking through the nose" though this does not actually happen. Rather, the resonating capacity of the sinuses adds "nasalization" to the sound.

The most important means of modifying sound in the upper vocal tract is the tongue. Some portion of the tongue is placed in conjunction with some part of the roof of the mouth. The changed shape of the mouth's interior produces a different sound. The "articulators" in this process are the tip (apex), front and back (dorsum) of the tongue. The "points of articulation" are the upper lip, upper teeth, gum ridge (alveolar ridge), hard palate and soft palate (velum). An additional possible articulator is the lower lip. Remember, the *articulator* is placed against the *point of articulation*. (See the diagram of the "oral cavity".)

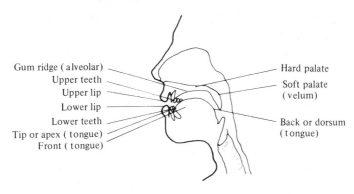

Gum ridge (alveolar)
Upper teeth
Upper lip
Lower lip
Lower teeth
Tip or apex (tongue)
Front (tongue)

Hard palate
Soft palate (velum)
Back or dorsum (tongue)

The oral cavity

LOL–B*

Another means of modulation besides nasalization and articulation is breath release. Stops, as we learned before, are sounds made by stopping the breath behind an obstruction—e.g. the two lips or the tongue tip on the gum ridge—and then suddenly releasing the breath as a puff. The sounds made *without* stopping the breath are called continuants. Fricative continuants are made by a steady rush of air through a narrow opening. This opening is formed by an articulator and a point of articulation. Like all other continuants, these fricatives can be prolonged; stops cannot. Affricates begin like stops with a partial obstruction, but end like fricatives: "j", "ch". They are called continuants although you can prolong them only slightly. The other continuants are called resonants. Resonants employ very little emission of breath. Instead, the static air column resonates behind some unchanging stoppage (for example, the closed lips). There are three types of resonants: the nasals (velum lowered, stoppage in the mouth), the lateral ("l") and the median ("r").

There is one more way to modulate sound, and we have already mentioned it: voicing, the vibration of the vocal cords.

Inventory of Consonants

All consonants are combinations of these various kinds of modulation. Some consonants are voiced stops, others unvoiced. Some voiced stops use the tip of the tongue against the gum ridge, and so on. A complete inventory of the consonants needs no further descriptive features than we have already had.

Stops include voiced and unvoiced bilabials (two lips closed), apico-alveolars (tip against gum-ridge) and dorso-velars (back against velum). The symbols for these stops are: /b/ (baby), /p/ (pit), /d/ (death), /t/ (toil), /g/ (God), /k/ (kite).

Fricatives include voiced and unvoiced labio-dentals (lower lip against upper teeth), inter-dentals (tip of tongue against upper teeth), apico-alveolars (tip against gum ridge), fronto-palatals (front of tongue against hard palate) and unvoiced glottal (mouth open, no constriction, rush of air through space between open vocal cords—the *glottis*). The symbols for these are: /v/ (very), /f/ (fine), /ð/ (the), /θ/ (thing), /z/ (zoo), /s/ (so), /š/ (sheep), /ž/ (azure), /h/ (hate).

Affricates include voiced and unvoiced fronto-palatals (front of tongue against hard palate). The symbols for affricates are: /ǰ/ (jeep), /č/ (cheap).

The resonants include the nasals, median, and lateral. These are all necessarily voiced. The nasals include the bilabial (two lips closed), the apico-alveolar (tip against gum ridge) and the dorso-velar (back against velum). The symbols for the nasals are: /m/ (men), /n/ (no), /ŋ/ (as in sing).

The median symbol is /r/ (race) and the lateral symbol is /l/ (late). (See the diagram of the consonant inventory.)

Finally we should mention that two sounds, often associated with letters "w" and "y", behave rather like consonants but are articulated more like vowels. These "semi-vowels" can be grouped with consonants for some purposes, but we will describe their articulation with that of vowels in the next unit.

	Stops		Continuants						
			Fricatives		Affricates		Resonants		
	Voiced	Unvoiced	Voiced	Unvoiced	Voiced	Unvoiced	Nasal	Lateral	Median
Bilabial	/b/	/p/					/m/		
Labio-dental			/v/	/f/					
Inter-dental			/ð/	/θ/					
Apico-alveolar	/d/	/t/	/z/	/s/			/n/	/l/	/r/
Fronto-palatal			/ž/	/š/	/ǰ/	/č/			
Dorso-velar	/g/	/k/					/ŋ/		
Glottal				/h/					

Inventory of consonants in English

Variation and Function

Although the introduction of all this terminology may make the subject seem complicated, there are actually not very many consonants. The fact that their number is limited makes sound production easier. Yet the combination of a limited number of consonants still allows for the creation of a very large number of words.

The features of consonants that we have described here are also limited. If we extended our description into more minute details, we could describe an infinite number of different consonants, and even an infinite number of differences within the limits of *each* consonant type. The consonants we have described, therefore, are *classes* of consonants. Though /b/ may be said in many variations, it is accepted always as /b/ by English speakers; it is this that enables alliteration to work. All the particular productions of /b/ are accepted as symbols of the whole class /b/.

Variations other than those we have described are not perceived simply because they are never used to distinguish words. The sole purpose or *function* of variation in sound is to distinguish words. Only some possible variations are used to distinguish words; others are not, and these variations are called non-functional. For example, the forcefulness of breath release or "puff" is a possible variation which is not used in English to distinguish words; but in some other languages it is. Traffic lights may come in several shades of green, but all are recognized in the English-speaking world only as the signal to "go".

The test for a functional difference in sound is made by finding "minimal pairs" such as "big" and "pig", "hiss" and "his", "lick" and "look", "lack", "lock", "lake", "leek". If the sound change, such as voicing in "his", makes a new word of "hiss", then it is a functional difference, and one of the limiting features which deserves to be described.

Unlimited variation, however, is not irrelevant. In alliteration the many non-functional variations in sound provide a pleasing variety within a pattern. Unlimited variation in sound also extends the possibilities for onomatopoeia, because the function of different sounds here is not to discriminate meaning, but rather to reflect patterns already set up by the lexical meaning and the context. Sound becomes a factor in the poem on its own merits, not just as a signaller of words.

If we return to lines 1 and 2 of "God's Grandeur" we are now in a position to see more clearly the onomatopoeic effects. If we set aside the resonants and the vowels which are always voiced, the difference in the number of unvoiced consonants in the two lines is striking. Only /č/ (charged) and /θ/ (with) are unvoiced in line 1, but every one is unvoiced in line 2. Even in the resonants themselves there is a pattern. There are four /r/ consonants in line 1 and three of these occur in the first three stressed syllables. The effect of this patterning is almost like alliteration in helping to organize the rhythm of the poem. In line 10 also, "There lives the dearest freshness deep down things", an onomatopoeic effect is achieved by patterning the voiced and unvoiced consonants. The line contrasts the idea of "freshness" with the idea of depth. The first and last words in this line both begin with "th", but the first sound is /ð/, a voiced sound. If we ignore the resonants, which like the vowels are distributed through the line, the line begins with a number of voiced consonants: /ð/, /v/, /ð/, /d/. A change occurs in the middle of "dearest" which is also the most unexpected and most emotional word in the line. The word "dearest" begins with a voiced consonant /d/ but ends with a cluster of unvoiced consonants /s/, /t/, and is followed immediately by three more in "freshness": /f/, /š/, /s/. This contrasting chorus of unvoiced consonants in the middle of the line combines with other linguistic features to echo perfectly the sense. The contrast is completed by the voiced alliterating /d/s of "deep down". Onomatopoeia occurs as the result of many other sound effects too, as we shall see in the following units; but in many of these also, the lowly consonant will play its part.

III. APPLICATION: the Consonant and the Canadian Poet

You are now in a position to identify a consonant sound in terms of its articulation. You also have seen how a poet like Hopkins, or like the anonymous author of *Beowulf*, uses such articulations in establishing and varying a rhythmic pattern. The rhythm may be set up by a repeated consonant (actually a class of slightly different sounds), or even by just a repeated component of consonant articulation, like the voicing aspect of different consonants in line 1 of "God's Grandeur". In the following poem, a famous Canadian poet rings some new changes on the Old English poetical style. Note carefully the distribution of consonants.

ANGLOSAXON STREET

Dawndrizzle ended   dampness steams from
blotching brick and   blank plasterwaste
Faded housepatterns   hoary and finicky
unfold stuttering   stick like a phonograph

Here is a ghetto   gotten for goyim   5
O with care denuded   of nigger and kike
No coonsmell rankles   reeks only cellarrot
attar of carexhaust   catcorpse and cookinggrease
Imperial hearts   heave in this haven
Cracks across windows   are welded with slogans   10
There'll Always Be An England   enhances geraniums
and V's for Victory   vanquish the housefly

Ho! with climbing sun   march the bleached beldames
festooned with shopping bags   farded flatarched
bigthewed Saxonwives   stepping over buttrivers   15
waddling back wienerladen   to suckle smallfry

Hoy! with sunslope   shrieking over hydrants
flood from learninghall   the lean fingerlings
Nordic nobblecheeked   not all clean of nose
leaping Commandowise   into leprous lanes   20

What! after whistleblow!   spewed from wheelboat
after daylong doughtiness   dire handplay
in sewertrench or sandpit   come Saxonthegns
Junebrown Jutekings   jawslack for meat

Sit after supper   on smeared doorsteps   25
not humbly swearing   hatedeeds on Huns
profiteers politicians   pacifists Jews

Then by twobit magic   to muse in movie
unlock picturehoard   or lope to alehall
soaking bleakly   in beer skittleless   30

Home again to hotbox   and humid husbandhood
in slumbertrough adding   sleepily to Anglekin
Alongside in lanenooks   carling and leman
caterwaul and clip   careless of Saxonry
with moonglow and haste   and a higher heartbeat   35

Slumbers now slumtrack   unstinks cooling
waiting brief for milkmaid   mornstar and worldrise
Toronto 1942

—Earle Birney

Numbers of Earle Birney's devices for evoking the Old English poetry do not directly relate to consonants at all, of course. In the first place, the locating of "Anglosaxon Street" in the "Toronto" of "1942" establishes the poem as an inside joke for Canadians, and for anyone else who thinks, rightly or wrongly, that Toronto's "Cabbagetown" is the only English-speaking ghetto in North America. Birney's wonderful fantasy suggests that White Anglo-Saxon Protestants, when poor and ghettoized, reincarnate the heroic tribalism depicted in *Beowulf* and other remnants of song from pre-Norman England. And that is why his poem, like *Beowulf*, enjoys archaic word-formation ("Dawndrizzle", "plasterwaste", "housepatterns"), archaic phrase-formation ("the lean fingerlings/Nordic nobblecheeked   not all clean of nose/leaping Commandowise   into leprous lanes") and archaic clause-formation (". . . housepatterns . . . unfold stuttering   stick like a phonograph"). Archaic lexis is actually less numerous than grammatical archaism ("farded", "-thewed", "handplay", "-thegns", "alehall", "Anglekin", "carling and leman", "clip").

Try out your grasp of consonant function in poetry by performing the following tasks:

1. Identify the alliterating consonant in single alliterating lines, the two alliterating consonants in double-alliterating lines.
2. Compare the abundance of alliteration in Birney's poem with the norms for alliteration in Old English poetry stated above (p. 13).
3. Identify lines in which alliteration is obscured by spelling conventions in modern English.
4. Identify places where a sound-rhythm emerges, not from repeated consonants, but from a repeated feature of articulation in otherwise dissimilar consonants.

IV. QUESTIONS FOR REVIEW

1. Can you give a meaning to each of these terms?

rhythm	affricates	centre
rhyme	diaphragm	dorsum
Petrarchan sonnet	trachea	continuants
sestet	larynx	resonants
octet	vocal cords	nasals
metre	lower vocal tract	lateral
alliteration	upper vocal tract	median
onomatopoeia	velum	bilabial
stress	nasalization	apico-alveolar
Old English	articulator	dorso-velar
caesura	point of articulation	labio-dental
voicing	alveolar ridge	inter-dental
voiced	hard palate	fronto-palatal
unvoiced	soft palate	glottal
stops	apex	minimal pair
fricatives	front	

2. Can you describe all the processes which you use in the formation of a single voiced stop consonant, starting with the contraction of the diaphragm? Of a voiceless stop consonant? Of voiced and voiceless fricatives? Of the affricates? Of the resonants?

3. The following symbols represent particular consonants. What is the articulatory name of each of these consonants?

    (a) /f/ (e.g. /f/ means *unvoiced labio-dental fricative*)

(b) /g/	(i) /k/	(p) /z/
(c) /ŋ/	(j) /d/	(q) /š/
(d) /b/	(k) /n/	(r) /h/
(e) /m/	(l) /ð/	(s) /ǰ/
(f) /l/	(m) /č/	(t) /p/
(g) /s/	(n) /v/	(u) /θ/
(h) /t/	(o) /r/	(v) /ž/

4. What is the difference in the sound of /t/ in "top", the sound of /t/ in "stop" and the sound of /t/ in "trade"? In what sense are these different sounds? In what sense are these the same sound? What could

you deduce about the effect of surrounding sounds on /t/? Do you think there is a minimal pair in the inventory of English words which distinguishes any of the different ways of articulating /t/ in "top", "stop" and "trade"?

5. In the following passage, the quality of consonants, the repetition of particular consonants and the repetition of a particular component in consonant articulation (e.g. voicing, fricative) all play important roles in reinforcing the literal sense of the text. Can you show how this is done?

And the shrill girls giggle and master around him and squeal as they clutch and thrash, and he blubbers away downhill with his patched pants falling, and his tear-splashed blush burns all the way as the triumphant bird-like sisters scream with buttons in their claws and the bully brothers hoot after him his little nickname and his mother's shame and his father's wickedness with the loose wild barefoot women of the hovels of the hills. It all means nothing at all, and, howling for his milky mum, for her cawl and buttermilk and cowbreath and welshcakes and the fat birth-smelling bed and moonlit kitchen of her arms, he'll never forget as he paddles blind home through the weeping end of the world. Then his tormentors tussle and run to the Cockle Street sweet-shop, their pennies sticky as honey, to buy from Miss Myfanwy Price, who is cocky and neat as a puff-bosomed robin and her small round buttocks tight as ticks, gobstoppers big as wens that rainbow as you suck, brandyballs, winegums, hundreds and thousands, liquorice sweet as sick, nougat to tug and ribbon out like another red rubbery tongue, gum to glue in girls'curls, crimson coughdrops to spit blood, ice-cream cornets, dandelion-and-burdock, raspberry and cherry-ade, pop goes the weasel and the wind.

—Dylan Thomas, *Under Milk Wood*

UNIT 2

Vowels: Articulation and Function

I. ANALYSIS: the Auditory Poetry of Dylan Thomas

DO NOT GO GENTLE INTO THAT GOOD NIGHT

Do not go gentle into that good night,   1
Old age should burn and rave at close of day;
Rage, rage against the dying of the light.

Though wise men at their end know dark is right,
Because their words had forked no lightning they   5
Do not go gentle into that good night.

Good men, the last wave by, crying how bright
Their frail deeds might have danced in a green bay,
Rage, rage against the dying of the light.

Wild men who caught and sang the sun in flight,   10
And learn, too late, they grieved it on its way,
Do not go gentle into that good night.

Grave men, near death, who see with blinding sight
Blind eyes could blaze like meteors and be gay,
Rage, rage against the dying of the light.   15

And you, my father, there on the sad height,
Curse, bless, me now with your fierce tears, I pray.
Do not go gentle into that good night.
Rage, rage against the dying of the light.   19

—Dylan Thomas

When a poet writes, he is commenting on his own situation in life, responding with his own concerns to the particular world in which he finds himself. For Dylan Thomas this response meant playing many roles: the poor country boy in love with poetry who struggles to find recognition, and ends up as a famous Welsh bard; the tavern ruffian, drinking and

26

womanizing his way to an early grave; the poetic prophet expounding and exemplifying his philosophy of beauty and death. The role of the bard is a familiar and traditional one in Wales, and so also is that of the tavern ruffian. The search for beauty that ends in death has come down to us from prehistoric times through the ancient Greeks. To these ready-made forms, Thomas easily adapted rich poetic gifts and an intense sensuality.

Dylan Thomas and G. M. Hopkins

Thomas' poem makes a good comparison with Hopkins', for in both we find an adaptation of traditional forms of poetry and traditional philosophies to personal purposes. Both poems exploit rhyme, metre and traditional stanza patterns; but both modify and expand these elements. Thomas and Hopkins were essentially religious poets, but Hopkins was a rigorously trained Christian theologian, and Thomas a natural pagan. Both men were profoundly sensual, but for Hopkins the beauty of life and nature was less significant than the God immanent to it. For Thomas this beauty was all there is: man's life is a tragedy of passing time.

The poem "Do not go gentle into that good night" is the poet's address to his dying father. It is written in the form of a "villanelle" with only two rhymes throughout and employing two refrains. The villanelle is an old French form with its origins in Italian part-songs like the madrigal. Because of the use of a traditional form, the address is formal; but because of the features that resemble songs—rhyme and refrain—it is also lyrical and musical. The villanelle, like the sonnet, is a vehicle suited to the expression of strong, personal feeling.

But the poem is also an argument which holds out for a certain course of action against an alternate course: that one should go violently, not gently, to one's death. The poet says at the end that his father's curse as he died would be a blessing to him, because it is appropriate for man to go fiercely to his doom—it reaffirms the value of life to the living. The argument is given in the form of four examples of four kinds of men responding to death ungently, each for different reasons, but reasons leading to the same end. Wise men rage because their wisdom has no power to illuminate the darkness which they know is inevitable. Good men rage as they sink because their good deeds can find no harbour against death's storm. Wild men rage because their good times have, ironically, only hurried death's onset. Grave men regret, near death, that they did not enjoy life more.

Beneath this obvious message of the poem there are ambiguities. Despite the exhortation to resist death, death itself seems to have value. It is a "good" night. Wise men know that "dark is right". Against that darkness, joyful actions glow "like meteors", which otherwise would be unremarked. A certain place is, although sad, a "height"—something above a normal experience. The message, then, is two-fold: this orphic voice celebrates beauty *and* death. It is life's nature to resist death; yet death is fundamental to the life which originates in it, shines most beautifully against its black backdrop, rages against it and dies again into it. Death has value, too.

In "God's Grandeur" there is no similar paradox. Life and nature are fecund, eternally returning because underlying them is an infinite plenitude of life and light. Life emerges out of life and returns to life. There is no struggle with, and no necessity to struggle with, death; for there is no death in an ultimate sense.

Just as in "God's Grandeur" the theme of the world "charged" with the grandeur of God was reflected in even the smallest elements of language, so also is Thomas' paradoxical theme of life in death here. In discussing that poem, we focused on the consonant. Here, we will be focusing on the vowel.

First, let's review all the formal ways in which, in poetry, sounds may be repeated in the syllable. The syllable is structured as a "nucleus" (usually a vowel) and an "envelope" (the consonants). The envelope may be entirely absent, absent before or after the nucleus, or entirely present.

Repetition is repetition of every sound in the syllable, although these might be spelled differently: hey/hey, hey/hay.

Rhyme is repetition of the vowel, but with a different previous consonant, and the same end consonant: f<u>eat</u>/b<u>eat</u>/sw<u>eet</u>. The previous consonant may be omitted in one of a rhyming pair, but not both since that would produce repetition: f<u>eat</u>/<u>eat</u>. The end consonants of *both* rhyming members of a pair may also be omitted: fl<u>ea</u>/t<u>ea</u>/<u>ee</u>.

Alliteration is basically repetition of the previous consonant, with or without vowel repetition or repetition of the end consonant—but not with both: <u>f</u>eat/<u>f</u>ate/<u>f</u>eel/<u>f</u>ee/<u>f</u>ew.

Assonance is repetition of the vowel but with a different end consonant, and the same, or different, or no previous consonant: f<u>ea</u>t/f<u>ea</u>r/b<u>ea</u>d/<u>ee</u>l.

Consonance is basically repetition of the end consonant, but with a different vowel and the same, or different, or no previous consonant: fea<u>t</u>/figh<u>t</u>/ha<u>t</u>e/i<u>t</u>.

The effects of vowel patterning in the poem can be seen in three areas: rhyme, assonance and onomatopoeia.

Vowel Patterns: Rhyme

Because the poem is a villanelle, the two sounds that repeat in the rhymes, "-ight" and "-ay", are especially important. These sounds are associated with significant meaning in their first appearances, for the first is carried by the word "night", the second by "day". If we look at the distribution of these two rhymes in the poem, we find the "-ight" rhyme occurs at the end of 13 lines in the poem, the "-ay" rhyme at the end of 6, with the word "night" closing 4 of the 19 lines: an overwhelming dominance of death. Yet the first word that rhymes with "night" is "light"; and the paradox of this contrasting meaning is reinforced subsequently with "right", "bright", "flight", "sight", and "height"—all concepts opposed in some way to the negative "night". Thus the single most powerful formal feature of the poem, its rhyme scheme, consistently underlines Thomas' paradoxical theme. The contrast of night and day (death and life) also seems to be reinforced by the contrast between the sounds of the words. "Night" ends in a consonant stop, while "day", as a vowel sound, stays open and prolongable.

Vowel Patterns: Assonance

The nuclei of the rhyming syllables are vowel sounds which also appear in significant positions elsewhere in the poem, as we discover when we examine assonance. Assonance is to vowels what alliteration is to consonants. In Old English poetry all vowels whatsoever that appeared as the first sound in a word were considered formally assonant with each other. They were incorporated in the formal structure of verse in the same way as alliterated consonants were. Our modern use of the term, however, refers only to the repetition of the *same* vowel, no matter where it appears in the word. If assonance occurs on a stressed syllable it is more powerful in its rhythmic effect, just as alliteration is.

Assonance, like alliteration, depends on the *perceived* identity of certain vowels, although these vowels may in fact have different sound characteristics. Vowel articulation is modified by the consonants before and after: thus the nuclei in "old" and in "close" are slightly different. As with alliteration, assonance occurs between *classes* of vowel sounds.

To continue our previous analysis, the vowel sounds which form the nuclei of the rhyming syllables of the poem, "-igh-" and "-ay", also appear significantly in the second line of the poem, which introduces the "-ay" sound as part of the second rhyme, and in the third line, which introduces the second refrain. In the second line of the poem the pattern of assonance goes like this:

Old áge should búrn and ráve at clóse of dáy.

The "-ay" sound appears three times, each time in a stressed syllable; and in addition there is further assonance with the "-o-" sound which appears twice. Since the first line is relatively free of assonance, our attention is drawn, consciously or subliminally, to the importance of sound patterning in the poem, and to the special significance of the sound "-ay". This is a significance immediately reinforced by the third line:

Ráge, ráge against the dýing of the líght.

The "-ay" sound is repeated twice more, in a repeated, stressed syllable. In addition, this line, the second refrain of the poem, picks up the "-igh-" sound abandoned in line 2. The line ends with its repetition in accented syllables:

dýing . . . líght.

If we look at the meaning patterns that parallel these sound patterns we find at the beginning of the line the strongest possible protest, life in its most energetic manifestation: "rage". The line ends, however, with the "dying of the light" that supported that protest.

Other assonantal effects in the poem include line 4 where the triple complex of assonance and rhyme "though"/"know", "men"/"end", "wise"/"right" parallels the idea of balance and complexity in intellectual argument; line 7 where the cluster of "-igh-" sounds at the end of the line extends the sound of "cry"; line 8 where assonance combines with alliteration to produce a complex pattern in sound:

Their frail deeds might have danced in a green bay;

line 10 where the assonance of the first and last vowels of the line helps to present the line as a single unit; line 11 where the rhyme of "they"/"way" anchors the last half of the line, as the alliteration of "learn"/"late" (linked to "they"/"way" by assonance) anchors the first; lines 13 and 14 where the cluster of "-igh-" sounds surrounded by the "-ee-" sounds ties the two lines together; and line 17 where the strong assonance of "me", "fierce" and "tears" combines with the strong consonance of "curse, bless" and "fierce". Both sound patterns share the item "fierce", an effect that runs parallel to the lexical juxtapositions of "curse, bless" and "fierce tears".

Vowel Patterns: Onomatopoeia

As we have already begun to see, vowels, like consonants, have their place in onomatopoeia: the quality of a stretch of text whose sounds seem in some way to parallel context, though there can never be a one-to-one correspondence of sound to sense. Lines 1 and 2 are excellent examples.

They contrast in sense and rhythm and vowel structures. Line 1 falls into two halves with parallel rhythms:

Do not gó géntle / into that góod níght.

The line is divided in its rhythmic impulse as it is in its meaning. The negative "not" contradicts the imperative "go gentle". The expression "good night" ironically stands for "death". Line 2 is a single unit with a steady and emphatic beat:

Óld áge should búrn and ráve at clóse of dáy.

In addition, line 2 employs a great deal of assonance to structure vowel sound in a firm way. Line 1 does not. Instead we find *partial* or suggested sound patterns. The sounds of the first half of the line (Do not go gentle) are similar to those of the last half (into that good night) but the similarity is undercut rather than emphasized. The first words of each half of the line rhyme (Do/to) but these are not stressed syllables. The next two words show consonance (not/that) but again are not stressed. The next two words alliterate and are stressed (go/good). The strength of this is startling, but is immediately denied by the following words which are utterly different in sound (gentle/night). The absence after the initial "Do/to" of any repeated vowel sounds contrasts strikingly with line 2. The sense of line 2 is also reinforced onomatopoeically, not only through assonance but also through a repeated tensing of the musculature characteristic of these vowels and some others, and through the extension of the vowel sound by following continuant consonants: "Old age should burn and rave at close of day". The line ends on a vowel, which can also be extended.

   In the first two lines of the poem not only is the theme introduced, but also the kinds of sound structurings that will support that theme throughout the poem. In the first two lines of the last stanza a similar contrast between gentleness and determination is echoed in the sound patterns. The second line of this stanza has very strong patterns of assonance and consonance, as we have seen:

Cúrse, bléss, me now with your fiérce teárs, I práy.

Among the strongest of these is the assonance of the consecutive stressed words "fierce tears". The first line has nothing to compare with this strength.

   These two lines are also remarkable in the poem as a whole because they are the only lines where Thomas uses the first-person pronouns, betraying his own involvement in his argument. The emphasis seems to be still on the father, the "you" he is addressing, but two of the first-person pronouns are in assonance, although they are unstressed syllables: "my" with "height" in the first line; "me" with "fierce tears" in the second. The involvement with his father's moment of truth is clearly revealed by the last two words of the second line, the ironic (in the absence of Eternity) "I pray". The connotations of "father", "height", "bless", and "pray" create a religious aura around this section of the poem, making the plight of the pagan Thomas apparent. Is it only coincidence that the two syllables "I pray" contain the two most prominent vowel sounds of the poem, those associated with "death" and "life"? In Thomas, it seems, they will stand forever in perfect juxtaposition.

II. FRAMEWORK: Production of Vowel Sounds

As YOU remember from Unit 1, sound production is originated by the contraction of the diaphragm, the subsequent compression of air in the lower vocal tract, and (optionally) the excitation of the vocal cords. The sound is modulated in the oral cavity by the juxtaposition of articulators like the tongue and lower lip to points of articulation such as the upper lip, the teeth, and the roof of the mouth. The sounds so produced are called consonants and are classified according to the modulation techniques used. Each separate technique adds an essential feature to define the consonant. Despite the degree of variation possible within these defined classes of sound, there is sufficient similarity to make contrasts between words possible.

One feature of consonants which is not in the strictest sense part of articulation is voicing. In voicing the vocal cords are actively vibrating in the air stream. Some consonants are voiced: /b/, /d/, /g/, /v/, /ð/, /z/, /ž/, /ǰ/, /m/, /n/, /ŋ/, /l/, /r/. Other are not voiced: /p/, /t/, /k/, /f/, /θ/, /s/, /š/, /h/, /č/. *All vowels are voiced.*

Some consonants are modulated by using the tongue as the articulator: /d/, /g/, /t/, /k/, /ð/, /z/, /ž/, /θ/, /s/, /š/, /ǰ/, /č/, /n/, /ŋ/, /l/, /r/. Others are not: /b/, /p/, /v/, /f/, /h/, /m/. *All vowels are articulated by deployment of the tongue.*

Articulation of the Vowels

The crucial characteristic of vowel production is the position of the uppermost curvature of the tongue. This is so because, in general, vowels are produced by a resonating air column whose exact audible quality is a function of the internal shape of the oral cavity as created by the tongue position. When the tongue's curvature is relatively forward in the mouth, "front" vowels result. The *height* of the curvature distinguishes the different front vowels. The "high" front vowels are: /i/ "seat", /ɪ/ "sit". The "mid" front vowels are: /e/ "sate", /ɛ/ "set". The "low" front vowel is /æ/ "sat".

When the tongue's curvature is relatively back in the mouth, "back" vowels result, which are also distinguished by the height of the curvature. The "high" back vowels are: /u/ "boot", /U/ "put". The "mid" back vowels are: /o/ "or", /ɔ/ "taught". The low back vowel is /ɑ/ "top". Not all speakers may produce all the same vowels in this group. There are many British Commonwealth and North American regional variations, especially in the vowels /i/, /e/, /u/, /ɑ/. Speakers in the southern United States may employ diphthongs (see below) in place of the first three of these vowels. The /o/ vowel also presents a special difficulty in exemplification, since it rarely occurs in Modern English in isolation, but usually in conjunction with a sound modification known as a "back glide", of which more later. In "or" the glide tends to be obscured by the following /r/ consonant.

When the tongue's curvature is in the centre of the mouth, "central" vowels are produced. The "high" central vowel is represented by the second syllable of "Cuba" (/ə/). In North American English, it usually appears in unstressed syllables only. The "mid" central vowel is /ʌ/ "putt". The "low" central vowel is /a/ "pop". Some speakers may have either /a/ or /ɑ/, but not both. Such speakers will pronounce "top" and "pop" as rhymes. The following diagram correlates the tongue positions and the vowel inventory.

		Front	Central	Back		
	Closed	/i/ "beet"		/u/ "boot"	Closed	
High			/ə/ "a(bout)"			High
	Open	/ɪ/ "bit"		/U/ "put"	Open	
	Closed	/e/ "bait"		/o/ "or"	Closed	
Mid			/ʌ/ "cut"			Mid
	Open	/ɛ/ "bet"		/ɔ/ "taught"	Open	
Low		/æ/ "bat"	/a/ "cot"	/ɑ/ "fa(ther)"		Low

Diagram of vowel articulations

Secondary Vowel Characteristics

Some other features of vowel articulation are called "secondary" vowel characteristics. "Aperture" is one of these. The different vowel articulations are associated with different degrees of openness of the mouth (the distance between the jaws). In general, the higher the vowel, the more closed the aperture. But for each "high" and "mid" pair, one of the vowels has a relatively more closed and one a relatively more open aperture. The high (relatively) closed vowels are /i/ (front) and /u/ (back). The high (relatively) open vowels are /ɪ/ (front) and /U/ (back). The mid (relatively) closed vowels are /e/ and /o/; the mid (relatively) open are /ɛ/ and /ɔ/. It is customary to refer to this contrast simply as "closed" and "open", with the understanding that we are talking about the *relative* degree of aperture in each pair of front or back vowels at a particular height. (See vowel diagram.) Thus the definitions front, central, back combined with the possibilities of closed and open in the classes high and mid give us the possibility of twelve vowels, of which the four front and four back vowels have been distinguished so far in our description.

"Rounding" is another secondary vowel characteristic. Different vowels are partially the result of different lip-roundness or puckering. In general, back vowels are rounded, and front vowels "retracted". The higher the back vowel the more rounded it is. Hence, the high back vowel /u/ as exemplified in "boot" is the most rounded.

As is well known to ventriloquists, both aperture and rounding are less essential than the position of the curvature of the tongue in the oral cavity, in that the vowels can nearly be articulated without them.

"Duration" is another secondary characteristic of vowels. The terms "long" and "short" should be taken to mean relative duration in real time. The absolute duration of vowels is really a function of stress timing which will be discussed in the next unit. But in general, the vowels /ɪ/, /ɛ/, /æ/, /a/, /ɔ/, /U/ tend to be *perceived* by most people as shorter than /i/, /e/, /ɑ/, /o/, /u/, everything else being equal. The "closed" vowels are longer than the "open". Hence, /u/ in "boot" is perceived as longer than /U/ in "put".

"Tension" is another secondary characteristic of vowels. The musculature involved in the sound production is more tense for some vowels than for others. Tense vowels are the "long" vowels /i/, /e/, /ɑ/, /o/, /u/. The others are called "lax".

Contrasts in all four of these secondary characteristics may contribute to extended assonantal and onomatopoeic effects, and so these characteristics are as important for our purposes as the distinctions between vowels themselves. For example, in line 2 of Thomas' poem—"Old age should burn and rave at close of day"—the /o/ and /e/ vowels are both long, stressed, closed and tense, which results in a markedly extended, tension-filled line. In addition, the stressed vowel in "burn", for Thomas' British pronunciation, is one that North Americans do not have; and it is also long, stressed, closed and tense.

Diphthongs

The syllable, as we have said, consists of a vowel nucleus and a consonant envelope. The nucleus is the peak of air compression, what is known as the breath "pulse"; and so it is also the peak of auditory prominence. The nucleus is also a carrier of voicing and of changes in pitch. (As any singer will tell you, one "sings" on the vowels.) It is the nature of the whole syllable that really defines the vowel. Whether preceding or following consonants are present, whether they are voiced, whether the syllable is stressed, whether the syllable carries a change in tune: all affect the vowel sound.

Syllables may also be constructed with diphthongs. A diphthong consists of two different vowel positions plus the movement between them. Diphthongs may be seen as comprising the nucleus and the "posterior", or following part of the envelope. In this latter case the glide or movement from one vowel position to the other functions like a consonant. Compare the minimal pair "pot"/"pie".

It is the movement of the tongue's curvature from one place to another in the oral cavity that produces the "glide". The glide referred to here is always an upward movement of the tongue (from low or mid to high), but can be either to the front or to the back. The "front" glide is a gliding of the tongue bulge from /a/ (in some speakers /ɑ/) or from /o/ (in some speakers /ɔ/) towards the position of /i/. The "back" glide is from /o/ or /a/ (in some speakers /ɑ/) towards the position of /u/. Both these glides are called "off-glides". Notationally we will represent the diphthongs as /aɪ/ ("buy"), /ɔɪ/ ("boy"), /oU/ ("bow") and /aU/ ("bough"). Additional diphthongs may be encountered in various regions of the Commonwealth and North America. Speakers in the southern United States tend to have front-glide and back-glide diphthongs which they use in place of the simple vowels /i/, /e/, /u/. See the following diagram of the diphthongs.

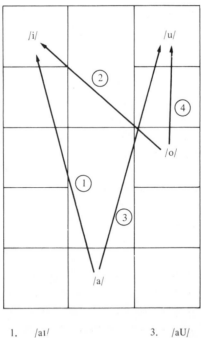

1.	/aɪ/	3.	/aU/
2.	/ɔɪ/	4.	/oU/

Diagram of diphthong articulations

Semi-vowels

Some consonants resemble vowels in articulation. The voiced consonants resemble vowels since they involve vocal-cord vibration. Resonant consonants resemble vowels in being modulated resonations of the nasal and/or oral cavities: /m/, /n/, /ŋ/, /l/, /r/. But two other consonants resemble vowels since they are *glides from* the /i/ or /u/ positions to any one of several vowel positions; notationally these are /j/ as in "yet", "yonder", and /w/ as in "win", "wombat". These are called "semi-vowels". They are also called "on-glides" because they glide *from* the /i/ or /u/ positions onto simple vowel positions, whereas diphthongs, the off-glides, glide off the simple vowels toward the /i/ or /u/ positions. Semi-vowels, like the resonants and other voiced consonants, are phonetically like vowels, that is, in the features of their sound production; but they *function* in the syllable like consonants, being usually classified as part of the envelope, rather than the nucleus. To explain why they are so classified requires first a review of the concept of "functionalism".

The purpose of consonants, vowels and diphthongs is to form different arrangements of sound to serve as symbols for concepts. The inventory of significant sounds must necessarily be a limited one, or the whole process becomes futile. Thus, limits to individual variation are tacitly agreed on by speakers of a given language and everything within those limits is classed as one sound for functional purposes. This functional sound is called a "phoneme", and it is really a class of all variants within its limits, these variants being called "allophones".

Since semi-vowels occur at the front or "prior" part of the envelope in the syllable, they occupy the same place as other consonants. If we investigate semi-vowels using the minimal pair technique outlined in the previous unit, we find that they contrast only with consonants ("yet"/"bet", "win"/"tin"). That is why they function like consonants although they are articulated similarly to vowels and diphthongs.

By definition, the infinite variety of variation within the limits of the phoneme does not change one phoneme into another. Some of that variety is the product of the influence of neighbouring sounds. For example, the quality of a glide is affected by the simple vowel adjacent to it. This kind of variation, although not affecting meaning since it does not change the recognition of the phoneme, does contribute—like the secondary characteristics of vowels—to assonantal and onomatopoeic effects.

Analysis of the building blocks of language, speech production, is necessarily a subtle and sensual business requiring both a knowledge of the body and a trained ear. The poet has these abilities in another sense. He may not classify as he writes, but his body does respond as he repeats his own words, and his ear makes subtle distinctions. Poets probably arrange their vowel sequences as the result of both how the vowels "feel"—the physical sensations of articulation—and how they sound—the more conventional perceived assonances. There seems to have been a shift in contemporary poetry away from alliteration and assonance, the generally perceived sound patternings, toward more subtle combinations. This has resulted from a de-emphasizing of an overtly poetic register in favour of something that is *perceived* as closer to "ordinary" speech. In fact, this disguised poetic register is as highly organized as the traditional one; it is simply subtler. The general public, in consequence, tends to be mystified and prefer the old "real poetry". It does take a fairly sophisticated knowledge of vocal characteristics to show the sound patterns in a subtle contemporary poem. We ourselves have limited our discussions to poems employing more obvious features. Nevertheless, you now have the knowledge and the vocabulary to describe the features of vowels that you can hear. Can you hear them?

III. APPLICATION: Sound patterning in Byron

REPETITION, rhyme, alliteration, assonance and consonance all play a part in the very rich tapestry of sound woven by Lord Byron in the following poem:

SHE WALKS IN BEAUTY

She walks in Beauty, like the night   1
    Of cloudless climes and starry skies;
And all that's best of dark and bright
    Meet in her aspect and her eyes:
Thus mellow'd to that tender light   5
    Which Heaven to gaudy day denies.

One shade the more, one ray the less,
    Had half impair'd the nameless grace
Which waves in every raven tress,
    Or softly lightens o'er her face;   10
Where thoughts serenely sweet express
    How pure, how dear their dwelling-place.

And on that cheek, and o'er that brow,
    So soft, so calm, yet eloquent,
The smiles that win, the tints that glow,   15
    But tell of days in goodness spent,
A mind at peace with all below,
    A heart whose love is innocent!   18

—Hebrew Melodies, 1815

Byron is describing simultaneously a black-haired, black-eyed beauty, and the bright moon; a sensually beautiful woman and her innocent purity. The charm in her, and in Byron's poem, lies in the combination of opposites. Somewhere behind this poem lies the old earth-centred world-view which divided the universe into the two regions above and beneath the moon. Beneath the moon lies the mortal, natural world; above it, all is eternal, unchanging. For man, standing "below" on the mortal earth, the moon "above" is the symbol of purity. Women, also, were seen as "pure" above, but "natural" below. The romantic poets rebelled against these rigid divisions, and here we see Byron's attempt to combine nature and purity, above and below, "dark and bright" into one unity of beauty. His, like

Dylan Thomas', is essentially a pagan attempt to see bright life as more beautiful when set against the darkness of mortality, as the moon is beautiful against the clear night sky, as a woman's brow seems whiter against raven hair, and her eyes brightest when blackest.

Just as the theme of Thomas' poem was supported by vowel patterning, so is Byron's. Can you show:

1. The richness of the over-all sound patterning?
2. The use of rhyme in combination with other elements of sound patterning to reinforce the idea of the combination of opposites?
3. The use of assonance within individual lines, and also to bind lines together?
4. The function of vowel sounds in creating onomatopoeic effects in individual lines, for example, the third line of stanza 2?

IV. QUESTIONS FOR REVIEW

1. Can you give a meaning to each of these terms?

vowel	duration
nucleus	tension
rhyme	breath pulse
alliteration	diphthong
consonance	front glide
assonance	back glide
front, central, back vowels	off-glide
high, mid, low vowels	on-glide
secondary characteristics of vowels	semi-vowel
aperture	phoneme
rounding	allophone

2. What is the crucial characteristic of vowel production? How is a diphthong produced? A semi-vowel? Can you produce all the sounds in the two vowel charts? Are any of the sounds *not* distinguished in your idiolect? Are other vowel sounds distinguished which are *not* on the chart?

3. Give an example of: a low front vowel, a high back vowel, a mid front vowel, an open high front vowel, a closed mid back vowel, a low central vowel, a closed high front vowel.

4. For one line of Byron's poem in which assonance and repetition do *not* occur, chart the vowels according to the diagram of vowel articulations. Is there a pattern in this sequence? Is the pattern onomatopoeic? Can you find a line in which the sequence of vowel sounds is onomatopoeic, in addition to any onomatopoeic effects produced by repetition, rhyme, or assonance?

5. The following poem has fun with language in many ways in order to make fresh again its eternal theme. Can you describe the fun it has with vowel patternings? The joke involves fulfilling expectations in an unexpected way.

LOVE IS MORE THICKER THAN FORGET

love is more thicker than forget   1
more thinner than recall
more seldom than a wave is wet
more frequent than to fail

it is most mad and moonly   5
and less it shall unbe
than all the sea which only
is deeper than the sea

love is less always than to win
less never than alive   10
less bigger than the least begin
less littler than forgive

it is most sane and sunly
and more it cannot die
than all the sky which only   15
is higher than the sky

—E. E. Cummings

6. Discuss the theme of this poem, and how the vowel patterning
   supports it.

UNIT 3

Stress, Juncture and Tune

I. ANALYSIS: Rhythm and Measure in a Modern Poem

ACQUAINTED WITH THE NIGHT

I have been one acquainted with the night.   1
I have walked out in rain—and back in rain.
I have outwalked the furthest city light.

I have looked down the saddest city lane.
I have passed by the watchman on his beat   5
And dropped my eyes, unwilling to explain.

I have stood still and stopped the sound of feet
When far away an interrupted cry
Came over houses from another street,

But not to call me back or say good-bye;   10
And further still at an unearthly height,
One luminary clock against the sky

Proclaimed the time was neither wrong nor right.
I have been one acquainted with the night.   14

—Robert Frost

The task in writing a poem of alienation is to produce an absence of expressed emotion together with the suggestion of mighty emotions unreleased. One solution is to mechanize activity, thus suggesting power without life, activity without self-will. The repetitive action of walking is a good example of this. If we add to this action a hint of aimlessness by stopping the march for a moment, and then having it go on as before, we have a good image of what it is like to feel no sense of purpose, but be possessed by the need to act. Frost reinforces this image through the careful manipulation of sound patterns to echo the rhythm of mechanical, purposeless walking.

43

Robert Frost

Frost is an American poet who, like Dylan Thomas, acted out the same archetypal roles in both his literature and his life. Frost played the New England Yankee, the farmer famous for his poems of rural life, and for descriptions of common scenes that suggest metaphysical conceptions: woods with snow falling, people on a beach staring out to sea, a crossroads. This was despite the fact that he made his reputation in sophisticated London and was most definitely an aware and professional writer, rather than the intuitively wise farmer he seemed. Yet he did live the rural life of a farmer in after-years; and this plain role is reflected in his poetry through understatement, and in the suggestion of speech rhythms in traditional metres.

"Acquainted with the Night", however, is an urban poem, and more contemporary than traditional in its theme. Yet the understatement is there in the first line in the word "acquainted"; and it is in the commonplace term "night", used for something that is complex and frightening, whether it is despair or isolation or—as in Dylan Thomas' poem—the knowledge of inevitable extinction.

Where "God's Grandeur", faced with the spoiling of the world, revealed cause for optimism in the constant replenishment of that world by God, and where Dylan Thomas found a form of consolation in death as the necessary complement to life, this poem is concerned simply to express the feeling itself: despair, repetition, isolation, alienation. No solution is offered; the poem ends as it began. Like the previous two poems, however, this poem employs an argument structure. It states a thesis, produces a series of examples, and restates the thesis. But the thesis does not attempt to illuminate the nature of the world or of human existence. It is simply a statement about one individual's experience. Perhaps this is a gesture away from alienation, towards solidarity—the sharing of a human experience with others. Yet, ironically, the experience shared is of isolation.

The structure of the poem oddly combines the forms of the sonnet and the villanelle. Like an Elizabethan sonnet it has 14 lines and a final couplet. Like a villanelle it is built of 3-line stanzas, and ends with a refrain. The rhymes that form a chain, one stanza to another, reinforce the sense of sequence in both the argument form and the walking activity described. Yet the stanzas remain separate units since their beginning and ending lines rhyme. In a way, the poem ironically reverses the movement of the sonnet, since, though it raises the possibility of something happening, this turns out to be simply more of the same; the poem closes with the same situation it begins with, rather than leading to a resolution. Perhaps this reversal is reflected in the fact that it divides thematically into a sestet and octet, rather than the usual sonnet's octet and sestet.

The poem is also unusual in beginning with four consecutive one-sentence lines. This establishes a repetitive pattern that is reinforced in turn by a degree of lexical repetition and grammatical parallelism. It is against this strongly established monotony that the abortive attempts to make a human contact are staged.

Supra-segmentals

However, our particular interest here is with sound, in so far as it supports the sense, and this time not with sound broken into its smallest units—consonants and vowels known as "segmentals"—but with the features of more extended sound patterns: the so-called supra-segmentals. There are three of these. *Stress* is a contrastive device that depends on the unequal prominence of consecutive syllables. Contrast "bláckbird" with "bláck bírd". *Time* in language is both real and apparent. The real time that it takes to say a given syllable depends partly on the vowel selected, but also partly on the distribution of stress, of which more later. Apparent or perceived time may be exemplified by the perception of boundaries between morphemes. Contrast "night rate" and "nitrate". It is not so much a differing pause between the syllables, as a change in the "t" and "r" pronunciations that makes the distinction. *Tune* in language is pitch change. Contrast "He went home" with "He went home?". The first ordinarily has falling pitch, the second, rising. All of the supra-segmentals are ordered in Frost's poem to produce specific effects supporting his theme.

Stress Rhythm

Stress and time together produce rhythm, which is stress at regular intervals. Traditionally, rhythm is analyzed by comparing the actual stresses of a poem's language to an idealized model. For example, the model for iambic pentametre is: /˘´/˘´/˘´/˘´/˘´/. Using the traditional two-stress system for now, the first line of Frost's poem may be analyzed as:

/Í hăve/ been one/ ăcquáint/ ĕd wǐth/ thĕ níght/.

The following rules apply. Divide the line into five two-syllable feet. Only one, but not necessarily any, syllable per foot is stressed. The last foot may have any number of unstressed syllables, but must have one stressed one. Comparing the ideal with the actual, we find three feet coincide. The trochee when it occurs in the first foot is a permissible variation, as is the foot without a stress. Enough feet conform to the ideal to establish it as a pattern, but only in our minds. It is the double perception of pattern plus conformity or exception that makes this sort of scansion interesting intellectually. The catch is that only the actual can be voiced or heard. If we distort the actual to capture the ideal, we falsify language. All too many readers of poetry do just that.

Fortunately, the poets themselves seem to write poetry with their bodies, not their minds. Our task now is to learn to scan Frost's lines so that we get a rhythmic pattern equivalent to what we actually feel, which is also a pattern distinctively different from the patterns of prose and speech. Let us look first at the patterns of prose and speech. We use, when we speak, two different kinds of sound-producing impulses. There is a "chest" pulse produced by contraction of the chest muscles for formation of an ordinary syllable. There is also a stronger "stress" pulse produced by an especially strong contraction of the chest muscles. This forms a stressed syllable.

In English the stress pulse which makes the stressed syllable is "isochronous", that is, it is produced at regular intervals in real time. But the chest pulse is not isochronous, since we may have any number of unstressed syllables between the stressed ones.

For example, tap out with a pencil:

"Thís ĭs thĕ hóuse thăt Jáck búilt"

making a louder tap for the stressed syllables. Now tap again, without tapping for the unstressed syllables. Do you feel the regularity of the stressed syllables? They carry rhythm because they occur at regular intervals in time. This rhythm is present in speech, prose and poetry. What sets verse apart from the others is an increased tendency to regularity in the distribution of the unstressed syllables. In perfectly regular verse metre, the number of unstressed syllables between the stresses would always be the same. Most verse tends to such regularity, without actually achieving it.

But now for the surprise. Because stress is a function of stress pulse rather than articulation or voicing, it is possible to have *silent* stress; and indeed in Frost's poem silent stress is one of the major features that make it so effective. In

/Í hăve bĕen /óne ăc /quáintĕd /(X̆)wĭth thĕ /níght/

the silent stress is indicated by "(X)". The difference between this and traditional scansion is one silent stress. That may seem unimportant until we see the beauty of using a system that describes rather than prescribes.

Compare this actual reading with the distortion produced by the attempt to approach an "iambic" ideal:

/Ĭ háve/ beĕn óne/ ăcquáint/ ĕd wíth/ thĕ níght/.

This is a reading too often heard. (See the diagram on the next page for a complete analysis of the poem; stressed syllables are underlined.)

Diagramming actual stresses, of course, requires a performance text; and that requires choices of pronunciation; and that in turn requires interpretation, since the position of a stress helps to determine meaning. We have chosen a slow, serious performance, since that seems to reflect the sense. A faster performance might become humorous like the speeded-up walking of old movies. We have also decided to stress the initial "I" of the first and last lines, which emphasizes that the poem is making a personal assertion. To stress "have" instead would have the effect of insisting on the truth of the statement: "I *have* been one . . .". This interpretation seems less likely since it requires some context not provided, and seems shrill rather than solemn. Following our diagram you should be able to make out our reading, and hence our interpretation. Shifting the stresses produces a different interpretation. Hence assigning stress, within reasonable limits, is really a matter of deciding what you want, just as an actor or director decides on a given reading of a line within the limits of a play.

The silent stresses still require some explanation, particularly the ones at the beginning of the lines. Traditionally, the ends of lines suggest a pause either of real or apparent time (cf. "juncture" below). This pause is enhanced if it coincides with major grammatical boundaries. We have already noticed the extreme use of this effect in the first four lines of the poem. But the real point is that this silent pause may carry a stress. That stress is marked at the beginning of the next line. This locates it in a convenient position, because several unaccented syllables at the beginning of that next line may be members of the foot initiated by the final silent stress of the previous line. (By convention, in this type of analysis the foot is considered to run from a stressed through any intervening unstressed syllables up to, but not including the next stressed syllable.) A caesura, a pause in the middle of the line, may also carry a stress.

The major effect of stress in Frost's poem, as we have assigned it, is to make of each line a "measure", for aside from lines 1, 2, 12 and 14, there are six stresses in every line. The other requirement for a "measure" is that the ends of the lines be marked; and here they are marked both by rhyme and by silent stresses (though for convenience we have placed that silent stress at the beginning of the following line). Assonance, and a monosyllabic foot (if not occurring before in the line), may also mark the end of a measure. Such a single monosyllabic foot does end lines 1, 9, 10, 13, 14. The

Stress and tune in "Acquainted with the Night"

1.	I have been	one ac	quain ted	(X) with the	night. ↘	
2.	(X) I have	walked	out in	rain – ↗	(X) and	back in	rain. ↘
3.	(X) I have	out	walked the	fur thest	ci ty	light. ↘
4.	(X) I have	looked	down the	sad dest	ci ty	lane. ↘
5.	(X) I have	passed	by the	watch man	(X) on his	beat ↗
6.	(X) And	dropped my	eyes, ↘	(X) un	will ing to ex	plain. ↘
7.	(X) I have	stood	still and ↗	stopped the	sound of	feet ↗
8.	(X) When	far a	way	(X) an in ter	rup ted	cry ↗
9.	(X) Came	o ver	hou ses	(X) from a	no ther	street, ↘
10.	(X) But	not to	call me ↘	back or	say good-	bye; ↘
11.	(X) And	fur ther	still	(X) at an un	earth ly ↗	height,
12.	One	lum i na ry	clock a	gainst the	sky ↗	
13.	(X) Pro	claimed the	time was	nei ther	wrong nor	right. ↘
14.	I have been	one ac	quain ted	(X) with the ↘	night.	

establishment of this measure contributes powerfully to the repetitive effect of the poem. (We might note in passing that modern poetry often does *not* use such an auditory measure, substituting instead other kinds of prosody.)

A second major effect flows from the extensive use of silent stress. Every line except 11, 13 and 14 ends on a silent stress. In addition, eight of the fourteen caesuras carry silent stress. This is an effect impossible to detect using traditional metrics. The abundance of silent stresses effectively slows the pace of the poem.

The use of a monosyllabic foot is also striking in its effect. If this occurs anywhere but in conjunction with a silent stress it means that two consecutive syllables must be stressed. The necessary extension of these syllables in real time, in combination with appropriate lexis, further slows the pace of the poem. The effect occurs in consecutive lines 2, 3, 4, 5, and is emphasized by grammatical parallels as well. The effect occurs elsewhere in different lexical contexts, consequently with a different impact. In line 7 it is associated with an account of coming to a halt. In line 12 the lexis suggests isolation, as single stress follows single stress. In lines 2, 6, 8, 11 a second adjacent stress is silent; and this produces a pause in the movement of the poem, a pause that effectively parallels the lexis at these points. At the end of all lines except 11, 13, 14, the monosyllabic foot followed by a silent stress creates the most powerful rhythmic effect in the poem.

Tune

Tune also is important to this poem. There are five basic tunes in English, and they may occur in a single syllable or stretched over many. Variations in tune discriminate meaning. For example, "Oh" with a moderate rise in pitch (tune #3) may express initial receipt of information; with falling pitch (tune #1), disappointment; with fast-rising pitch (tune #2), puzzlement ("Oh?"); with a fall and then a rise (tune #4), excitement ("Oh?"); with a rise–fall (tune #5), dismay. In declarative sentences there is typically a fall at the end (tune #1) to signify the end. In an interrogative sentence there is typically a rise at the end (tune #2). A moderate rise (tune #3) indicates something unfinished, more to come, and is frequently associated with a dash. The fall–rise (tune #4) is an extreme version of the interrogative. The rise–fall (tune #5) is an emphatic version of finality. Tunes may override other signals; for example, a rise may convert a declarative to an interrogative.

Like stress, the assignment of tune to a written text is a function of interpretation; but again this is true only within limits. There are obviously more and less plausible interpretations. The most effective use of tune in Frost's poem is in fact a function of grammar and depends for its effect on the monotonous background of silent stresses which occur after the end of nearly every line. Through the first four lines this silent stress coincides with the end of declarative sentences and so also with falling tune; but in line 5 the sentence does not end, so the falling tune is suspended until halfway through line 6. Nevertheless, the silent stress after the end of the line does occur. The effect is of a delayed ending. The tune is expected, does not come, and then comes at last in the next line. The same thing happens through lines 7 and 8 where the tune does not drop, despite the presence of the silent stresses, only to drop finally at the end of line 9. In lines 11 and 12 the same thing happens, the tune not dropping despite the silent stress at the end of line 12, until the end of line 13. The consecutive falling tunes at the ends of lines 9 and 10, and 13 and 14 restore the pattern begun in lines 1–4.

A similar effect can be seen in miniature in line 2 where a moderate rise on the first "rain" is followed by a fall at the end of the line, echoing the fall at the end of line 1. An alternative reading could produce, of course, falls at the ends of lines 7, 8, 11, 12, rather than low rises. Such an interpretation would be even more repetitive and slow paced.

We have tried here to make a point about the poem—that it depends very largely for its effect on the consistent patterning of supra-segmentals—and a point about rhythm—that traditional scansion is inadequate for describing what is really happening in the poem. Rhythm is a physical phenomenon. Writers write, as we dance, and as Frost's persona walks, with our bodies. That heavy figure in the night is known by the rhythm of his steps, a heaviness and a rhythm that perhaps we all have known, so that at the end of the poem we, too, say, "*I* have been one acquainted with the night."

II. FRAMEWORK: the Supra-segmentals in Poetry

VOWELS and consonants are called segmentals because they are segments of the stream of voice production. Supra-segmentals can co-exist with a single segmental or stretch over several. They have a phonemic function because variations in them produce variations in meaning. Contrast "I like it" with falling tune to "I like it?" with rising tune.

The supra-segmentals are generally considered to be stress, juncture and tune. Time is an important aspect of stress and juncture in literature, where rhythmic patterns can be significant. Stress is the "beat" in poetry and prose, and time measures the regular rhythm of this beat, forcing us to slow down or speed up syllables and produce appropriate kinds of pauses in order to keep the beat. Tune is the melody of pitch change, which in literature becomes significant aesthetically as well as semantically.

But first consider the phonemic functions of supra-segmentals. Stress and juncture, like tune, are functional. Stress as a minimum contrast is illustrated by "a blackbird":

$$\text{/ə blǽk bə̀rd/}$$

versus "a black bird":

$$\text{/ə blǽk bə́rd/.}$$

The symbol / ´ / signifies primary stress, /ˆ/ secondary, / ` / tertiary and /ˇ/ weak stress. Juncture may be illustrated by "night rate" /naɪt-ret/ versus "nitrate" /naɪtret/. /–/ signifies here an unreleased final stop. The /r/ phone is different as well in "nitrate", sounding rather like /č/. We can hear these differences and the differences produce different meanings. Juncture, especially as it affects production of allophones, may well be significant in literature. For one thing, the relative ease of passage from syllable to syllable has onomatopoeic possibilities. For another, the kind of juncture which is associated with word boundaries ("night rate") gives the illusion of pause; this pseudo-pause may function in a line of verse just as if it actually took place in real time.

Stress

All literature originates in the midriff! Syllables are perceived as peaks of prominence in the breath stream. These peaks are produced by irregularly spaced contractions of the diaphragm. A peak of contraction produces a peak of prominence. This phenomenon we have called the "chest pulse". In addition to these peaks of prominence, at regular intervals in time occurs a "super-peak" of prominence called "stress". The distinguishing features of stress are complex, for it is not quite equivalent to loudness. Because of their occurrence at roughly regular intervals, the movement from stress to stress is called "isochronous rhythm".

A line of poetry therefore will have stressed syllables at intervals roughly equal in real time. A convenient unit of measure is the "foot" which consists of an initial stressed syllable plus unstressed syllables up to the next stressed syllable. The number of syllables in a foot may vary from one (the stressed syllable) to many.

Ideally, a foot of one stressed syllable is just as long in real time as a foot of two syllables. It follows that the syllables themselves in a two-syllable foot are each half as long as the syllable in a one-syllable foot. This idea is not entirely realized because of the tendency of some vowels to be inherently longer than others, and because of human inability to maintain perfect rhythm.

In literature, the most important special effect of isochronous rhythm is the contrast between syllables of different length in time, that is, the contrast in the relative speed of their pronunciation. The single syllable in a single-syllable foot is emphasized and isolated by its contrast with the quicker syllables of adjacent polysyllabic feet. For example, the single syllable foot "God" that ends the first line of Hopkins' poem attains a prominence through this effect in keeping with its significance in the poem, a prominence and significance maintained by the rhymes with "God" in succeeding lines. In line 2, /shóok/fóil/ contrasts two such monosyllabic feet with the previous rhythm of polysyllabic feet in a similar support of significant meaning. Such speed contrasts reinforce other effects, such as rhyme, assonance, alliteration and syntax. The effect of monosyllabic feet in Frost's poem has already been discussed.

The two-term system of stress or non-stress is itself an idealization. We have now actually distinguished four audible levels: primary, secondary, tertiary, weak:

$$/é \ ê \ è \ ĕ/.$$

The question, spoken with normal emphasis,

"Hôw's thĕ bábỳ?"

illustrates all four possibilities. Thus the perception of isochronous rhythm is itself an abstraction from all the phenomena of stress. The perception of auditory phenomena often makes different sounds sound similar. As we have said, phonemes are realized by various allophones.

Stress is no exception. The perception of stronger stress is relative to weaker stress. Usually, tertiary and weak stress are perceived in a two-stress framework as non-stress. Primary is usually perceived as stressed. This leaves secondary stress as the movable one, realizing stress or non-stress according to its environment. For example, "shook" in "God's Grandeur", like most attributive adjectives, takes secondary stress. But alliteration and rhythmic pattern influence its classification as *stressed* in a two-term system.

Traditional metric description, however, uses very different principles to arrive at its classifications of stressed and unstressed. This system is inherited from classical and romance poetry. The foot in such a system is either a rising or falling one, that is, ending or beginning with a stressed syllable. Feet are also classified by the number of unstressed syllables in them, and lines by the number of feet. Iambic pentameter (the metre of all three poems that have begun our Units so far) is a rising metre, with a two-syllable foot, and five feet in a line. The anapestic metre also rises, adding another unstressed syllable before the stressed one. Trochaic and dactylic are falling metres of two and three syllables respectively.

The problem is that these classification systems originated with languages that were not stress-timed, like English, but which instead were "syllable-timed". In these, a beat does not fall at equal intervals, so all syllables preserve a more or less natural duration. There is no quickening or lengthening of syllables to fit the equal units of real time that stress-timing calls for. Consequently the classical ideas of fixed long and short syllables had validity, and a metric analysis based on them worked much better in those languages than its adaptation does in English. In classical metres, there were very few irregularities in the foot, so that the ideal metre was also nearly always an accurate description of what was actually happening.

In adapting this traditional system to English, the long syllable was seen as equivalent to a stressed syllable, and the short syllable to an unstressed syllable. We must observe, however, that actual isochronous rhythm only tends to realize a traditional metre. One problem is that silent stresses have no place in traditional metres. Another is the fact that in natural speaking we do speed up and slow down syllables. If verse is designed according to the traditional ideal it begins to sound artificial and repetitive. Consequently the contrast between actual and ideal metre must be felt as an important ingredient in structure. The variations become as significant as the conformities, and a whole system of "permissible" variations, "loose" and "exact" metres, theories of caesura, etc., has grown up to enable English poets to write in rhythms resembling the way they speak!

In classical and romance languages metrical analysis is almost a description of what is actually happening. In English the same kind of analysis is an ideal model against which the actual must be measured. Metre is no longer purely physical, but instead an uneasy tension between mind and body which frequently results in some artificiality of articulation to make the ideal manifest. English verse in some sense is distorted towards a different group of languages in order to be realized according to the traditional model. No wonder the history of English verse consists of a series of rebellions in the direction of speech, prose, or the language of the common man. There is a similar tension in lexis between the development of an artificial "poetic" vocabulary which imitates the ancients and a return to plain style.

Pause

Time in verse has several aspects. One is the isochronous interval between stresses that can be counted to produce English measure. Another is the consequent variability of syllable length from foot to foot. Another is the interesting possibility that some pauses carry a silent stress, or pulse. That is, the isochronous stress pulse need not produce an audible syllable. In verse, this pause is identified with the strong caesura or the "end-stopped" line.

All pause has a subjective aspect. It is not only a matter of actual silence, but also the perception of silent stress, the modification of sound to produce "juncture", and so on. In verse, the *perceived* time of any pause can vary from zero to a full foot. In English verse, the caesura, or pause in the middle, is traditionally felt in every line. There may even be two caesuras; and marking the caesuras is part of traditional metrics. There is a pause also at the end of the line. If it is a slight one, the line is said to be "enjambed". This happens when there is no marked grammatical boundary at the end of the line. When the pause is long, the line is said to be "end-stopped". This pause coincides usually with a major grammatical boundary.

Medium duration pauses may really be silent stresses. Shorter pauses are usually just juncture. We perceive juncture as pause but in fact it is only a lengthening or holding of word-terminal consonants and vowels plus a shortening of the immediately following initial consonant or vowel. In line 4 of Frost's poem, "I have looked down the saddest city lane", the caesura pause after "down" is really juncture. The "n" of "down" is held and "the" is speeded up. This brings the word-boundary to our attention but we *perceive* it as a pause.

The decision, when analyzing verse, as to where a pause occurs, or whether it takes a silent stress or not, requires a reading, and an interpretation. Try it various ways and note the differences. Does it seem appropriate or artificial? The more prominent the grammatical boundary at the end of the line, the longer the pause, but this is not the only factor. A "silent lift" (unstressed pause) is possible. Since a caesura is present in all lines of any length, its placing is usually deduced from the grammar and from punctuation signals. A caesura will also take a beat in order to keep the beat off adjacent words of minor significance. For example, in line 2 of the poem the caesura after the first "rain" is marked by a dash, and takes a beat to keep the beat off the following "and". A beat on "and" would distort its meaning by giving it too much emphasis. Whether caesuras carry silent stresses or silent lifts or are simply "juncture", may depend on the established tempo. A faster reading of Frost's poem might eliminate some silent stresses but it would also distort the meaning since a speed-up gives the poem a slightly comic air.

To summarize, the possibilities at caesura are: a foot with stressed silence; a silent lift (unstressed silence); juncture ("night rate"). The stylistic effects of these choices are those of pattern and variety in caesura placement and caesura length. For example, the very short caesura of line 10 in Frost's poem (after "back") contrasts with the fairly marked caesuras of the lines of the preceding stanza. This line is very close to an ideal iambic, alternating unstressed and stressed syllables. The resumption of the regular rhythm after the lines with strong caesuras is appropriate to the meaning. Remember, it is not the impact of a single one of these effects, but rather their coincidence with others that combines with lexical content to produce literature.

Tune

"Pitch" is a word used in linguistics to refer to the level of the voice, high or low. It is an objective reality which can be heard by the ear or measured by instruments. It does not necessarily change when different syllables are made. A "tune" is a change in pitch that accords with some preconceived standard pattern of change. A tune is always associated with one syllable especially, which is called the "tonic" syllable. The tonic syllable is the syllable of greatest pitch change in any tune and it is always a stressed syllable. A tune may be confined to the tonic syllable, or it may stretch over several following syllables as well. If some pitch change occurs before the tonic, this change is called the "pretonic", and is not considered part of the tonic segment.

Because it carries the greatest pitch change, the tonic syllable stands out. The choice of this syllable is very important for the meaning of the clause since its location can signal that a lexical element is *contrastive*. For example, in the phrase "the *green* chair", the tune on "green" makes "green" the contrastive item (contrasting "red" perhaps). The last lexical item in a clause is usually the item that carries the tonic: in our example, "chair". The tonic syllable is the stressed syllable of the key word.

Reading a written text implies selecting the appropriate tune; it also implies selecting the most contrastive word. For example, there are several possible readings for Frost's line, "Whose woods these are I think I know". The tonic syllable could be "think", or "I" or even "woods" or "whose" or "are" or "these". However, since this is the first line of the poem we have no context by which to decide if any of these possiblities are appropriate. The safest interpretation then is to place the tonic on the last stressed syllable, "know". This is the normal pattern, and being normal it fits Frost's low-key, neutral style of poetry, of understatement.

Different contexts imply different variations in tune *type* as well as variations in placement. The five different kinds of tune times the number of stressed syllables in the clause give the number of possible meanings of the clause. One begins to understand the difference between speaking and writing. When we write letters we frequently underline one word to show it carries the tonic and thus to change the meaning. J. D. Salinger uses italics in the conversations of *Franny and Zooy* for the same purpose.

If a piece of writing is unmarked for tonic, it probably falls on the last lexical word with a stress in it. This is an ordinary contrast since it is the last item in the clause that is normally "new" by contrast with what came before the clause. The shifting of the tonic forward makes some earlier item "new" by contrast with whatever information came before. Normally a clause takes one tune; however, it is perfectly possible to put a tune on every stress, such as mothers do in extreme outrage:

"You are going to bed!"

Besides the five kinds of tunes and the possibility of putting them in different places, each tune has various kinds of pretonics, and there are meaningful variants within tunes as well. All these multiply the possible meanings of clauses; but since we are primarily interested in written texts, which cannot carry such signals directly, we have to get at these possiblities through *context*. Because we know the situation the text describes, we can realize the appropriate tune to present the meaning we perceive. The variations in basic tunes are so complex that long personal training is required to distinguish them all readily. Let one example suffice. For tune #1 ("falling") there are the possibilities of the tune beginning (the "onset") at relatively high, middle or relatively low pitch. In the sentence, "I don't think so", the neutral reading would have middle onset. High onset indicates a slight emphasis equivalent to "common sense tells me it's not the case, but additional data might change my mind". Low onset indicates a slightly deprecating response: "I'm not anxious about this and so it would be vulgar to pursue it further".

Probably every poem has a number of legitimate interpretations in choices of tune, tonic and pretonic, each choice realizing a slightly different meaning. If, for you, there is one ideal meaning for the poem, then there is one ideal way of reading it also.

The selection of tonic and tune type may also be used to establish patterns in successive clauses. Variation from the established pattern then makes a significant contrast. Line 6 of Frost's poem with its two #1 tunes contrasts with the previous three lines' single tunes. These tune patterns can coincide with other phonological patterns and serve to reinforce the lexical content, as the significant pause after the first #1 tune in line 6 demonstrates. In line 6 of "God's Grandeur",

"And all is seared with trade; bleared, smeared with toil",

the three rhyming words are lexically related and all bear the same #1 tune. The tonic, which normally would fall on "trade" and "toil", has been shifted in both the clauses by suggestion of the rhyme and the lexical connections. "Trade" and "toil", of course, retain some emphasis because of their positions last in their clauses, and because they alliterate. The line is an excellent example of "loaded" language. It bears a burden of sound.

The length of the tone group—the stretch of text from the end of one tune to the end of the next—is also important. By back-to-back stress and the use of silent lifts and silent feet, a poet can suggest a relatively large number of tone groups, and so load or slow his line or his poem. On the other hand, he can produce extra long tone groups conveying flow or effortlessness. These "meanings", of course, have to be reinforced by the lexis to emerge as genuine onomatopoeic effects. Compare lines 2, 6, 7, 10, each with two tone groups, with the other lines. In line 2 there is a reversal of direction; in line 6, unwillingness; in line 7, a cessation of the walking pace; in line 10, a presentation of two alternatives. In each case the tonic interrupting the flow of the line supports the sense.

Listening to the supra-segmentals of a poem is more than ear-training; it is also training in, and appreciation of, the possibilities of meaning. Reading a poem with precision requires individual decisions about meaning. Reading a poem according to an abstract, traditional metrical system produces by contrast a sing-song, ritualistic effect, emptying the poem of individual meaning. The supra-segmentals are there to add and specify meaning. They are the reason a poem frequently seems to spring to life, to reveal new possibilities, when it is read aloud by someone who understands what he is reading.

III. APPLICATION: the Supra-segmentals in "Dover Beach"

DOVER BEACH

/ . The / sea is / calm to- / night.
The / tide is / full, the / moon lies / fair
U / pon the / straits; / . —on the / French / coast, the / light /
/ Gleams, and is / gone; the / cliffs of / England / stand, /
/ Glimmering and / vast, / out in the / tranquil / bay. /   5
/ Come to the / window, / sweet is the / night- / air! /
/ Only, from the / long / line of / spray
Where the / sea meets the / moon-blanch'd / land, /
/ Listen! you / hear the / grating / roar
Of / pebbles which the / waves draw / back, and / fling,   10
At / their re / turn, / up the / high / strand,
Be / gin, and / cease, and / then a / gain be / gin, /
With / tremulous / cadence / slow, and / bring
The e / ternal / note of / sadness / in. /

       Sophocles long ago   15
       Heard it on the Aegean, and it brought
       Into his mind the turbid ebb and flow
       Of human misery; we
       Find also in the sound a thought,
       Hearing it by this distant northern sea.   20

       The Sea of Faith
       Was once, too, at the full, and round earth's shore
       Lay like the folds of a bright girdle furl'd,
       But now I only hear
       Its melancholy, long, withdrawing roar,   25
       Retreating, to the breath
       Of the night-wind down the vast edges drear
       And naked shingles of the world.

Ah, love, let us be true
To one another! for the world, which seems   30
To lie before us like a land of dreams,
So various, so beautiful, so new,
Hath really neither joy, nor love, nor light,
Nor certitude, nor peace, nor help for pain;
And we are here as on a darkling plain   35
Swept with confused alarms of struggle and flight,
Where ignorant armies clash by night.

—Matthew Arnold

"Dover Beach" was written about 1851, yet it is in both theme and form very like a modern poem. Arnold, like Frost, seems to be describing a moment of despair when he doubted the goodness of the world or any purpose in it. In form, the lack of a measure resembles free verse, and the irregular spacing of the rhymes suppresses their effect. In addition, although the poem may be scanned in traditional metre as iambic, Arnold has taken advantage of all the permissible variations (e.g. trochee in first foot, feet with no stress, feet with double stress) to create a rhythm closer to speech and less regular than expected in the verse of his day. The effect is to make the poem less formal, more personal and individual.

Yet the apparent lack of structure in the poem is actually neither new nor true. The tradition of irregular measure and rhyming is an old one in the English ode, and Shakespeare's verse offers only one of many examples of free iambics. The poem does rhyme and scan and every line has either five, or four, or three feet—not two, one or six.

So far we have looked at the poem in traditional terms, and probably in the terms Arnold himself considered it in. When we look at the supra-segmentals of the poem in terms of descriptive linguistics we see much more. The impression of formal verse is given more strongly the more closely the unstressed syllables conform to a pattern. We have marked the stresses for the first section of the poem. Look at the number of unstressed syllables in each foot. The number varies from zero to three. The irregularity of the feet stands out at once. Which areas of the first section are most regular? Is there a relationship between this regularity and what is being said at these points? Remember that to mark the stresses we must have first produced a performance text which is, of course, also an interpretation. Read the first section aloud according to our marking. How would you describe our interpretation? Do you have a different one?

Traditional prosody also does not consider pitch. Again for a certain performance text, we have marked the tonic syllables and the type of tune for the first section of the poem. What patterns do you see? What justifies shifting the tonic syllables forward in line 6? Mark the supra-segmentals and discuss them in relation to theme for the rest of the poem.

IV. QUESTIONS FOR REVIEW

1. Can you give a meaning to each of these terms?

supra-segmental	two-stress system
real time	rhythm
perceived time	measure
juncture	scansion
stress	prosody
isochronous	caesura
silent stress	morpheme
chest pulse	end-stopped
stress pulse	enjambed
silent lift	traditional metre
phoneme	foot
allophone	long and short syllables
pitch	onset
tune	context
tonic syllable	stress-timed language
pretonic	

2. What are the names of the five basic tunes? Can you create examples of each? What are the general meanings for each?

3. In the following sentence what changes of meaning occur as a result of shifting the tonic syllable forward to each word in turn? "She told me to go."

4. What are the ideal models for iambic, trochaic, anapestic, and dactylic metres?

5. For the following sentence what differences of meaning occur when the sentence is pronounced with low, middle, or high onset and falling tune. "Alright, Jack." What variations in meaning occur when other tunes are used?

6. Do you remember the sentence illustrating the four levels of stress? Create a similar sentence. What names are given to these four levels?

7. Write out an interpretation for the following line with (1) an iambic scansion, (2) a trochaic scansion: "Whose woods these are I think I know."

8. For the following poem mark the stresses, using a two-term system and including silent stresses, if any. Mark the tonic syllables and the type of tune they carry, and divide the lines into feet. Does this poem have a "measure"? Are the ends of the lines marked by sound patterning? How? What is the effect of Hopkins' own stress markings? Are there other possible readings of the lines he has marked? What is the effect of these other readings? Discuss the theme of the poem and how it is related to the rhythm and the patterning of tune.

SPRING AND FALL: *to a young child*

Márgarét, are you gríeving

Over Goldengrove unleaving?

Léaves, líke the things of man, you

With your fresh thoughts care for, can you?

Áh! ás the heart grows older

It will come to such sights colder

By and by, nor spare a sigh

Though worlds of wanwood leafmeal lie;

And yet you wíll weep and know why.

Now no matter, child, the name:

Sórrow's springs áre the same.

Nor mouth had, no nor mind, expressed

What heart heard of, ghost guessed:

It ís the blight man was born for,

It is Margaret you mourn for.

—G. M. Hopkins

9. What features of style in this poem are familiar to you from the previous poem by Hopkins we have looked at?

Chapter Two **Graphology**

WHEN we perceive language in a written medium, the thing we perceive in the most direct sense is shape and colour. This should be obvious to us from the experience of looking at language in a non-Roman alphabet which we have not been taught to understand—Arabic perhaps, or Cyrillic. Even if the colour of the characters is intended only to distinguish them from the background, the rhythmic repetition of exotic and incomprehensible figures fascinates the eye. But in reading our own language, the majesty of alphabetic design is usually lost to us. As in the case of spoken language, the elements of the medium escape our attention because we are so intent on the meaning they convey. Due to long familiarity, written symbol has become transparent to meaning; we have forgotten that immediacy of experiencing written characters which is known only to those who are just starting to learn to read.

In literary language, however, it often happens that the written medium possesses features which are part of literary meaning. Chapter One showed us something like this happening in the spoken medium, when alliteration, onomatopoeia or some other phonological feature contributed to the effect of the text. In written literature it is possible for the medium to convey a literary effect based upon design in the visual field. Except in rare circumstances this is not done by experimentation in the design of letters. Rather it is the product of novelty in layout, manipulation of sense lines, or even the clustering of alphabet symbols into non-verbal patterns.

The terms "phonology" and "graphology" together represent the whole substance-related level of language—the level of language phenomena in which we perceive language in a physical medium. Phonology, as you have learned, refers to the encoding of meaning in sound. Graphology refers to the encoding of meaning in visual symbols.

UNIT 4

Graphology and Design

I. ANALYSIS: Three Modern Poems

```
she    loves   me                        1
she    loves   me    not
she    loves
she    loves   me
she
she    loves


she                                      7
```

—Emmett Williams

This is a poem you must see to understand, for you cannot hear it. The pleasure in the poem comes from solving its visual problem: what is the pattern that produces the poem? The answer to this question also makes clear the poem's theme. We have seen that sound patterning can reinforce a poem's meaning, but so can design, layout, spelling and lettering. It is also true that any spoken performance of a poem says more than can be written down; here we have a poem that says more than can be read aloud.

The poem starts from the old daisy-stripping augury, "she loves me/she loves me not", repeated until the daisy has been plucked. The puzzle here is what the answer was. If we write out the whole sequence we can see. (Brackets have been placed around the missing pieces.)

```
she loves me
she loves me not
she loves (me)
she loves me (not)
she (loves me)
she loves (me not)
(she loves me)
she (loves me not)
```

This gives us a preliminary answer to our question, for if an even number of lines are filled in, the answer must always be, "she loves me not". The

answer to one further question removes all ambiguity: what is the principle
by which words were deleted?

The answer to this question is found when we see that the poem, whether
read aloud or seen on the page, has a "stripping" effect like the stripping
away of daisy petals. Each subsequent repetition of the two base lines of the
poem is diminished by one word. But this basic pattern leads in turn to the
creation of others. Thematically we see that our lover becomes progressively more at a loss for words. If we read each line as an attempted description
of one phase of the relationship, we find our lover gradually rejected and
his mistress eventually preferring her own company.

Other formal patterns are produced as well. If we start at the bottom left
of the original, with "she", and read diagonally upward to the right the
remaining isolated words, we find "she loves me not". The deletion of just
these words contrives to leave this fatal statement isolated. It is this
statement that makes the poem impossible to read aloud. Seeing this
pattern completes the divination, a fact confirmed by Emmett Williams'
own principle that the structure of a concrete poem is all-important, that the
visual element is not mere gloss on a poem, but fundamental to its meaning.

The visual element can also be used to reinforce and emphasize verbal
meaning in a poem, just as we have seen sound patterning working to
produce certain onomatopeic effects in previous poems. Indeed, the
influence of this reinforcement may be so pervasive as to lead one to
wonder if there would be a poem at all without it. The following poem is an
extreme example of this kind of reinforcement:

> dying is fine)but Death   1
>
> ?o
> baby
> i
>
> wouldn't like   5
>
> Death if Death
> were
> good:for
>
> when(instead of stopping to think)you
>
> begin to feel of it,dying   10
> 's miraculous
> why?be
> cause dying is

perfectly natural;perfectly
putting   15
it mildly lively(but

Death

is strictly
scientific
& artificial &   20

evil & legal)

we thank thee
god
almighty for dying

(forgive us,o life!the sin of Death   25

—E. E. Cummings

In this poem graphological effects are used to "jazz up" (and we use the phrase advisedly) a fragment of a playful, enthusiastic, pseudo-theological monologue. E. E. Cummings was an unconventional painter and poet living in Greenwich Village who had an interest in jazz and speech rhythms as well as in visual patterns. Syncopations in all of these forms come together in this poem.

Our perception of jazz connotations in the poem's design is cued by the first 3-line stanza which uses a jazz phrase and rhythm: "o/baby/i". This stanza also draws attention to the importance of typography in the poem by its unusual use of punctuation: "?". An unusual use of punctuation also occurs in the first line of the poem where one of its indicators—the capitalization of "Death" which is sustained throughout the poem—also relates to the jazz parallel. "Death" is established as a keynote; and it operates somewhat like the fragment of tune that a jazz improvization is organized around, and keeps returning to, through all its variations. The closed bracket of the first line, without a preceding opening bracket, together with the opening bracket without a following closed bracket of the last line, indicates that the whole language sequence is part of an ongoing, larger work, just as a jazz variation may take off from some already established theme and return to it later.

Here, unlike the case of the daisy poem, we can create a spoken text that reproduces most of the poem—*if* we interpret the signals to "play it by ear" properly. However, the text does not make explicit a given reading; it only suggests the sort of thing that might work. Instead, we are encouraged to enjoy what is happening in the design, to enjoy the visual rhythms produced.

The major visual rhythm is carried by the stanza pattern with its 1-line, 3-line alternation. It is this strict formal structure that enables Cummings to play his games with language, just as the formal musical structure of jazz gives individual musicians the opportunity to play their improvizations without creating chaos.

These two stanza patterns are filled in with different variations. The one-line stanzas vary from prosaic "bridges" between three-line stanzas (stanzas 3, 7), to more complicated structures employing the use of a bracket (stanzas 1, 5, 11, 13), to the single climactic use of the key word, "Death" (stanza 9). The three-line stanzas play with variations on the long-line/short-line theme. Stanzas 4, 8, 12 use a short middle line to contrast with longer surrounding lines. Stanza 2 reverses this. Stanza 6 uses progressively shorter lines, stanza 10 approximately equal lines (reflecting its content).

The lines themselves offer still more graphological play. Lines 6 and 14 begin and end with the same word balanced around a central item, lines 11 and 20 with the same letter or symbol. Lines 16 and 21 are balanced into two halves by similar looking and sounding words. Line 21 is also balanced around an ampersand. The first and last lines are divided into halves, the first by a bracket, the last by an exclamation point. The short lines, 8 and 12, are divided by punctuation and grammar into two halves in a striking way.

It is a relief, after all this typographical hype, to stand back and just read the *words* of the poem, in which we find an inventive and colloquial argument in favour of process against stasis. Since we've just been through a highly invigorating process ourselves we come to this theme with experience. Cummings, through his active use of design, has engaged us in reading poetry, in an act of language, in the act of living which is the act of dying, just as jazz music or pop art engages us. We cannot read this poem only with our mind's eye. Our senses are involved. We have escaped "the sin of Death".

The interrelationship of the graphological and the phonological which Cummings' poem suggests through the possibility of a "jazzy" spoken version to augment its "jazzy" design, is one central question in modern poetry. The interrelationship of the graphological with formal patterns of lexis and grammar is another. Consider this poem:

NANTUCKET

Flowers through the window   1
lavender and yellow

changed by white curtains—
Smell of cleanliness—

Sunshine of late afternoon—   5
On the glass tray

a glass pitcher, the tumbler
turned down, by which

a key is lying—And the
immaculate white bed   10

—William Carlos Williams

William Carlos Williams was a New Jersey doctor who was associated with the Imagist movement in early twentieth-century literature. The poets of this movement sought to produce a poetry which concentrated on the visual. They rejected the poetry of the ear, and they rejected the poetry of argument, or of any large rhetorical pattern. They created instead a poetry of visual frames, of a succession of isolated, though related, images. The poem passed from image to image to create its effect, but without connecting these images in argument form. Each image exists in a splendid, isolated intensity. The development of this kind of poetry is intimately related to the development of *vers libre* or "free verse" because free verse depends on a visual rather than an auditory signal to define its line endings.

Besides the graphological indications of the line endings, and the division into five stanzas, there are also some graphological indications of grammar in this poem. The poem is written in five sentences, each sentence beginning with a capital letter and ending with a dash, except the last which has no dash. It is when we try to discover the principle by which the line-endings are determined that we become first puzzled, and then aware of the importance of graphology in this poem. This principle is not grammatical as we can easily see in the last stanza where the last sentence is begun in the middle of the penultimate line. Neither is it some traditional phonological principle of measure such as number of stresses or syllables or feet. There are different numbers of these in the lines.

The mystery is solved only when we realize that the whole poem is a visual design to which the patterns of grammar (and hence the phonological patterns of tune and juncture) and the patterns of lexis are related. This relationship changes through the poem and it is through seeing this pattern of change that we can grasp the poem's significance. Indeed, the key word in this poem is "changed" in line 3. Just as the white curtains impose a pattern on the flowers outside the window, so the visual arrangement into lines and stanzas imposes a pattern on the formal elements of the poem—its grammar and lexis. This pattern "changes" the meaning of the poem, just as the curtains changed the way the flowers were seen.

Working through the poem line by line will show us the pattern of change. The first two line endings coincide with significant grammatical divisions and hence with associated phonological patterns of tune and juncture. We may say that graphologically the line endings substitute for commas we might expect to find here. The end of line 3 also coincides with a significant grammatical division, here marked by the dash. Lines 4 and 5 again coincide with significant grammatical units, their beginnings marked by capitals and their endings marked by dashes. A convention seems well established. But line 6 which initiates the second half of the poem also initiates a change in that convention. It ends with a grammatical division but one that we normally do not mark with a comma. Line 7 definitely does not coincide with a significant grammatical division. The division, marked by a comma, occurs in the middle of the line, and the end of the line initiates a new grammatical item without finishing it. Lines 8 and 9 continue this pattern, line 9 more extremely than 8 since the grammatical division in the middle of the line is that between sentences. The end of line 10 again coincides with a significant grammatical division, although the beginning does not.

The pattern of grammatical and graphological coincidence strengthens in the first half of the poem, and then is shattered in the last half. Something has changed. It is important to note that this change in patterning could not be detected if the poem were read aloud since we would have no way of knowing where the lines end. Nor could we detect the contributory lexical pattern made by the items occupying the last positions in the lines. In lines 1 through 7 these are all lexical items. In lines 8 and 9 they are grammatical, and in line 10 lexical again.

What is the meaning of this "change"? It is only in the second half of the poem that we see the effect of the visual pattern. Something is different about the second half of the poem. That difference is in our mode of apprehending the poem. Suddenly it will not do simply to hear the poem. We must also see it. We must put the accustomed formal patterns of grammar with their related patterns of tune and juncture together with a pattern of line endings that, as is apparent by the end of the poem, is completely arbitrary. What does this mean?

Williams' theme is the sense of mystery in the ordinary. It is announced in the first three lines of the poem. Our way of perceiving by the end of the poem is different from that with which we began. The prosaic "cleanliness" of line 4 becomes the resonating "immaculate" of line 10. The apparent grammatical ordering of the line endings vanishes. Near the end of the poem the lines end in mysterious grammatical items—"by which", "and the"—instead of lexical items. The pitcher and tumbler, the key, the bed, all seem to take on symbolic overtones, inviting some hidden experience. Definite colours—"Lavender" and "yellow" have become "white". The focus of vision is no longer "through the window", but in the room. The stillness of a vision replaces activity. The "immaculate white bed" promises eternal rest.

Of course, the mystical content of the poem is also ironic. This is, after all, the vision of a motel room seen by a tired traveller. But it *is* a vision and the last line is mysterious and mystical, an immaculate conception. The reduction of the particular to an abstract pattern, an arbitrary formal structure, results in the particular world taking on new meaning. The key, the bed, the glass pitcher are framed and suspended, as in a cubist painting. The framing gives them importance. The eternal traveller confronts his place of eternal rest. The poem is entitled "Nantucket" because that is a particular place, like Oshkosh or Hawaii. But this kind of experience can happen anyplace, so there is also no significance in it being Nantucket.

This is an amazing little poem. It is as apparently innocent and as deceptively full of meaning as Chaucer's tales. But the most amazing and "modern" thing about it is that its effects are achieved by graphological means. This is not the same poem when read aloud. This poem, and many other modern poems, is an inner meditation, a private experience. It is not a rhetorical activity designed to move an audience to action or response. The existence of such private poetry reflects a change in the situation of poetic communication. This poem is not a speech to a large group about social rules, but a private inner voice whispering to an individual about his own moment-by-moment existence, his "being". The rise of the novel, itself dependent on low-cost printing and universal literacy, created a new "private" audience which the experimental modern novelist attempted to exploit through effects not reproducible by reading aloud: Joyce's visual puns, Virginia Woolf's use of brackets, the development of an "interior monologue" meant to be heard in the head. Similarly, modern poetry has exploited graphological effects as the ideal tool to take a reader inward to the real situation of the poet's message, the individual experience of being human.

II. FRAMEWORK: Visual Design in the Written Medium

LANGUAGE is meaningful and uses conventional signs. It is also a series of events. As you have learned, a language event has three aspects. The first is substance. The signs must have some kind of physical existence, whether it is noise or marks. The second is form. The signs must have some kind of consistent and conventional patterning. The third is situation. The signs must take place in a context which gives them meaning. The utterance "No!" has substance and conventional form but is puzzling without a situation.

The formal aspect of the language event can be exemplified by grammar, and lexis—the dictionary meaning of words. Grammar and lexis account for most of the "shape" language is in. By a pattern we simply mean a recurrence of some phenomenon with the same conventional meaning. Grammar recurrences are recurrences of things like clauses, like the sequence subject–predicator–object, like pronouns. Lexical recurrences are recognized more simply as the same shape with the same meaning: bird, running, white.

The situational aspect of language, despite what we've just said about the conventional meaning of form, may change the meaning of the language event. "No!" may mean delighted affirmation in certain situations of ecstatic surprise. Double entendres work by reminding us of two contexts at once, one of which is vulgar or obscene. In fact, the formal, conventional meaning really just means the most probable contextual meaning.

Context is an abstraction from the total situation of just those elements that affect meaning. In the same way form is an abstraction from some kind of physical substance, usually noises or marks. In language some physical substance is organized to provide tokens or signs for representing formal patterns. Our preceding units on phonology have described the organization of sound. This unit will deal with graphology, the organization of space into written symbols.

Literature and the Aspects

Related to the aspect of substance are two choices of medium, the phonological and the graphological. Each is oriented to different situations and each creates different complexes of formal patterning. Spoken English is therefore not the same as written prose, formally as well as in medium; and poetry written to be recited is not the same as poetry written for sight-reading. Prose can employ complex grammar or a consistently

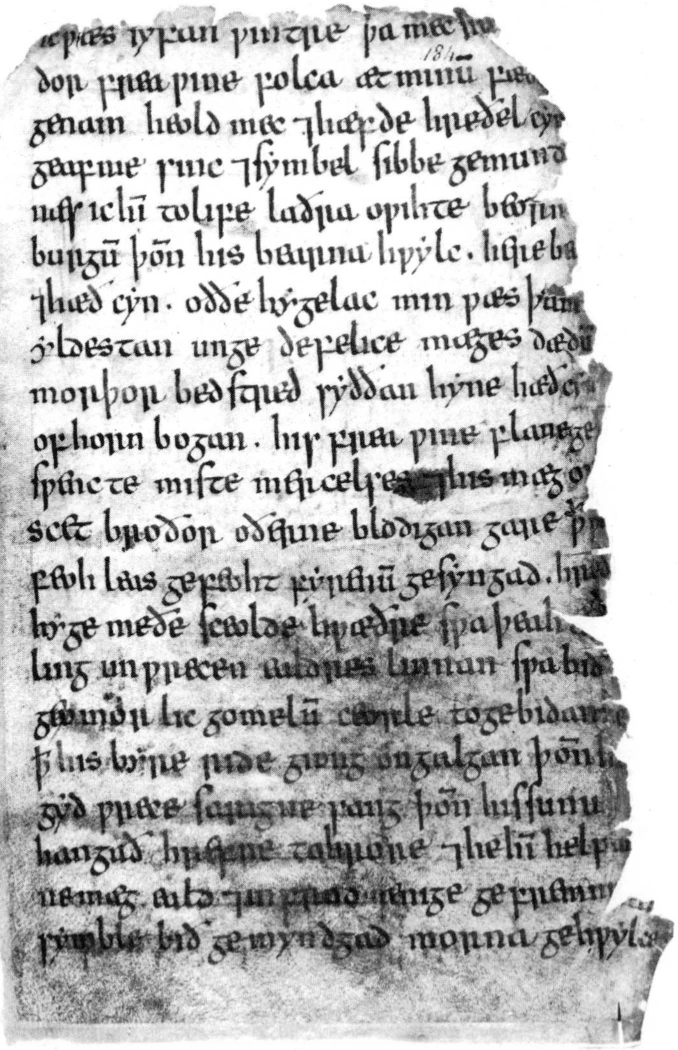

Page from the Beowulf Manuscript (Fol. 184a)

Ic wæs syfanwintre,   þā mec sinca baldǫr,
frēawine folca   æt mīnum fæder genam;
hēold mec ond hæfde   Hrēðel cyning,
geaf mē sinc ond symbęl,   sibbe gemunde;
næs ic him tō līfe   lāðra ōwihte,
beorn in burgum,   þonne his bearna hwylc,
Herebeald ond Hæðcyn   oððe Hygelāc mīn.
Wæs þām yldestan   ungedēfelīce
mæges dǣdum   morþǫrbed strêd,
syððan hyne Hæðcyn   of hornbogan,
his frēawine   flāne geswencte,
miste mercelses   ond his mǣg ofscēt,
brōðor ōðerne   blōdigan gāre.
þæt wæs feohlēas gefeoht,   fyrenum gesyngad,
hreðre hygemēðe;   sceolde hwæðre swā þēah
æðeling unwrecen   ealdres linnan.
   Swā bið geōmorlīc   gomelum ceorle
tō gebīdanne,   þæt his byre rīde
giong on galgan;   þonne hē gyd wrece,
sārigne sang,   þonne his sunu hangað
hrefne tō hrōðre,   ond hē him helpe ne mæg
eald ond infrōd   ænige gefremman.
Symble bið gemyndgad   morna gehwylce

Transcription of *Beowulf* Text (ll. 2428–50)

"correct" grammar, and use written symbols such as numbers and various punctuation devices. Sight poetry may depend more on design, the pattern of black on white, than on auditory patterning. Concrete poetry, like "She loves me", can't even be translated effectively into the phonological medium.

Historically, the development has been from the phonological to the graphological, from *Beowulf* to Virginia Woolf. A preliterate society creates both its language and its literature solely in the phonological medium. An early literate society still does not distinguish between written and spoken literature. Its people see writing only as a record of the phonological. Old English verse, for example, was recorded like prose, with one line run into the next. The sight-line for poetry was invented later. Pure sight poetry is a very modern invention and probably cannot exist without something approaching universal literacy, which is itself very recent. Preceding is a page from the *Beowulf* manuscript, reproduced beside a modern transcription into type face and proper sense lines. Notice how much more of the phonological patterning is made clear in the modern transcription. It is only a step from this kind of visual organization of phonological data, to a visual organization that carries meaning without reference to the phonological: "She loves me".

Graphology

The science of phonology which we have been explaining in Units 1, 2 and 3 describes the organization of sound into usable tokens for the representation of language events. A hypothetical science of graphology would describe the organization of space into usable tokens. These tokens would include writing symbols such as the alphabet and the number system, punctuation, and designs. Examples of conventional design are the writing of poetry in lines, the writing of prose in paragraphs. The three poems we looked at in part I each show a different design and our commentary was largely devoted to analyzing and understanding the principles behind each design. With this understanding comes a clarification of meaning, just as we saw happen when we analyzed phonological patterning in the earlier poems.

In phonology, usable tokens—recognizable patterns with conventional meanings—are abstractions from a whole class of actual utterances. These usable tokens are called phonemes. In graphology the usable token (for example, a letter) would again be an abstraction from a variety of possible formations. (How many ways can you write "A" and still be understood?) The phoneme/allophone distinction has its parallel in the grapheme/allograph. That is, we can say "r" in many different ways, all recognizable as "r"; and we can write "r" in many different ways, all recognizable as "r". This parallel is not limited to individual sounds or letters, however. Just as there are supra-segmentals in phonology, so there is "design" in graphology: paragraph division, sentence punctuation, headlining, italics, brackets, use of white space, diagram conventions, page size, type size, etc. All these aspects of design have conventionalized meanings.

But besides the fact that phonology and graphology each have their own conventionalized set of symbols, or tokens, there are also conventionalized relationships between the two sets. Spoken English does not use punctuation, and written English does not use tunes. But we feel punctuation and tune are related because they tend to try to give us similar information. Historically, punctuation was developed as a stand-in for different kinds of junctures and tunes, but now punctuation stands as an independent graphological system with its own rules.

Design in Practical Writing

Besides the conventional symbols, all of us are familiar with larger patterns of graphology which we can call "design". The use of various type sizes and type styles has meaning in legal documents and on letter-heads. The placement of blocks of writing, the shape of the blocks, or paragraphs, is similarly meaningful. We've all learned to beware of "the fine print".

This Indenture

made (in duplicate) the   21st   day of   September   19 82

Between   _____, Professor, and
                        _____, his wife, both of
            the Borough of North York, in the Municipality of
            Metropolitan Toronto, as joint tenants and not as
            tenants in common,

                                            herein called "the Assignor,"
                                                of the FIRST PART,

                            AND

            _____, wife of
                                    and the said
            _____, both of the Borough of
            North York, in the Municipality of Metropolitan Toronto
            (formerly of the City of Toronto, in the County of York)

Meaningful design of a more advanced kind is used to supplement writing in a technical work, such as this book with its diagrams and analyses. Notation in mathematics, logic, physics, chemistry and so on, is really a graphological expression of a different language. Graphs, charts, blueprints are on the borderline between sophisticated design in graphology and outright pictures.

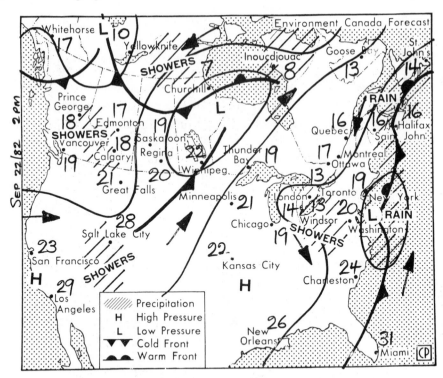

Indeed, it could be argued that when composition and symbolization become conventionalized, a picture *is* language transmitted graphologically. It has been argued that medieval paintings, and even whole cathedrals, were just such meaningful linguistic structures.

Much modern advertising, of course, is designed to utilize the full resources of the graphological medium, and in turn this has resulted in the educating of the general public to the full possibility of graphological design. Reading a contemporary poster is frequently a sophisticated exercise in design interpretation. Type size and style, logos, spacing, white space, line-length rhythms, are all employed. Often advertising blends pictures with graphological design, raising graphology to the level of art (if not literature!).

Design in Written Literature

Ordinarily, language in its formal aspect takes its meaning from reference to conventionalized situations. A word means something in a certain context. And ordinarily language seen in its substantial aspect takes its meaning from reference to formal patterns. A sound or mark is significant to the degree it helps create language patterns. But design taken beyond the

basics of writing and punctuation can leap directly into a relationship with situational meaning, without referring to the aspect of form. An example is the arrow on a one-way street.

This leaping-across aspect of language can also be seen in phonology in the phenomenon of onomatopeia. Suggestive sounds in the appropriate context refer to situations directly. They do not just serve as codes for words. Similarly a letter or punctuation or spacing can refer to situation directly in poetry, without realizing a formal pattern.

At the beginning of the twentieth century some poets explored new possibilities for design in graphology. They sacrificed the phonological effects of regular metre to achieve the freedom to make interesting designs out of line lengths, rather than just using the line to reflect the phonological patterning. This "poem" by Guillaume Apollinaire illustrates their work:

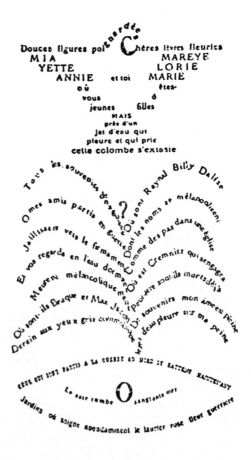

La Colombe Poignardée et le Jet d'Eau
(The Wounded Dove and the Fountain)

The visual aspect of the line length was often as crucial in *vers libre* as the phonological or the formal (grammatical or lexical) aspect.

The arrangement of a poem into lines on the page is purely visual although it can suggest phonological pauses, or even tunes. Some free-verse poets are willing to give up these phonological possibilities in order to have greater freedom in visual arrangement. For example, the shorter the line, the more emphatic is its spatial relationship to other lines. Look at the visual effect of the short line, "Death", in Cummings' poem, or of the progressively shorter lines in Emmett Williams'.

Concrete poetry is a logical extension of this interest in referring directly to situation through design. A concrete poem in the strictest sense would avoid the formal aspect entirely and use letters and punctuation strictly as free designs. The following poem comes very close to that ideal condition:

au pair girl

                pair g\
                au pair
                ir girl a
                ∪ pair gir
                pair girl
                au pair girl
            girl au pair gi
           au pair girl au pa\
        girl au pair girl au
        jirl au pair girl au p
        girl au pair girl au
        ir girl au pair girl
        au pair girl au pa'
        rl au pair girl

—Ian Hamilton Finlay

The development of Imagism seems to be part of this attempt to refer directly to experience without the interference of the formal aspect. It is analogous to the contemporary attempts to paint "light" rather than "theme". Concrete poetry is one result of the Imagist impulse. A second result is the development of a kind of poetry that specifies its line and stanza divisions graphologically, thus introducing a new kind of patterning to poetry. Such poems are not as effective when read aloud. A modern poem must be looked at in two ways: to see what graphological patterns are

present, and to see what phonological patterns are. This second development leads to an interesting result. Traditional phonologically-based poetry
using rhyme and rhythm is a recognizable distortion of spoken language.
Paradoxically, the graphologically-organized poetry can be much closer to
spoken language! It depends upon graphological rather than phonological
means for the extra linguistic patterning that makes poetry more intense
than speech.

Verse and Poetry

The definition of "verse", as opposed to speech, or to prose, depends on
the substantial aspect of the language event. Verse used to be distinguished
from prose or speech by a phonologically perceived "measure", its division
into line units defined by a certain number of feet, and sound patterns that
marked the ends of the lines. A similar situation exists now with regard to
"free verse". It is marked as "verse" only graphologically, by the fact that
its right-hand margin is not justified, as prose is.

The term "poetry" has undergone a similar change. It has always been
used to describe a particularly moving or intense use of language whether
that be in the substantial form of verse, prose, or speech. But what is
"moving" or "intense" has changed also. Some immense structuring of the
universe, apparent in the largest as well as in the smallest movements of
creation, was once fundamental to poetry. This was the basis of "sublime"
poetry. Now such larger theories of existence are dismissed as didactic or
pompous and it is the particular alone, the details of the surface of life, the
small nuances of the moment that are seen as significant and so poetic. The
basis of poetry is no longer the sublime conception that stands behind the
particular but the individual human experience. Are these shifts in the
definition of verse, from phonological to graphological, and the definition
of poetry, from abstract to particular, related?

If we return to "Nantucket" with this question in mind we can see that
the shift of medium from phonological to graphological that becomes clear
in the course of the poem is the carrier of a corresponding shift in poetic
experience from outer to inner, from the abstract public structure of the
world to the particulars of individual perception. The poem begins outside
the "window" with the sensations of the world without. The phonological
medium is asserted in the jingling sound of the opening couplet:

"Flówĕrs thrŏŭgh thĕ/wíndŏw/ /Lávĕndĕr aňd/yéllŏw."

But then intervenes the "white curtains" and this changes everything. The
phonological medium begins to fade although a hint of the couplet is
retained in the second stanza through the end-stopping and through the

alliteration and near consonance of "curtains" and "cleanliness". A second sense—smell—is asserted, a much closer, more intimate sense. By the third stanza the phonological structuring of the couplet is gone, and we have begun a description of a new visual landscape: inner space, the interior of the room. We are also using a new mode, graphology, to structure this description. This inner world is luminous ("sunshine of late afternoon"), mysterious ("a key") and full of associations ("immaculate"). It is a series of exact images that are not explained, presented in the form of a list of separate items noted by the author. This non-commenting note-form is one of the literary indications of interior monologue. The images succeed each other without the grammatical signs of an argument structure. "And" in the last stanza simply signals the end of the list of sensations, of observations. By this point we are entirely inside Williams' mind, as he is entirely in the room. He is no longer explaining to us but simply communicating his feelings and sensations. He is no longer speaking to us, but simply allowing us to receive his perceptions. And he has framed those perceptions in a graphological structure that gives them significance but that cannot be realized by the spoken voice. The silence of this poem, of this room, of this mind, is absolute.

III. APPLICATION: Design as Symbol in Modern Poetry

MOST prose literature that you will encounter incorporates features of
design in only the most trivial sense: the left margin is conventionally even,
the right margin is either even or ragged, headings are marked with
contrastive sizes of type, italics are used to call attention to certain words or
phrases, and so forth. The graphology of prose texts is usually regulated by
convention only: the standard alphabet, the standard system of punctuation, standard spellings.

In poetry, however, you know that you find a greater variety and
freedom in design features, if not in graphology. Even conventional poetry
distinguishes a large variety of types by stanza forms, and these forms have
their own appearances in page layout. In modern poetry, we have recognized a principle of freedom and experimentation in design: the poet is
allowed to be as much a designer as a word-smith. Once this is allowed, the
poetry is inseparable from the appearance. To understand the inventiveness
of the poem is partly to understand why words and lines have been placed
where they are in the visual field.

In the following poem, verbal description and layout are wedded for a
single purpose. Ideally, this is how the combination of techniques should
work in modern poetry.

The pennycandystore beyond the El   1
is where I first
                    fell in love
                              with unreality
Jellybeans glowed in the semi-gloom   5
of that september afternoon
A cat upon the counter moved among
                              the licorice sticks
                    and tootsie rolls
            and Oh Boy Gum   10

Outside the leaves were falling as they died

A wind had blown away the sun

A girl ran in
Her hair was rainy
Her breasts were breathless in the little room   15

Outside the leaves were falling
and they cried
Too soon! too soon!   18
—Lawrence Ferlinghetti

Ferlinghetti is an American poet partly indebted to a tradition which flows through Walt Whitman. His subject, as here, often involves the urban scene, popular amusements, the archetypal events of common, everyday life. This poem turns on a not-very-subtle association between "penny-candy", "jellybeans", "licorice sticks" on the one hand, and "love", "girl", "breasts . . . breathless" on the other. But the overtness of the suggestion of sexual gratification is calculated. It is consonant with the abruptness of onset and the power of puberty, that famous transition from "pennycandy" to "love".

Lying behind the sexual drama of the candy counter is also an evocation of romanticism. The "unreality", "semi-gloom", "september", "leaves . . . falling . . . died" echo the longings of romantic melancholy, the yearning for the unobtainable, by which frustrated sexual desire is often sublimated. Both the "jellybeans" which "glowed" and the "girl" whose hair was "rainy" represent the object of romantic longing; but what is crucial to the poem is the suggestion that the conversion of romanticism to sexuality in adolescence is a kind of death. The poet saves his romanticism, however, by making this experience of death itself a contribution to the image of the romantic otherworld: "Outside the leaves were falling . . . Too soon! too soon!". This is in keeping with his announced theme of falling "in love/with unreality".

The evocation of romantic nostalgia is thus deliberately spread over the elements of modern, urban, democratic triviality: the elevated tracks, the candy counter, "tootsie rolls" and "Oh Boy Gum".

Design features are very prominent in this poem. If you really understand how this poem is meant to work, then you should be able to give satisfactory answers to the following questions.

1. What are the major sectional boundaries of the poem, and how do these boundaries relate to the spacing between sense lines and the grouping of sense lines?
2. What contribution to meaning is made by the isolation of certain sense lines, and of certain groups of sense lines?
3. Why are each of three groups of sense lines (ll. 2–4, 8–10, 16–18) composed of shorter stretches of text, arranged in a cascade?
4. What is the function of punctuation (and its lack) in this poem?
5. To what degree is line-end a visual feature?
6. What is the special relationship between design and sense in ll. 13–15?
7. To what degree would the effectiveness of the poem be impaired by moving all sense lines flush up against the left-hand margin?

IV. QUESTIONS FOR REVIEW

1. Can you give a meaning to each of these terms?

imagism	allograph
graphology	notation
language event	logo
substance	*vers libre*
form	concrete poetry
situation	verse
context	free verse
grammar	"sublime"
lexis	interior monologue
grapheme	

2. We have agreed that every language event, every utterance, has three aspects; can you name them? Explain how each more abstract aspect is made actual by the next less abstract aspect.

3. Why does "concrete" poetry lose its effectiveness if it is read aloud and not seen with the eye?

4. Show how the distinction between the phoneme and the allophone could be matched by a distinction between the grapheme and the allograph.

5. How does English spelling demonstrate the independence of phonological and graphological representations of formal items?

6. We have agreed that onomatopeia represents a leap directly from the substance aspect of an utterance to the situational aspect, that is, that sound can contribute to contextual meaning without the intermediacy of the formal level. Explain in principle how letters, spacing and other aspects of design may contribute to contextual meaning by means of a similar leap over the formal level of language.

7. Characterize the basic principles of *vers libre*, the Imagist movement, and concrete poetry. In what ways do these movements in poetry differ?

8. Can you think of any way in which the history of design-consciousness in poetry is linked to the technological and economic history of writing?

9. The following is a highly regarded example of Imagist poetry. Features of design which are present in the poem include the absence of punctuation, the presence of stanza grouping, segmentation into sense lines, and the arbitrary distribution of various formal items into various sense lines. To an unusual degree, some of these features have little or no relationship to phonology or grammar. Explain how this poem works to produce its intended effect, paying particular attention to the design features.

THIS IS JUST TO SAY

I have eaten   1
the plums
that were in
the icebox

and which   5
you were probably
saving
for breakfast

Forgive me
they were delicious   10
so sweet
and so cold   12

—William Carlos Williams

Chapter Three   **Grammar**

WE CANNOT attach referential meaning to individual sounds or letters. Rather it is the function of individual sounds or letters to group together in sequences—and it is the sequences, whether as short as a word or as long as a sentence, which carry referential meaning. We notice in speaking or reading that many such sequences frequently repeat themselves. This is most noticeable in the case of words and short groups of words. But you will also note the frequent repetition of parts of words, and the occasional repetition of whole clauses and sentences. Each sequence carries a referential meaning. The core of this meaning remains constant through the repetitions, despite changes in context.

We can think of these repetitions as patterns. A text is a complex of patterns, and each pattern carries meaning. Because language is patterned in this way at a more abstract level than phonology or graphology, we give this level of abstraction the name "Form". The level of Form has two components, grammar and lexis, each including different kinds of patterns. Grammar patterns are more general than those of lexis and ultimately fewer in number. Grammar patterns include categories like word, clause, sentence, Subject, Complement, noun, adverb, and even sets of words like "and", "if", "you", and so forth. Each of these categories and sets is abstracted from the regular repetitions found in texts. Clauses as such, for example, recur repeatedly in texts; Subjects as such recur repeatedly in clauses; often the Subject is "you". Each of the categories and sets referred to also has a meaning. Often this meaning is very general, but without these meanings, we would have nothing intelligible to say or write.

Lexis, on the other hand, includes repetitions with very particular meanings. Lexis is simply a collective name for "lexical items", i.e. words as they are catalogued in the dictionary—a lexicon. The categories of grammar, being very general, give us only the skeleton of a text. Grammar can tell us that someone is doing something to someone else, but it is the lexical items which tell us whom or what these general roles refer to.

Literature, we have learned, makes extraordinary use of ordinary language. As a part of this capacity, literature makes extraordinary use of ordinary grammar. You will find that the description given to the grammar patterns of ordinary sentences holds good for sentences created at any level of sophistication. You will also see that imaginative writers find in ordinary grammar patterns a potential for producing literary effects of the most profound kind. In Units 5, 6 and 7 we will examine the literary use of clauses and word groups. In Unit 8 we will explore the literary potential of grammatical contrasts.

UNIT 5

Grammar of the Clause

I. ANALYSIS: the Play of Grammar in Donne and Hemingway

The bell doth toll for him that thinks it doth; and though it intermit again, yet from that minute that that occasion wrought upon him, he is united to God. Who casts not up his eye to the sun when it rises? But who takes off his eye from a comet when that breaks out? Who bends not his ear to any bell which upon any occasion rings? But who can remove it from that bell which is passing a piece of himself out of this world? No man is an island, entire of itself; every man is a piece of the continent, a part of the main; if a clod be washed away by the sea, Europe is the less, as well as if a promontory were, as well as if a manor of thy friend's or of thine own were. Any man's death diminishes me, because I am involved in mankind; and therefore never send to know for whom the bell tolls; it tolls for thee.

—John Donne, *Devotions Upon Emergent Occasions*

Once in camp I put a log on top of the fire and it was full of ants. As it commenced to burn, the ants swarmed out and went first toward the centre where the fire was; then turned back and ran toward the end. When there were enough on the end they fell off into the fire. Some got out, their bodies burnt and flattened, and went off not knowing where they were going. But most of them went toward the fire and then back toward the end and swarmed on the cool end and finally fell off into the fire. I remember thinking at the time that it was the end of the world and a splendid chance to be a messiah and lift the log off the fire and throw it out where the ants could get off onto the ground. But I did not do anything but throw a tin cup of water on the log, so that I would have the cup empty to put whiskey in before I added water to it. I think the cup of water on the burning log only steamed the ants.

—Ernest Hemingway, *A Farewell to Arms*

A gifted writer always puts himself into his work, but sometimes the gifted writer creates in a single, short, dense passage a symbol of his whole personality, or of his outlook on life. Both Donne and Hemingway have created in these two passages epitomes of their styles and of their whole presence in literature.

John Donne

Dr. John Donne was already renowned in his lifetime (1573–1630) as a poet, preacher and ecclesiast (Dean of St. Paul's Cathedral). His *Devotions* are a series of meditations on sickness and mortality that drew inspiration from one of his own grave illnesses. On his sick bed he began to notice the bell of the church adjoining tolling the daily funerals of his parishoners. He began to reflect that these funerals served to remind him of his own death, which might soon ensue, and that for all he knew he might even then be dying and the bell be tolling for himself. That in turn brought him to consider the question of his involvement in other people's lives, which is essentially the same question that Hemingway was to meditate 300 years later.

In this passage Donne asserts that a personal connection with the bell depends on a person's attitude (". . . doth toll for him that thinks it doth . . ."). But if a man does choose to be involved in other persons' lives—if he takes this first step, to become involved in mankind—then he is also involved in God, for God unites all men and all things. Moreover, says Donne, every man is involved in every other man whether he chooses to recognize it or not (". . . every man is a piece of the continent . . ."), because what every man does affects the rest. The news of one man's fate is therefore as significant to every man as the daily rising of the sun, as interesting as the appearance of a comet, as arresting as the sudden pealing of bells. A man may choose not to know this—to deny his connection with his fellow men, and so with God—but the man who does deny it is foolish (". . . never send to know . . . it tolls for thee.").

For Donne, the moral universe is very structured. The human race are related to God as a father above, and to each other as brothers and sisters below. Human society is a network of interconnecting values unified in the source of all value, God. For an outlook like Donne's, value is everywhere: one thing is always better than, as good as, or worse than another, depending on its role in mutual human involvement, and involvement with God. Even the construction of Donne's clauses reflects this outlook. In a structured world of value, language must be supple enough to reflect a reality which is intensely varied; and it must also be capable of bringing the most distantly related things together into overriding unity.

One of the first things we are apt to notice about Donne's text is its reliance on parallelism. In the stretch of text "Who casts . . . out of this world?" four sentences occur. Each sentence consists of one *indepen-*

dent (or *main*) clause and one *dependent* (or *subordinate*) clause of some kind:

Who casts . . . to the sun/ when it rises?
But who . . . from a comet/ when that breaks out?
Who bends . . . to any bell/ which upon any occasion rings?
But who . . . from that bell/ which is passing . . . this world?

The sense of climax which is achieved in the last clause, which makes the connection between sun, comet, bell and the theme of involvement, is achieved because it comes at the end of a series of parallels. In fact, there are two series of parallel clauses produced in these four sentences. First, there is the series of independent clauses, and second, the series of dependent clauses.

The effect of this structuring into parallel grammatical items is to produce a block of text which seems very ordered and regular, despite the fact that what is conveyed in the text as a message is very far-flung and fanciful. The news of a death is compared to the rising of the sun, the sudden appearance of a comet, the unexpected ringing out of a bell; and finally the death is compared to the loss of a member of one's own body. The imaginative energy of these images is tightly confined within the parallel clauses. A structure which can contain so many phenomena and yet remain so unified in its overall design is a microcosm of Donne's moral universe.

A second feature of Donne's text which is very prominent is its reliance on subordination. We have noticed that the parallelism of the four central sentences in this passage depends on the two series of independent and dependent clauses. The rest of the passage also abounds in dependent clauses, always initiated with words that signal their subordination: ". . . *that* thinks it doth . . .", ". . . *though* it intermit again . . .", ". . . *that* that occasion wrought upon him . . .", ". . . *if* a clod be washed away by the sea . . .", ". . . *as well as if* a promontory were . . .", ". . . *as well as if* a manor of thy friend's or thine own were . . .", ". . . *because* I am involved in mankind . . .". Such subordination is a highly specific ordering of information. Each of these subordinate clauses offers related information about the message of a main clause. These subordinate clauses define a person or thing, disallow an objection, present a necessary condition, or specify a cause. In all cases this ordering of information into *subordinate* or *main* clause indicates a sense of hierarchy and value.

The rhythm of the very first sentence in the passage ("The bell doth toll . . .") demonstrates how the patterning of subordination produces an interesting climactic effect within a larger symmetry. In its gross structure, the sentence consists of two independent clauses, linked by "and". The first independent clause contains a dependent clause, ". . . that thinks it doth

. . .", which finishes the larger clause. The second independent clause is preceded by a dependent clause, ". . . though it intermit again . . .". The effect of arranging the independent clauses in this way is to begin and end the sentence with the messages of main importance, and to sandwich in the circumstantial information between them. The sentence therefore seems to fall into two balanced halves, with the order of *independent, dependent* reversed in the second half to produce a sense of symmetry. But the second half also contains another dependent clause ". . . that that occasion wrought upon him . . .", which delays the Subject and Verb of the independent clause, ". . . he is united . . .". This affects the impression of balance produced by the symmetry of the sentence, but the effect is not so much to spoil the symmetry as to give the feeling of onward movement, of climax. The climax is the achievement of a delayed goal, the final member of the four-fold symmetry in the pattern: main-message; subordinate-message/ subordinate-message; (subordinate-message) main-message. The intrusion of the extra subordination which delays the return to the main-message makes that return all the more satisfying.

Over all, we are given the feeling that a great ordering power is at work producing these symmetrical structures. This achievement of order in his sentences and paragraphs reflects Donne's belief in the unity of God's creation. It is that unity that makes sense of every individual's death.

Ernest Hemingway

The protagonist of *A Farewell To Arms*, Frederic Henry, has reached out for happiness in life by falling in love and begetting a child. Now he has just been informed at the hospital that his child was born dead, strangled by the umbilical cord. The fate of the child seems to him like the fate of the many men he has seen killed in the Italian campaign of the First World War. All men are born only for death, all men are in some sense destroyed by their own begetting. In the passage quoted above, Frederic is introspectively relating the futility of individual human existence not only to the futility of nature, but also to himself, to the futility he feels as the doomed witness of life.

In the incident of the ants, Frederic was the cause of the catastrophe, the comprehending spectator to the catastrophe and the potential saviour of the catastrophe. He is in the same position generally in life. Simply by continuing to live a human life but especially by begetting another human life, Frederic contributes to the ongoing absurdity which he feels life is. But by coming to a comprehension of life's absurdity, Frederic has achieved an understanding of the human position from a point outside it. He can observe humanity with the same cool superiority with which he had once watched the ants swarming and dying in the fire. And Frederic, of course, can always choose to play the messiah in human life by taking a moral position, by taking action: by fighting a just war, by fathering a child, by taking pity on the suffering. This choice is neither more nor less absurd, more nor less valuable, than not acting.

The abruptness and indifference with which their potential saviour chooses only to steam the ants is soon to be matched by Frederic's later actions. He will leave the hospital to have his dinner at a nearby café. His appetite will not be diminished. Watching the ants die, he simply wanted whiskey. About to watch the child's mother die too, he still requires food. His life will simply go on. The narrator of the story—the ultimate cause of, witness to and saviour of Frederic's particular catastrophe—makes Frederic's dinner as important an event as any other in the story. All events for this spectator are equal. Value has been suspended.

The construction of the clauses in the Hemingway passage is as indicative of the world those clauses represent as the clauses of the Donne passage were. If we compare the two, we at once notice that the extraordinary parallelism of the sentences in the Donne passage is absent here. The co-ordinating conjunction "and" is frequently used, sometimes "but", and once "then"; but the clauses which these conjunctions link together form no beautifully elaborated symmetrical patterns.

What is prominent in the Hemingway passage instead is an almost monotonous co-ordination of clauses. Most of the eleven "ands" link together main clauses, much as a child might in telling a story. The recitation of events has the structure of a list.

But a more important result of this use of "and"—also of "then" and "but"—is to reduce the possibility of anticipating a connection between events. After "and" anything can happen. It simply attaches together independent clauses. As a matter of fact, about half of the events that do occur after "and", "but" and "then" in this passage are surprises: the log turns out to be full of ants; the ants turn out to swarm toward the fire, not away; then they run for the end; the survivors of the fire turn out to be suffering from sensory disorientation; the spectator turns out to have messianic leanings; but the leanings lead only to steaming the ants, and so forth. The point is that the co-ordination of main clauses within a sentence makes for about the same narrative rhythm as if each clause formed a single sentence. The main clauses describe events. The events merely happen one after another.

The sentence which most represents the rhythm established here is the sentence in the middle of the paragraph which sums up and repeats the events that have already been described:

> But most of them went toward the fire
> and then back toward the end
> and swarmed on the cool end
> and finally fell off into the fire.

The potential for parallelism like that of the Donne passage is here but the parallels in these clauses are not as elaborated and varied, and there is a good deal of mere repetition (e.g. "fire", "end"). The simplicity and obviousness of this pattern adds to the impression of a child telling a story, without enough sophistication or sense of narrative to build to a climax, able only to list events in chronological order.

Although parallel structure has been replaced by repetition, subordinate clauses, as in Donne, abound: ". . . As it commenced to burn . . .", ". . . where the fire was . . .", ". . . When there were enough on the end . . .", ". . . their bodies burnt and flattened . . .", ". . . not knowing where they were going . . .", ". . . that it was the end of the world (etc.) . . .", ". . . to be a messiah and lift (etc.) . . .", ". . . where the ants could get off onto the ground . . .", and so forth. However, the quality of the subordinations is very different without the overriding framework of parallel constructions that Donne created to contain them. In Hemingway, the circumstantial information tends simply to accumulate rather than to take its place in a unified and ordered pattern.

Moreover, as the following sentence shows, Hemingway can produce an effect much the same as monotonous co-ordination, not just with main clauses, but with subordinate clauses as well:

> I remember thinking at the time
> that it was the end of the world and a splendid chance
> to be a messiah and lift the log off the fire and throw it out
> where the ants could get off onto the ground.

Although everything after "remember" is subordinated to the "I remember" clause, Hemingway still manages to include in this highly sophisticated structure—in lines 2 and 3—examples of "and" linking phrases and clauses of equal value, so that the sense of mere series, even here, predominates over the possibility of any more sophisticated scheme of order.

Hemingway's moral cosmos has a structure, for every cosmos has a structure. The sense of mere sequence in the events of his narratives is a microcosm of that universe, and it is matched by a similar sense of sequence in the grammar of those narratives. It is not a simple kind of writing, in the sense of some simple contrast with the balance and complex subordination of Donne. Both men are gifted writers after all. Rather, it is a marshalling of the resources of language into a different order, to show a different thing. Hemingway's concern is to emphasize that there is no innate value or order in events themselves; they just happen. Donne's concern is to show how, through the concept of God's unity, value and order can be achieved.

II. FRAMEWORK: Structure and Function in the English Clause

The Rank-Scale

To understand the structure of the English Clause we need to understand the terms *rank-scale* and *unit-complex*. The concept of the rank-scale is that every sentence in English is made up of a set of compartments. The largest compartment is called *clause*; the next largest, *group*; the next largest, *word*; and the smallest, *morpheme*. At least one example of each compartment exists in all sentences.

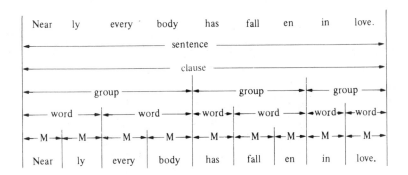

In this *sentence* we have one *clause*, the *clause* has three *groups* within it, and each of the *groups* has two *words*. Some of the *words* ("nearly", "everybody", "fallen") have two *morphemes* (*M*), and others ("has", "in", "love") have only one each. But we could also have a sentence in which there was but a single clause, a single group, a single word, and a single morpheme.

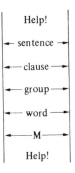

It is important to insist that clause, group, word, and morpheme are all present in every sentence, always, because that permits us to be perfectly consistent in the method of describing sentences. This way, we never have to argue whether such compartments are really present in any particular sentence—we just assume that they are and work from there.

The Unit-Complex

The concept of the unit-complex is that two or more of these compart-ments, or units, may be attached together to do the work of one. For example, we get a *clause-complex* when two or more clauses are attached together to perform a single function. This is the very top of the rank-scale, so we may say that the normal function for *all* clauses is always the same—to make up sentences.

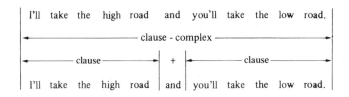

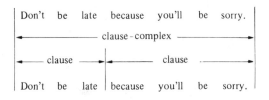

There are similar unit-complexes at the group, word, and morpheme ranks. The simple units within a unit-complex at any rank may be related to one another in two different ways. They may be parallel to one another in their importance and impact, or one may be subordinate to the other in importance and impact. To keep such relationships straight, we represent parallel or "independent" simple units as "α" and subordinate or "depen-dent" simple units as "β" in unit-complexes:

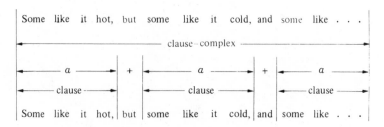

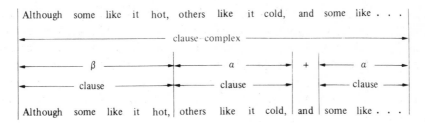

For reasons which will be made clear in Unit 7, individual clauses and other simple units are labelled "α" even when they occur alone, unaccompanied by another unit of the same rank. In the first of the two sentences diagrammed just above, all three clauses offer information of about equal importance. Another term for this parallelism is *parataxis*. Such structures are said to be *paratactic* structures. In the second sentence, however, the first clause is different in its impact from the next two clauses. The initial word, "although", serves as a signal that what follows is conditional information, that is, information which is only circumstantial to the matters of main interest, the information of the next two clauses. Another word for this subordination is *hypotaxis*. Structures conveying this relationship are said to be *hypotactic*. Hypotaxis in clause complexes is signalled by a number of special words: although, if, unless, because, for, etc. Even some stock phrases are used to do this job: due to the fact that, even if, etc.

The Five Functions of Groups

But now, in order to discuss the structure of the clause itself, we must examine the several different functions that groups have in a clause. Normally clauses have only a single function, to make up sentences. They differ only in their relationships with each other—hypotactic or paratactic. Of course, groups, too, have one main function—to make up clauses—but they also perform several different functions within clause structure, and each of these functions is given its own name:

SUBJECT	actor, or who or what is being talked about
PREDICATOR	the action, or the "talking about"
COMPLEMENT	the object of action, or an identification with subject
ADJUNCT	manner, time, signals for hypotaxis (and sometimes parataxis)
Z	"extra" groups which name the auditor, or anticipate another group

The symbols for these names are S, P, C, A and Z.

The groups which perform these different functions are sometimes easy to identify and sometimes hard. They are easy to identify when, in addition to possessing the function in an obvious way, they also possess characteristic punctuation, place-order or form.

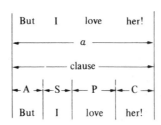

In this one-clause sentence, the group which fulfills the Subject function is *I*, just a one-word group. Apart from the obvious fact that *I* represents the "actor" in this situation, there are three other details about *I* which are highly characteristic of Subject groups. First, the *I* falls to the left of the group which carries out the Predicator function. Second, the *I* is not separated from the Predicator by punctuation. Third, the *I* form is used, not the *my* or *me* form. Now the Subject group does not always have to be to the left of the Predicator group, but it tends to be. Similarly the Subject group tends not to be separated from the Predicator group by punctuation. You would agree that Standard English always requires us to use *I, she, he, they, you, it* for Subject forms in pronouns, not *me, her, him, them, your, its,* etc. In this sentence all these details add up, and we identify the *I* as Subject without having to reflect too deeply on the precise nature of its function.

The *her* group is easily recognizable as the object of the Subject group's affections, thus "object of action" and Complement in function. It too has a characteristic place-order and form. Like most Complement groups, it comes after the Predicator group. As the object of some "action", it occurs in the *her* form, not the *she* form which would be characteristic of a Subject group.

The Predicator group *love* can of course be recognized as the "action", but it is also recognizable as the group between Subject and Complement groups, if these have already been recognized for what they are from characteristics other than place-order alone. The one-word group *But* is an Adjunct group in clause structure, and not the linking element "+" because its clause begins a sentence, and is thus not in a clause-complex with some preceding clause.

Other clauses are more difficult to analyze into group functions.

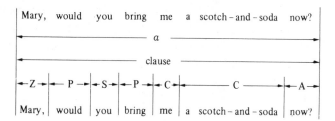

The assumption that there are only five functions in the clause in English is a useful point of departure, like the assumption that every sentence has at least one clause. Let's argue that *Mary* has the Z function because it names the auditor. *You* is thus the S because it is the one-word group which represents the actor. Of course *Mary* represents the actor too, and *you* in a sense names the auditor. But our assumption about five separate functions will make us want to keep them as distinct as possible. *Mary* is more a naming of auditor than a representing of the actor, and *you* is more a representing of the actor than a naming of the auditor. This will be clearer if you think about how such a sentence would be said aloud. Also note that *you* is not set off by punctuation, but *Mary* is.

Both *would* and *bring* have a hand in representing the action, but they are not separate groups. Together they make up a single group which does the one job of representing action. The P symbol is repeated in our analysis only because the S group interrupts the P group. In questions, it often happens that the S group interrupts the P group instead of preceding it.

Both *me* and *a scotch-and-soda* are C in function because both are in some sense objects of action. The second C is an object of the action of "bringing" in a more obvious sense than that of the first C. However, *me* represents someone who is also on the receiving end of this activity, and thus an object in a secondary sense. Finally A is the function of *now* because that one-word group gives us a time reference.

Bundles of Functions

When we go into the matter more fully, we find that each of the five named functions is actually a bundle of more subtle functions collected together because their activities are somehow related. Yet it is still fairly easy, given that there are only five named functions, to sort groups into the different categories. Let's look at them one by one.

The S Function

The S function thus embraces a number of different roles which a group may play. Some of these differing roles are illustrated in the following sentences.

I *drive* fast.	S: *I* (who is the actor, who is being talked about)
Harry *likes* potatoes.	S: *Harry* (who is being talked about)
Harry *was hit* by a potato.	S: *Harry* (who is being talked about, although the potato is the actor)
It's a potato!	S: *It* (which in a limited sense is being talked about)

In sentence number 3, *Harry* is now on the receiving end of the action, but still represents the S function because we still instinctively feel that the rest of the information in the clause is about *Harry*, rather than vice versa. This is less true of the S group *It* in sentence number 4; but we still feel that early occurrence in a clause is a sign of the main interest, so even the colourless *It* looks more like S than anything else. *Harry* in sentence number 2 cannot really be an actor, since "liking" does not look much like an activity. Rather this *Harry* is a participant in an emotion, and is still the main interest. Notice that S tends to occur before P, or interrupts P in questions.

The C Function

Any group which can occur as S in clause can also occur as C in some other clause.

It is I!	C: *I* (identification with subject)
The potato struck Harry.	C: *Harry* (object of action)
She threw Harry a potato.	C: *Harry* (secondary object of action)
	C: *potato* (primary object of action)
He returned it.	C: *it* (object of action)

The functions "identification", "primary object" and "secondary object" are really three different roles. As in the case of the slightly different S roles, it is convenient to give these slightly different roles a single name too. Complement function thus includes things or persons directly operated upon in a clause (traditionally "direct object"), things or persons benefited by or just in reference to an action (traditionally "indirect object"), things, persons, qualities identified as, or as part of, the Subject (traditionally "subjective completion", or "predicate nominative", etc.).

The P Function

The P function is usually a representation of action, but sometimes something is happening in the clause other than a real action. In the following sentences the P function also is revealed to be a bundle of different roles.

He moved his piece across the board.	P: *moved* (action, performed by "He", with "his piece" as object)
The piece was moved by Harry.	P: *was moved* (action, performed by "Harry", with "The piece" as object)
Harry played her a game of backgammon.	P: *played* (action, with "her" as secondary object, "a game of backgammon" primary)
She likes backgammon.	P: *likes* (action in a sense, with "backgammon" as primary object)
She is very intelligent too.	P: *is* (not action, just an equating of "She" with identifying characteristic)

Although "moving", "being moved" and "playing" are clearly actions, the three represent different slants on the notion of action. In the case of sentence 1, the S element is the performer of action; but in sentence 2, the S element is on the receiving end. In sentence 3 it seems as if the primary object is on the receiving end of the action; but when you think about it, you realize that "a game of backgammon" is a means of defining the action. A piece may be played, but only in a context which makes that play significant; and that context is the game. To play a game may be to move pieces, but it is hard to think of the game as undergoing action in quite the same way. Here we also see another one of the many functions belonging to C.

In sentence 4, "liking" is even less like an action that works upon some object. Rather it is simply feeling an emotion, or perhaps registering an intellectual preference. Another function for the primary object is revealed as the cause of such an emotion or preference. In sentence 5, "being" is not in the slightest an action, but functions much like an "equals" sign in mathematics. Yet all of these P elements which are not in the truest sense actions are still a means of "talking about" the S element.

The A Function

There are all sorts of Adjunct elements. The following sentences contain a sprinkling of the different types.

If he likes her, Harry takes her to dinner.	A: *If, to dinner* (signal of hypotaxis, and circumstance)
On the other hand, he usually enjoys himself.	A: *On the other hand, usually* (circumstance, and manner)
He looked her up in the phone book.	A: *up, in the phone book* (manner)

It is important to note that none of these A elements could be mistaken for S, P or C. In a sense, the A function is a bundle of almost all the functions left over after we cull out the most basic functions in the clause. Signals for hypotaxis, like *if* (and *when, although, supposing that, where,* etc.), are unambiguous in the main. Groups which represent circumstance, manner or time may sometimes seem hard to pin down, but it is important to realize that the A function embraces nearly everything which does a job additional to the jobs of S, P and C.

The Z Function

The Z element is less likely to occur in a clause than any of the other elements. There is usually something "extra" about the Z, but, as usual, Z is a term applied to a number of different functions.

My brother, he ain't too bright.	Z: *My brother* (unnecessary repetition, thought to be "incorrect")
He doesn't like it one bit, linguistics!	Z: *linguistics* (explanatory repetition, perhaps unnecessary)
Harry, you get to work!	Z: *Harry* (naming of auditor)
Check, waiter.	Z: *Check, waiter* (element in predicatorless clause, and a naming of auditor)

Each of the Z elements in these sentences just misses being some other element. *My brother* comes close to functioning as the S element, but its real purpose is to emphasize; *he* holds the place of topic, and so serves as S instead. The one-word group *linguistics* might have done as C element after *like*, but instead is used to explain *it*, which is very like the role played by *My brother* in the previous sentence. Both *Harry* and *waiter* might have done for S elements, but in sentence 4, *Harry's* real function is to get Harry's attention, and *you* does the Subject job. In sentence 5, the action is only implicit. This makes *waiter* functionally ambiguous, since "the waiter" may or may not be implicitly an actor. But he is certainly named. *Check* is even more ambiguous without a P element alongside it, so it becomes Z by default, because it is not clearly either S or C.

Rank-shift

All along we have been treating the S, P, C, A and Z elements as functions being performed by groups. In so far as clauses are supposed to be made up of groups, this is quite logical. But the following sentences make our procedure seem too neat (p. 103).

The first sentence is very ordinary. The elements in the clause are functions carried out by groups. But in the second sentence, *creamcheese,* an ordinary one-word group, is replaced with a whole clause. This clause,

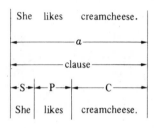

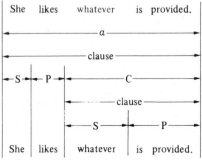

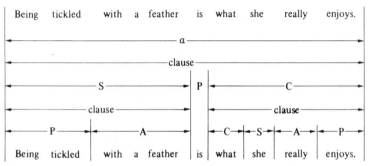

whatever is provided, contains groups carrying out their ordinary functions. But it itself is carrying out the role of a clausal element in the larger clause. This fulfillment of a clausal element function by a clause is different from the ordinary function of a clause, which is just to be an element in the larger unit, sentence, either as α or β. We have now found an exception to the rule of the rank-scale, which has previously assured us that clauses ought only to be made up of groups. Therefore the *She . . . provided* clause will be said to contain a *rank-shift*; that is, the *whatever is provided* clause is rank-shifted from clause status to group status because it helps to make up another clause. Notice that the third sentence is made up directly of one single clause, but that this larger clause contains two rank-shifted clauses, one in the S role and the other in the C role. The *Being tickled with a feather* clause is what is being talked about, and the *what she really enjoys* clause is an identification with the S element. The P element, as usual in such topic-identification constructions, just serves to equate S with C. Previously we identified β clauses as *subordinate*. Now we can label all rank-shifted clauses as *subordinate* too.

Back to Donne

With all these terms and definitions to hand, the task of explaining the rhetoric of a Donne or a Hemingway is much easier. We noticed that the four consecutive sentences from Donne's *Meditation* with which we began possess two series of parallel clauses; the first series is the independent clauses, the second the dependent. The independent clauses are all very similar in choice and arrangement of elements. The dependent clauses gradually expand in complexity and length, as measured both by actual text, and by the variety of their elements. The resulting structure is very pretty: within a basic four-square framework, a regularly paced variation proceeds to a suitable climax. The basic building-blocks of this nicely ordered composition are the clause unit and its constituent elements. Notice that the last two dependent clauses are not β clauses in sentence structure. Instead they are rank-shifted so as to fall within the structure of groups possessing the function Adjunct in the last two independent clauses. Unit 6 will make it easier to understand this distinction. (See the following diagram.)

	Who	casts not	up	his eye	to the sun	when	it		rises?		
				a				β			
	S	P	A	C	A	A	S		P		
But	who	takes	off	his eye	from a comet	when	that		breaks		out?
				a				β			
A	S	P	A	C	A	A	S		P		A
	Who	bends not		his ear	to any bell		which	upon any occasion	rings?		
				a							
	S	P		C ← A			S	A	P		
But	who	can remove		it	from that bell		which		is passing	a piece of himself	out of this world?
				a							
A	S	P		C ← A			S		P	C	A

III. APPLICATION: Rhetoric in Religious Prose

YOU can now see that the analysis of the language of Donne and Hemingway that we began with was based on the general principles of clause structure we have just discussed. These principles will hold good for the analysis of effects achieved in any writing which attempts to deploy the resources of the English clause. The following passage is such an instance.

4. Now there are diversities of gifts, but the same Spirit.

5. And there are differences of administrations, but the same Lord.

6. And there are diversities of operations, but it is the same God which worketh all in all.

7. But the manifestation of the Spirit is given to every man to profit withal.

8. For to one is given by the Spirit the word of wisdom; to another the word of knowledge by the same Spirit;

9. To another faith by the same Spirit; to another the gifts of healing by the same Spirit;

10. To another the working of miracles; to another prophecy; to another discerning of spirits; to another divers kinds of tongues; to another the interpretation of tongues;

11. But all these worketh that one and the selfsame Spirit, dividing to every man severally as he will.

12. For as the body is one and hath many members, and all the members of that one body, being many, are one body; so also is Christ.

13. For by one Spirit are we all baptised into one body, whether we be Jews or Gentiles, whether we be bond or free; and have been all made to drink into one Spirit.

—I Corinthians 12:4–13

Apparently it is the purpose of St. Paul to convince his readers that the church is one, that all members are on the same level of standing. (The theme may remind you of Donne's.) To do that effectively, St. Paul sets up a sustained contrast between the variety of people in the church (Jews, Gentiles, bond, free, the wise, the healers, etc.) on the one hand, and the basic unity of the Church on the other. You may find some of the terms unfamiliar, either because of their technical religious use, or because the text of this English translation belongs to the early seventeenth century. For example, "administrations" means "official functions", and "tongues" refers to the phenomenon called *glossolalia*, or "speaking in tongues" which may occur in the course of community worship. However, it is clear that St. Paul is contrasting variety with unity in several orderly series of clauses. Verses 4–7 make one series, 8–11 make another, and 12–13 make a third. The contrasts in each of these three series are presented in different ways. In addition, each series contains a great deal of parallelism; and the parallelism in each of these three series is presented in different ways, as well. Yet at the same time, the whole passage is drawn together by common structural devices (as well as by a common idea). It is also a very dynamic text, because it proceeds to a climax in verses 12–13.

Your job is to verify each of the statements we have just made about the construction of this passage, and the effects which its unique construction was calculated to achieve. Apply the principles of clause structure and clause-complexes which we have just discussed to prove the following statements:

1. The passage falls into three series, 4–7, 8–11, 12–13.
2. Contrasting ideas are represented in contrasting syntax.
3. Each series has a characteristic method of making contrasts.
4. Each series has a characteristic method of making parallels.
5. The whole passage possesses a structural unity.
6. The whole passage rises to a climax which is both conceptual and structural.

IV. QUESTIONS FOR REVIEW

1. Can you give a meaning to each of these terms?

rank-scale	clause-complex
unit-complex	subordinate
sentence	independent
clause	Subject
group	Predicator
word	Complement
morpheme	Adjunct
α	Z
β	actor
parataxis	action
paratactic	auditor
hypotaxis	identification
hypotactic	rank-shift

2. What are the various roles which together make up the Subject function? The Predicator function? The Complement function? The Adjunct function? The Z function?

3. Rewrite, combining the following pairs of independent clauses to make up clause-complexes, each having one α and one β. Add whatever signal words you require.
   (a) The plane is late. John arrives in the morning.
       (e.g. *If the plane is late, John will arrive in the morning.*)
   (b) You have egg on your face. You look funny.
   (c) Light a match. You can see how much gas is left.
   (d) Barnaby fell all the way to the bottom. It is a great shame.

4. Can you pick out the various groups which make up the following clauses? Can you assign to each group the appropriate function?
   (a) I like Paris in the springtime.
       (e.g. *I*: S, *like*: P, *Paris*: C, *in the springtime*: A)
   (b) Brother, can you spare a dime?
   (c) Sally and Patty and Mary and Herby came running, jumping, skipping and hopping down our street in the morning.
   (d) Let them eat cake.
   (e) Flowers are what I sent her, and regrets are what she returned.
   (f) All mimsy were the borogoves,/And the mome raths outgrabe.

5. The following passage achieves part of its very considerable effect by the manipulation of clausal elements, by the placing of clauses, and by the control of clause and group lengths. Can you show just how this is done? Discuss other relevant features of the language.

> There are many that I know and they know it. They are all of them repeating and I hear it. I love it and I tell it. I love it and now I will write it. This is now a history of my love of it. I hear it and I love it and I write it. They repeat it. They live it and I see it and I hear it. They live it and I hear it and I see it and I love it and now and always I will write it. There are many kinds of men and women and I know it. They repeat it and I hear it and I love it. This is now a history of the way they do it. This is now a history of the way I love it.

> —Gertrude Stein, *The Making of Americans*

6. You may be interested to learn that Ernest Hemingway and Gertrude Stein had a close relationship, he being instrumental in getting some of her writing published, and she "instructing" him in writing. Compare the clause structures and clause-complexes of this passage and the Hemingway passage. Can you detect a "Stein-ian" influence in Hemingway's prose?

7. The language of the King James version of the English Bible from which our *I Corinthians* passage was taken is the language of a time about a hundred years before Donne's *Devotions*. (The translators deliberately used some archaic forms.) Again, by comparing the clause structure and clause-complexes of both passages, can you detect a biblical influence in Donne's prose? The King James is the bible he most probably studied and meditated upon.

UNIT 6

Grammar of the Group

I. ANALYSIS: Two American Stylists

The day dawned bleak and chill, a moving wall of grey light out of the northeast which, instead of dissolving into moisture, seemed to disintegrate into minute and venomous particles, like dust that, when Dilsey opened the door of the cabin and emerged, needled laterally into her flesh, precipitating not so much a moisture as a substance partaking of the quality of thin, not quite congealed oil. She wore a stiff black straw hat perched upon her turban, and a maroon velvet cape with a border of mangy and anonymous fur above a dress of purple silk, and she stood in the door for awhile with her myriad and sunken face lifted to the weather, and one gaunt hand flac-soled as the belly of a fish, then she moved the cape aside and examined the bosom of her gown.

The gown fell gauntly from her shoulders, across her fallen breasts, then tightened upon her paunch and fell again, ballooning a little above the nether garments which she would remove layer by layer as the spring accomplished and the warm days, in colour regal and moribund. She had been a big woman once but now her skeleton rose, draped loosely in unpadded skin that tightened again upon a paunch almost dropsical, as though muscle and tissue had been courage or fortitude which the days or the years had consumed until only the indomitable skeleton was left rising like a ruin or a landmark above the somnolent and impervious guts, and above that the collapsed face that gave the impression of the bones themselves being outside the flesh, lifted into the driving day with an expression at once fatalistic and of a child's astonished disappointment, until she turned and entered the house again and closed the door.

—William Faulkner, *The Sound and the Fury*

Doctor Sax I first saw in his earlier lineaments in the early Catholic childhood of Centralville—deaths, funerals, the shroud of that, the dark figure in the corner when you look at the dead man coffin in the dolorous parlor of the open house with a horrible purple wreath on the door. Figures of coffinbearers emerging from a house on a rainy night bearing a box with dead old Mr. Yipe inside. The statue of Ste. Thérèse turning her head in an antique Catholic twenties film with Ste. Thérèse dashing across town in a car with W. C. Fieldsian close shaves by the young religious hero while the doll (not Ste. Thérèse herself but the lady hero symbolic thereof) heads for her saintliness with wide eyes of disbelief. We had a statue of Ste. Thérèse in my house—on West Street I saw it turn its head at me—in the dark. Earlier, too, horrors of the Jesus Christ of passion plays in his shrouds and vestments of saddest doom mankind in the Cross Weep for Thieves and Poverty—he was at the foot of my bed pushing it one dark Saturday night (on Hildreth & Lilley secondfloor flat full of Eternity outside)—either He or the Virgin Mary stooped with phosphorescent profile and horror pushing my bed. That same night an elfin, more cheery ghost of some Santa Claus kind rushed up and slammed my door; there was no wind; my sister was taking a bath in the rosy bathroom of Saturday night home, and my mother scrubbing her back or tuning Wayne King on the old mahogany radio or glancing at the top Maggie and Jiggs funnies just come in from wagon boys outside (same who rushed among the downtown redbricks of my Chinese mystery) so I called out "Who slammed my door (*Qui a farmez ma porte?*)" and they said nobody ("*Parsonne voyons donc*")—and I knew I was haunted but said nothing; not long after that I dreamed the horrible dream of the rattling red livingroom, newly painted a strange 1929 varnish red and I saw it in the dream all dancing and rattling like skeletons because my brother Gerard haunted them and dreamed I woke up screaming by the phonograph machine in the adjoining room with its Masters Voice curves in the brown wood—Memory and dream are intermixed in this mad universe.

—Jack Kerouac, *Doctor Sax*

Memory and dream are often intermixed in literature. The larger myth comes swelling out of remembered details of character and setting. Style is the secret of this metamorphosis, lifting language out of the ordinary, and so giving events a special significance as well. William Faulkner and Jack Kerouac are two American novelists known for their styles and for their ability to transform their regional backgrounds into universal experiences. Faulkner, in the last section of a mature work, raises an old negro servant into a giant image of her own religious conception of herself. Kerouac, in a long prose poem about his childhood, contrives to convey both the glowing sensual reality of youth and its concomitant guilty hallucinations. Both authors show through their prose styles the myth-making faculty of man. Both build their styles in these passages on an elaboration of the nominal group.

William Faulkner

William Faulkner was a southern novelist who used the specific settings of his own time and country to suggest the universals of existence. He is famous for a highly ornate rhetoric combining complex grammar and prosodic rhythms. One of his themes is decay, specifically the decay of the old white culture in the south as typified by the Compson family in *The Sound and the Fury*. All the members of this family are, one way or another, "crazed". Benjy, the second son, is a congenital idiot, symbolic of the whole family in his permanent infantile inability to see the world except in terms of himself. The eldest son, Quentin, is a suicide. The daughter Caddy, and her illegitimate daughter, also called Quentin' because of the incestuous feeling between Caddy and Quentin, sister and brother, represent the decay of honour into prostitution. The third son, Jason, is a furious materialist, but bound by pride to maintain the family as long as his neurotic mother lives. The father has died an alcoholic, having lived long enough to sell the remnant of what once was a large estate.

Dilsey, of the passage above, is the matriarch among the black servants of the Compson family. They have endured and supported the mad Compsons in their flight into oblivion through two generations. She represents a capacity for self-sacrifice, and for survival. She has seen the beginning of their end, and is to see their final disintegration as well. On Easter day, April 8, 1928, she has a vision in her church of her role as witness to the Compsons' tragic play.

The passage above describes the morning of that day. Dilsey is dressed in the clothes that she will wear to the Easter service. The day before, the idiot Benjy has had his thirty-third birthday. The night before, the illegitimate daughter, Quentin, has fled with a man from a travelling show after stealing 7000 dollars from the materialist Jason. Today, the tomb of our Lord is opened, and Dilsey comes forth. The passage depicts her as both a realistic and a symbolic presence. She appears from the cabin like Christ from the tomb, the uplifted hand, dressed in furs and royal purples, and even anointed with the "oil" of the sleety weather. There are suggestions of the crucifixion and the tomb in such words as "needled", "moribund", "skeleton", "bones", and of course in words like "fortitude" and "indomitable" and the climactic "guts".

The style of the passage is perfectly coincident with its themes: ornate, rich, regal and serious. This epic quality of style is what people expect from Faulkner. It can be funny when used to depict ridiculous scenes; but here it is not, coming at the end of a long book of tragic events. What holds this style together and gives it strength is its architectonic constructions. Both paragraphs, above, are punctuated to contain just two very long sentences each. Each of the four sentences consists of a number of groups and clauses, arranged in an interlocking complexity. Except for the second sentence of paragraph 1, each sentence is perfectly "correct" in its grammatical architecture.

The key to this architecture is the structure of the nominal groups and of the nominal group-complexes. The nominal group is an ordinary phrase used as the Subject, Complement, or Z element of a clause, or sometimes as an Adjunct element. Its internal structure consists of a head element and the optional elements, modifier (before the head) and qualifier (after). The nominal group-complex is the association of two or more nominal groups as one Subject, Complement, Z, or Adjunct element in clause structure.

Most of the first sentence in the first paragraph, above, represents a single nominal group-complex, made up of two nominal groups that together form the Subject element of the clause which is the sentence. The second nominal group (everything after the first comma) is appositive to the first ("The day"). Several clauses, initiated by "which", "instead of", "that", "when", "precipitating", "partaking of", are rank-shifted into this nominal group, prolonging and building it until it achieves the size and complexity necessary for Faulkner's conception.

The second sentence in the first paragraph and the first sentence in the second paragraph are about as long as the sentence we have discussed, and are also built up from nominal groups, but their structures are simpler. In the second sentence of paragraph 2, however, we return to the majestic structure of paragraph 1. Two sections, "unpadded . . . guts" and "the collapsed . . . flesh", are each nominal groups with rank-shifted clauses in them, as in the first sentence of the first paragraph. The opening of the door and the closing of it again as Dilsey retreats are thus both accompanied by a flourish of language.

Nominal groups are, in their nature, static, the names of things. Predicators are active, and descriptive of process. Here the nominal groups, inside their static selves, have expanded via the rank-shifted clauses into action and process as well. They have become deeper, full of Predicators. Similarly, on the level of meaning, the static picture of Dilsey at the cabin door is full of the background and movement of another symbolic figure. Dilsey has become an icon of the resurrected Christ. But she is an ironic icon for, like the groundhog at the end of winter, she looks but once and then returns to her tomb. There will be no resurrection for the Compsons, and hence no freedom for their servants.

Jack Kerouac

Jack Kerouac is as famous a stylist as Faulkner, and probably more influential. He singlehandedly made the "beat generation" famous through his book *On the Road*. His books are almost "automatic writing", written at top speed on a typewriter and uncorrected so as to capture the shifts and nuances of moment-by-moment experience. His style is designed to reflect the raciness of popular culture, the spontaneity of contemporary speech, and the blurred, fragmented flow of life in the young and hyped-up. His generation believed in turning on and experiencing "vision", the glimpse of something—perverse or holy—seen through the texture of everyday reality.

Doctor Sax is a novel about Kerouac's working-class childhood in the French (Canadian) sections of industrial Lowell, Massachusetts. Much of the story consists of the fantasies of childhood about the preternatural. These are woven into detailed portrayals of childhood friendships and heightened moments of experience. Doctor Sax is the archetype of the magician, the evil one, the mad scientist, he who stands behind the ordinary events of the world, orchestrating them into a dark significance. In the last passages of the novel he and all the dark fantasies are transcended as Kerouac's childhood is left behind.

The extract above introduces Doctor Sax to the novel as his earliest beginnings are recalled by the narrator. These lie in the necrophobic, necrophiliac feelings surrounding funereal symbolism in popular Catholicism, horror movies and crucifixion themes. But mixed with these glimpses of horror are fragments of domestic banalities, the little familiar routines— baths and radio programmes—that represent security to a child. The juxtaposition of horrific imaginings and mundane family realities is characteristic of childhood fantasy.

The style is racy and fragmentary, as the child's mind scampers to new and ever more vivid details. The style allows for the accumulation of discrete details, most of them bizarre. What makes this possible is the use of listing constructions in the passage. The first half of the paragraph is a long list of haunts. The second half begins as a list of domestic memories, then returns to haunts at the end. The constructions must be open enough and flexible enough to allow insertion of any sudden impulse or recollection for "Memory and dream are intermixed in this mad universe".

The listing technique is based on nominal group structures, both as lists of nominal groups and as lists at the modifier and qualifier elements of nominal groups. The qualifier elements are complex with lots of rank-shifting. The two sections "the dark figure . . . door" and "an antique Catholic . . . disbelief" exemplify this. Both are single nominal groups with embedded clauses and prepositional groups at the qualifier element. The prepositional groups themselves contain successively embedded nominal groups, and sometimes clauses, which produces the list effect. In addition, the first nominal group above is itself within the last item of a series of three nominal groups in a relationship: "deaths, funerals, *the shroud of that . . . door*". We have here lists within lists within lists, as the last item of each list is expanded into a new list, like opening yet another chinese box.

In addition to this there are more lists at the modifier element of the nominal group. These modifier strings are elongated: "an antique Catholic twenties film", "the dead man coffin", "W. C. Fieldsian close shaves", "a strange 1929 varnish red". More important even than the fullness of modification is the unusually high frequency of it. Not only are nominal groups modified heavily, many nominal groups are modified heavily.

The effect of Kerouac's style is to give an impression of anxious, amateurish piling up of experience, as though there is too much to say to get it all down easily. The strings of nominal groups in the prepositional groups, and clauses in the qualifier elements of nominal groups give additional detail without architectonics. The density of modifiers is amateurish because of the obviousness of this device; but the amateurishness is appropriate. Kerouac's hero is an excited, horror-ridden child, his brain teeming with fantasies, his senses tingling with stimuli, and without consistent, conceptual ways to organize this wealth of material.

Kerouac and Faulkner

Gothic fantasy runs through much of American regional literature, from *Moby Dick* and *The Scarlet Letter* to William Faulkner's stories of decaying southern families and Kerouac's hymns to experience and despair. Both Faulkner's and Kerouac's styles complement their themes. Faulkner's style tends to architecture with its long, counter-poised clauses embedded at the level of the group. This is in keeping with his epic symbolism and the way his books attempt to mirror mankind in the particular agony of the American south. Kerouac's prose is also elaborated at the rank of group, but his grammar, like his theme, is less deep. He is intent on capturing the moment-by-moment detail of life, and so both the modifier and qualifier elements of group structure are expanded to carry more material. The structure is left deliberately loose to allow the addition of more material as it occurs to him, without rewriting. Thus spontaneity is preserved. The attempt to get everything down without missing anything has led him, like Faulkner, to develop a style suitable to his vision. Both writers find their solutions in the elaboration of the nominal group.

II. FRAMEWORK: Nominal, Verbal and Adjunctival Groups

REMEMBER that the elements of clause structure are called Subject, Predicator, Complement, Adjunct and Z. According to the rank-scale these elements are normally realized by groups. When S, P, C, A, or Z is realized by more than one group, we have a group-complex. For example:

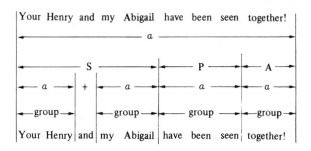

Note that we can use "α" and "β" notation to represent the members of group-complexes, just as we did to represent the members of clause-complexes. Such a group complex occurs in the second sentence of the first paragraph of the Faulkner passage, at C:

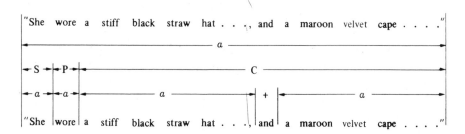

There are three different functional types of group. These are labelled according to which elements of clause structure they realize, and according to their own internal structure. The S, and C and Z elements, and sometimes the A element, are realized by "nominal" groups. The P element is realized by "verbal" groups, and the A element by "adjunctival" groups. These three different types of groups have different internal structures.

Nominal Groups

The same nominal groups realizing S can be used at C, and vice versa. Indeed, often the same nominal group can be found at Z, and even at A, though other types of group are possible there:

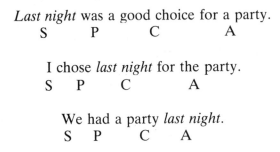

Nominal groups can always be strung together in complexes to make up a single S or C or Z or A. Sometimes nominal group-complexes occur within other complexes in a *recursive* structure. " Recursive" means having parts similar in form to the whole. The more recursive the complex, the greater *depth* of recursion. For example:

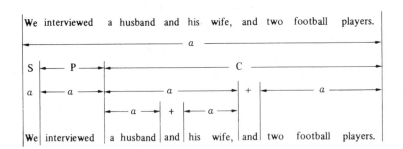

(Rank-shift is a different phenomenon but it also can contribute to the *depth* of grammatical structure, as we saw in the first sentence of the Faulkner passage with its many rank-shifted clauses at the qualifier element of the nominal group.)

The nominal group must have at least one word. The element realized by this word is the "head" (h) element. The nominal group may have elements before the head—the modifier (m) element—and after the head—the qualifier (q) element. A sequence of several words may realize a sequence of several modifier elements. A sequence of several different units may realize several qualifier elements. Here are some examples of the morphology of the nominal group:

really sick *from grief*   happy *enough*
  m   h   q   h   q

Your Henry   My friend *from Kansas*
  m   h   m   h   q

last night   The brothers *Grimm*
  m   h   m   h   q

Bob   All my children
 h   m m   h

These six men *from the West who arrived yesterday.*
  m   m   h   q   q

The h elements are classifiable by the type of word that realizes them. The most common classes are nouns (or "substantives") and pronouns, which can be classed together as "nominals". The other possibilities are "adjectives", "deictics" (words like "that", "these", etc.), "numerals" and "quantifiers" ("much", "many", etc.). Nouns can be distinguished at further delicacy as common (ants) or proper (Mary) and if common as countable (dogs) or mass (jam), and if countable as singular or plural. Pronouns can be sorted into personal (ours), relative (who), reflexive (myself), indefinite (anyone) and interrogative (what).

The ordinary exponent of a q element is a word because q is an element of group structure. Words at q may be nouns, pronouns, adjectives, even deictics, numerals, quantifiers, adverbs and verbs. We have to be careful when analyzing that we distinguish between a "defining" function, which is the q function, and an appositive function (α') which makes for a group-complex.

For example:

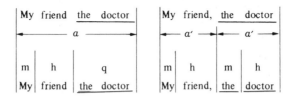

As in the example above we frequently find, rather than single words, whole nominal groups or prepositional groups rank-shifted at q. The prepositional groups are made up of a preposition (p) and a completive (c) and may be identified by the list of prepositions (to, in, out, of, from, by, for, over, under, etc.). Prepositional groups usually contain a rank-shifted nominal group as their completive element. For example:

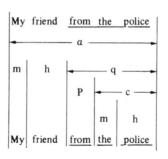

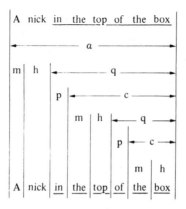

Clauses may also be rank-shifted at q. Common clauses appearing at q are relative clauses (who . . .), or clauses with participial predicators (verb forms usually ending in -ed, -en, -ing) in either the present or past tenses.

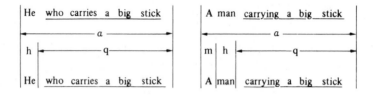

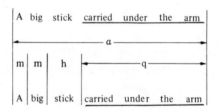

Such clauses may also occur at β in clause-complexes. Be careful to distinguish these from clauses at q. For example:

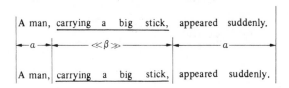

Note that a β clause may interrupt, rather than precede or follow, an α clause; and that when this happens we bracket the β symbol, while repeating the α symbol.

The q element in English may achieve great depth of recursion through rank-shift. As in the next example, rank-shifted elements at q may have rank-shifted elements in them or in their elements almost *ad infinitum*:

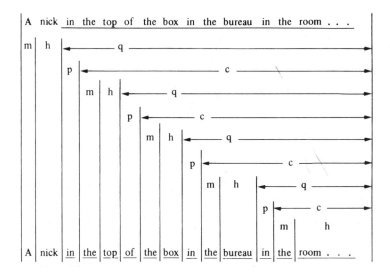

Faulkner, as pointed out in the analysis, makes full use of this option to build his effects. He uses rank-shifted clauses and clause-complexes at q, as well as groups and group-complexes to achieve depth of recursion. The nominal group which comprises most of the first sentence in the Faulkner passage above, "a moving wall . . . congealed oil.", begins a q structure with "of grey light . . .". The "light" has a q too, "out of the northeast" and "wall" has another q, the clause initiated by "which". This clause is interrupted by the β clause "instead of dissolving into moisture". Within the Adjunct occurs a rank-shifted group-complex "minute and venomous particles, like dust that . . ." which comprises the rest of the sentence. The "that . . ." clause is q in the second member of this complex. It is interrupted by the β clause starting "when . . ." and followed by another β clause started by "precipitating". The clause initiated by "partaking" operates at q in an even further degree of rank-shift. You will appreciate that this description is a little simplified.

The modifier element of the nominal group structure may be filled by four different types of words. "Adverb" words occur at m only when h is an adjective, deictic, numeral or quantifier word; as such the adverb is said to realize the adverb element (r). Adjective words commonly realize m, and as such are said to realize the "epithet" element (e). Nouns may also occur at m, and as such are said to realize the "nominal" element (n). The third type of element that m breaks down into is called the "determiner" element (d): modifier words which realize d include deictics, numerals and quantifiers. All these types of modifiers may occur alone or together. If the latter three occur together they are "place-ordered", that is, they tend to occur in a fixed linear sequence of d, e, n(h). Sequence thus helps to distinguish them at this higher degree of resolution. There are other clues about which type a word belongs to: adjectives are lexical, determiner element words are either numerical or purely grammatical (thus non-lexical) and nouns at nominal are elsewhere capable of taking plural forms when countable. Here are some examples:

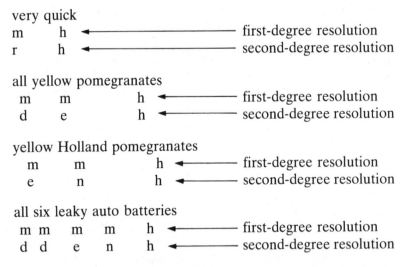

Even higher resolution reveals another sequence order of sub-types. At determiner, the ordered types are: d_1—"all", "both", "half"; d_2—articles, demonstratives; d_3—superlatives, ordinals; d_4—quantifiers, cardinals; d_5—comparatives, alternatives; d_6—"such":

All my finest six other such teacups (!)

d_1 d_2 d_3 d_4 d_5 d_6 h

At epithet there are the possibilities of e_1—size and shape; e_2—quality; e_3—age:

A big fat old grumpus
d_2 e_1 e_2 e_3 h

Such sequences are only normative, not inevitable.

You must be careful to note that rank-shifts occur in nominal groups not only at q element, but also at various modifiers. The most common of these can be found at the d or e elements, consisting of a determiner or adjective word itself modified by an adverb. That is, instead of a single word realizing elements d or e, we get a whole nominal group doing the same job:

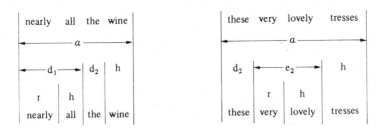

You must also be careful to distinguish between groups and complexes at the rank of word. Just as group-complexes are strings of two or more groups performing the same role in clause structure, word-complexes are strings of words performing the same role in group structure. A word-complex realizing some element in group structure is different from a rank-shifted group realizing the same element because the word-complex has no modifier-modified structure:

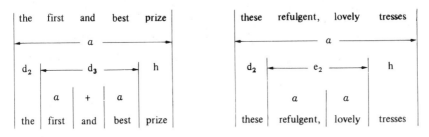

Verbal Groups

The Predicator element in the clause is always realized by the verbal group. Like nominal groups, verbal groups may be one word or several. Semantically, the verbal group indicates an action, process, or copula function. Action denotes visible or tangible activity ("run"), process denotes event ("see"), copula denotes the equation or linking of Subject and Complement ("is"). Verbal groups may show the polarity (positive or negative), the tense (present, future or past), the number (singular, plural), the person (1st, 2nd, 3rd), the aspect (perfective, progressive), the voice (active, passive) and the mood (indicative, infinitive, participial).

Like nominal groups, verbal groups may be joined in verbal group-complexes to realize a single Predicator. Potentially, if not very frequently, these complexes may develop recursive depth. For example:

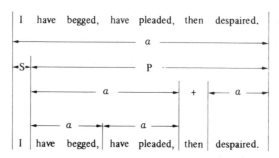

The verbal group must have one word, usually the head (h) element. It may have one or more auxiliary (x) elements. The word that realizes the head element carries the lexical meaning. The auxiliary words specifically convey future tense, aspect, passive voice and other effects.

Sometimes the auxiliary appears alone when the lexical element is "understood". Here are some examples:

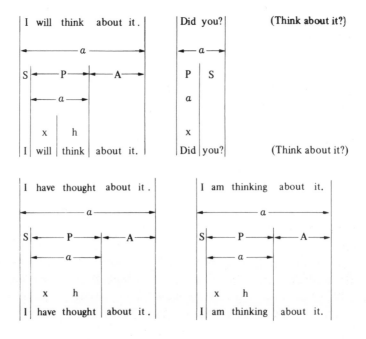

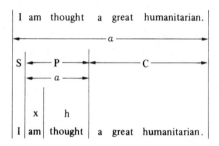

The x element may be distinguished into various types at higher resolution. These are the modal (x_m), perfective (x_{pe}), continuous (x_c) and passive (x_{pa}) types. The modal auxiliary may be known by the list of modal verbs: can, may, do, dare, need, ought, used, shall, will and so on. The perfective is carried by a form of the verb "have" (as in "I have thought . . ."), and the continuous by a form of "be" (as in "I am thinking . . ."). The passive is carried by a form of "be" (as in "I am thought . . .") or (colloquially) "get". Each type is followed by a characteristic form of the following verb: the modal by the "plain" or "to-" form (think, to think), the perfective and passive by the past participle form (thought, run, walked, shaken, been) and the continuous by the "ing" form (thinking).

When they co-occur the auxiliaries usually appear in the sequence x_m x_{pe} x_c x_{pa}. Each next auxiliary element has the form required by the preceding auxiliary. The head element will have the form required by the last auxiliary in the string. The negative word, if present, normally occurs after the first auxiliary.

will think	am thinking
x_m h	x_c h

have thought	am thought
x_{pe} h	x_{pa} h

I shall not have been being thought a great humanitarian.

x_m x_{pe} x_c x_{pa} h

Some strings of lexical verbs are neither auxiliary and head, nor verbal group-complexes, but are "phased" predicators. These consist of more than one verbal group, sometimes with a nominal group (as Z in clause structure) in between. But they are not separate predicators of separate clauses either. Phased predicators can be distinguished from auxiliary-head sequences because auxiliaries are realized by the special auxiliary words. They can be distinguished from predicators in rank-shifted clauses because phased predicators, after the first member, are non-finite in form ("plain", to-, or -ing); and any intervening nominal group which shows case will be in objective case (me, us, him, them, etc.)

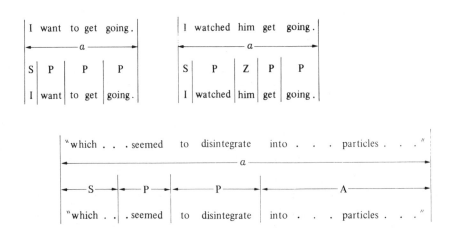

Adjunctival Groups

The Adjunct element of clause structure is carried by the adjunctival group. Semantically, these groups are adverbial or conjunctive. Accordingly, "adverb" words or "conjunctions" realize many of them. Like nominal groups and verbal groups, adjunctival groups may be strung together into complexes to realize the same Adjunct element. As with the other groups it is sometimes possible to produce recursive depth.

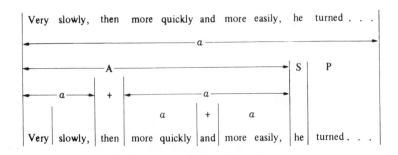

The basic structure of an adjunctival group consists of an obligatory head element and the infrequently used possibility of a modifier or qualifier. For example:

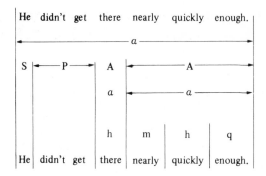

The type illustrated is called an "adverbial" adjunctival group, which has a conjunction or adverb word at head element, an adverb at modifier, and "enough" or a few other items at qualifier.

There is some overlap in the morphology of nominal groups and adjunctival groups. For one thing the adjunctival group exponent may be a nominal group which is simply being used as an Adjunct:

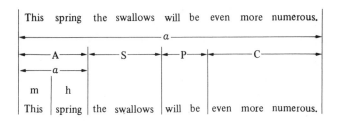

For another, a third possible type of adjunctival group exponent, the prepositional group, composed of two elements, preposition and completive, may take a rank-shifted nominal group at completive:

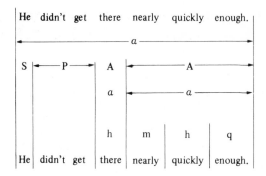

In analyzing, one must take care to distinguish the nominal group as Subject, Complement, or Z element from the nominal group as Adjunct. Also, one must be careful to distinguish the prepositional group as qualifier from the prepositional group as Adjunct. The prepositional group can even combine with the nominal group in a group complex with an α–α structure:

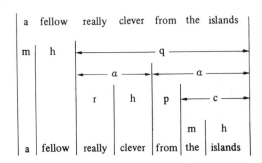

Adjunctival groups in the Faulkner passage are quite unremarkable but in the Kerouac passage they are sometimes the carriers of a large nominal group-complex: ". . . in his earlier lineaments in the early Catholic childhood of Centralville—deaths, funerals . . . door". In discussing a passage stylistically, you must remember that the nominal group structure may turn out to be any one of such various things as an adjunctival group, the completive of a prepositional group, the rank-shifted exponent of an element in another nominal group or an element of clause structure. When considering the effect of a group on style, you must also consider its function in larger structures.

In conclusion, if we return to the Faulkner and Kerouac passages, we find as much happening there at group rank as we found happening at clause rank in the passages from Donne and Hemingway. It is this ability to exploit the possibilities of language that makes certain writers memorable, and the study of their styles fascinating for students of language and literature alike. Whenever a man is gifted with a powerful and individual vision and seized by the urge to set it down, he will bend ordinary forms of language into new and more dramatic shapes. In no other way can the uniqueness of what he has to say be conveyed.

III. APPLICATION: the Centaur and the Nominal Group

IN *The Centaur*, John Updike has created a character based on the ancient Greek myth of Chiron, the teacher of Hercules. Chiron was the most humane representative of the race of centaurs, a species with the body and legs of a horse, but with a human torso, head and arms where the horse's neck should be. In war, the centaurs were archers, able to gallop and fire arrows at the same time. Chiron met his tragic fate trying to intervene in a quarrel, and getting a poisoned arrow in the leg for his efforts. Updike makes his centaur, who is also a teacher, representative of the compound nature of man: spiritual and animal, idealist and beast. Here is how he begins his novel:

> Caldwell turned and as he turned his ankle received an arrow. The class burst into laughter. The pain scaled the slender core of his shin, whirled in the complexities of his knee, and, swollen broader, more thunderous, mounted into his bowels. His eyes were forced upward to the blackboard, where he had chalked the number 5,000,000,000, the probable age in years of the universe. The laughter of the class, graduating from the first shrill bark of surprise into a deliberately aimed hooting, seemed to crowd against him, to crush the privacy that he so much desired, a privacy in which he could be alone with his pain, gauging its strength, estimating its duration, inspecting its anatomy. The pain extended a feeler into his head and unfolded its wet wings along the walls of his thorax, so that he felt, in his sudden scarlet blindness, to be himself a large bird waking from sleep. The blackboard, milky slate smeared with the traces of last night's washing, clung to his consciousness like a membrane. The pain seemed to be displacing with its own hairy segments his heart and lungs; as its grip swelled in his throat he felt he was holding his brain like a morsel on a platter high out of hungry reach. Several of the boys in their bright shirts all colors of the rainbow had risen upright at their desks, leering and baying at their teacher, cocking their muddy shoes on the folding seats. The confusion became unbearable. Caldwell limped to the door and shut it behind him on the furious festal noise.
>
> —John Updike, *The Centaur*

This initial paragraph does not indicate to the unwary reader that Caldwell is a centaur, nor that the situation is fantasy rather than realism.

Watching the author slowly and artfully revealing these two aspects of the story in the succeeding paragraphs is one of the pleasures of the book. However, you will not by now be surprised to learn that the style of this introduction is heavily involved with the rank of group. Like Kerouac, Updike here reveals a tendency to create lists to achieve the richness of sheer accumulation. Much of this listing involves the group, but, like Faulkner, Updike also depends for effects on the rank of clause, as well as on the rank of group.

1. Find some examples of what we have referred to as "listing".
2. Can you find any "lists" that involve just one type of unit, group or clause? How many members do these lists have?
3. Can you find a list which consists of two or more different types of unit?
4. Find a list which contains two or more α clauses, making a complex.
5. Find some lists which contain two or more α nominal groups, making a complex.
6. Can you find a list which contains two or more β clauses within an even more inclusive clause-complex?
7. What part do rank-shifted units play in listing effects?
8. Find some examples of listing effects within the modifier elements of nominal group structure.
9. In your own words, characterize the poetic effect which the lists of this paragraph achieve, and relate that effect to the situation which the paragraph attempts to describe.

IV. QUESTIONS FOR REVIEW

1. Can you give a meaning to each of these terms?

group	common noun	nominal element (n)
group-complex	proper noun	determiner element (d)
nominal group	countable noun	numeral
verbal group	mass noun	quantifier
adjunctival group	pronoun	verb
recursive	personal pronoun	copula
recursion	relative pronoun	polarity
depth (of recursion)	reflexive pronoun	auxiliary element (x)
head element (h)	indefinite pronoun	modal auxiliary
modifier element (m)	interrogative pronoun	perfective auxiliary
qualifier element (q)	appositive	continuous auxiliary
adjective	prepositional group	passive auxiliary
deictic	preposition	phased predicator
noun	completive	adverb
substantive	epithet element (e)	conjunction

2. Distinguish the groups in the following clauses, and classify each group (watch out for rank-shifts):
   (a) The fat old balloon man was panting from his long walk.
   (b) Not very long afterwards, the *Mary Deare* was found with no one on board.
   (c) My dear friend, you are the one who will pay for this mistake.

3. What structural elements are realized by the groups you distinguished and classified in Question 2? Which groups are rank-shifted?

4. Diagram the group-complexes in the following clauses:
   (a) In the first car we found three Europeans, a Scotsman, five Asiatics, a family from New Zealand, but no Americans.
   (b) All six witnesses and the defendant himself have testified to the same point.
   (c) A frightened suspect might freeze or might bolt, or could struggle and be injured.
   (d) Crunchies can be eaten in the morning, in the evening or just about any time.

5. What structural elements are realized by the group-complexes you diagrammed in Question 4?

6. Diagram the structures of the following nominal groups and nominal group-complexes, showing all structural elements at the highest degree of resolution:
   (a) the boy
   (b) a long-range Vickers gun
   (c) this primaeval forest
   (d) shoes and socks for little girls
   (e) the man who came to dinner
   (f) a week ago last Thursday
   (g) all the three other candidates
   (h) half this bottle of raspberry jam
   (i) 17 little new-born chicks
   (j) such quality as I've never tasted
   (k) and a one, and a two, and a three
   (l) *The Once and Future King*

7. Diagram the structures of the following verbal groups and verbal group-complexes, showing all structural elements at the highest degree of resolution:
   (a) will do
   (b) must have
   (c) will run, will be elected, and will serve
   (d) was being driven
   (e) will be hanged, might be drawn, and should be quartered
   (f) must have been being replaced
   (g) getting scratched
   (h) run and hide

8. Diagram the structures of the following adjunctival groups, showing all structural elements:
   (a) slowly
   (b) as slowly as you can
   (c) from my point of view
   (d) sufficiently well
   (e) just recently enough
   (f) from the bathhouse in the garden
   (g) six weeks ago
   (h) more temperately than I imagined

9. The style of the following passage shares a number of characteristics with the style of the Kerouac passage we examined earlier in this unit. Show how groups and group-complexes are used to contribute to the listing effects achieved, and relate those listing effects to the overall intention of the style.

   That's good thinking there, Cool Breeze. Cool Breeze is a kid with three or four days' beard sitting next to me on the stamped metal bottom of the open back part of a pickup truck. Bouncing along. Dipping and rising and rolling on these rotten springs like a boat. Out the back of the truck the city of San Francisco is bouncing down the hill, all those endless staggers of bay windows, slums with a view, bouncing and streaming down the hill. One after another, electric signs with neon martini glasses lit up on them, the San Francisco symbol of "bar"—thousands of neon-magenta martini glasses bouncing and streaming down the hill, and beneath them hundreds, thousands of people wheeling around to look at this freaking crazed truck we're in, their white faces erupting from their lapels like marshmallows— streaming and bouncing down the hill—and God knows they've got plenty to look at.

—Tom Wolfe, "Black Shiny FBI Shoes" in *The Electric Kool-Aid Acid Test*

UNIT 7

Univariate Structures, Rank-shift and Depth

I. ANALYSIS: the Mock-epic Sentence in *Tom Jones*

Black George now repaired to his wife, on whose prudent counsel he depended to extricate him out of this dilemma, but when he came thither he found his house in some confusion. So great envy had this sack [dress] occasioned that when Mr. Allworthy and the other gentry were gone from church, the rage, which had hitherto been confined, burst into an uproar and, having vented itself at first in opprobrious words, laughs, hisses, and gestures, betook itself at last to certain missile weapons, which, though from their plastic nature they threatened neither the loss of life nor of limb, were however sufficiently dreadful to a well-dressed lady. Molly had too much spirit to bear this treatment tamely. Having therefore—but hold, as we are diffident of our own abilities, let us here invite a superior power to our assistance.

Ye Muses, then, whoever ye are, who love to sing battles, and principally thou, who whilom didst recount the slaughter in those fields where Hudibras and Trulla fought, if thou wert not starved with thy friend Butler, assist me on this great occasion. All things are not in the power of all.

As a vast herd of cows in a rich farmer's yard if while they are milked they hear their calves at a distance, lamenting the robbery which is then committing, roar and bellow, so roared forth the Somersetshire mob an hallaloo, made up of almost as many squalls, screams, and other different sounds as there were persons, or indeed passions among them; some were inspired by rage, others alarmed by fear, and others had nothing in their heads but the love of fun—but chiefly envy, the sister of Satan and his constant companion, rushed among the crowd and blew up the fury of the women, who no sooner came up to Molly than they pelted her with dirt and rubbish.

Molly, having endeavoured in vain to make a handsome retreat, faced about, and laying hold of ragged Bess, who advanced in the front of the enemy, she at one blow felled her to the ground. The whole army of the enemy (though near a hundred in number), seeing the fate of their general, gave back many paces and retired behind a new-dug grave; for the churchyard was the field of battle where there was to be a funeral that very evening. Molly pursued her victory and, catching up a skull which lay on the side of the grave, discharged it with such fury that, having hit a tailor on the head, the two skulls sent equally forth a hollow sound at their meeting, and the tailor took presently measure of his length on the ground, where the skulls lay side by side, and it was doubtful which was the most valuable of the two. Molly then taking a thigh-bone in her hand fell in among the flying ranks, and dealing her blows with great liberality on either side, overthrew the carcass of many a mighty hero and heroine.

—Henry Fielding, *Tom Jones*

New genres, like new cities, often rise on the graves of the old. The novel as we know it grew out of the prose romance that grew out of the picaresque epic. It differs from the epic by being in prose, and from the drama by consisting of a series of loosely connected incidents rather than a tightly woven dramatic action. Henry Fielding, the author of *Tom Jones,* one of the identifiable progenitors of the modern novel, was aware of the origins of his new genre. He wrote a preface to an earlier work, *Joseph Andrews*, in which he defines his creation as "a comic epic poem in prose" and "a comic romance". Having defined what we call the novel by comparing it with its predecessors, he goes on to discuss what he means by "comic", thus describing one of the main branches of the modern novel: the social satire or novel of manners. *Pride and Prejudice, Vanity Fair, The Egoist* and *Ulysses* were to follow.

Fielding's discussion of his work involves considerations of form and style as well as content. He defines the subject of the comic romance as "the ridiculous" in human nature and carefully distinguishes this from the grotesque. He says that the ridiculous stems from one cause, affectation, or falsity of nature. This is the source of comedy: the discovery of what is false in human actions and characters. Fielding also talks about the burlesque style as a falsification of nature. It is the mating of a high style with low business. As such, the burlesque style may help reveal the ridiculous in the actions described.

For our purposes the passage above provides an excellent example of the idea of a variety of languages evolving from the specific uses to which language is put. The burlesque exhibited here cannot be effective without the reader's knowledge of a "high" or "heroic" style that includes invocations to the Muses, protestations of the author's inability to do credit to his overwhelming subject, and epic similes. But high style also involves the creation of "depth" through the use of complex grammatical structures. Without our previous association of grammatical depth with the seriousness and intellectual respectability of heroic themes, Fielding could not achieve the successful burlesque style that is part of his exposure of the ridiculous in human nature. Style, as well as genre, rises on the grave of the old.

Fielding and the Burlesque

Henry Fielding's life and writing career occurred in the early formative years of the novel. His contribution was a talent for light-hearted social satire, and the intellectual capacity for building formidable structures in both his sentences and his plots. *Tom Jones* is his most famous and accomplished creation. Tom Jones, the hero of the novel, is the first social picaresque hero of the British novel. Raised as a foundling on the country estate of an impossibly idealized eighteenth-century gentleman, he ends up some hundreds of pages later barely escaping the gallows at Tyburn after a rollicking jaunt through all the environments, mores and classes of rural and London life.

In common with the epic poem, the novel has a protracted story line, a quest theme and a heroic protagonist. In contrast to the serious epic, however, the hero is a rake, the adventures are all misadventures, and the quest continually misconceived. The plot and episodes are of a "ridiculous" nature, as the above passage exemplifies; the characters are largely drawn from low life; the sentiments and diction are ludicrous; and the style is a parody of the heroic.

Molly, in the passage above, is the daughter of Black George, who is gamekeeper to the eighteenth-century gentleman, Squire Allworthy, the foster-father of Tom Jones. Curvacious Molly has used her charms to acquire a number of upper-class lovers, Tom among them, and in the process has picked up both the airs and some of the clothing of a "lady". Unfortunately, she is also not a little pregnant. Her flaunting of both accomplishments at the village church has led to the jealous rage of the lower-class part of the congregation, with results that the passage details.

The slapstick attack on Molly in the churchyard has all the elements of low humour including making fun of the dead and of women fighting. The characters, "Black George", "ragged Bess" and "the tailor", are all comic buffoons. The portrayal of Molly as a "well-dressed lady" of "spirit" is just as obviously tongue-in-cheek. To these low elements Fielding has contributed the full force of his "high" style . The result is a burlesque or parody. According to Fielding himself the burlesque is an element of the comic romance but should be carefully limited since the intention of the genre is not to exaggerate but to describe realistically actual occurrences of the ridiculous in life. Parody is therefore limited to style. Furthermore, the genre of heroic poetry is not under attack here, but rather the ridiculous in life itself, as thrown into relief by the inappropriate "noble" style.

The apostrophe to the Muses occurs in the second paragraph of the passage and is accompanied by a reference to Butler's *Hudibras*, a famous mock-epic poem. The epic or extended simile follows in the next paragraph and is based upon an appropriately ridiculous comparison. The lexis also is appropriate to the high style but not to the actual situation portrayed: ". . . the rage, which had hitherto been *confined*, burst into an uproar and, having *vented* itself at first in *opprobrious* words . . . betook itself at last to certain *missile* weapons, which, though from their *plastic* nature they threatened neither the loss of life nor of limb, were however *sufficiently dreadful* to a well-dressed lady." The mob is pelting Molly with dung.

Epic Sentence Structure

But beyond these attributes of style it is the intricate and extended sentence structures that truly raise the language to the level of parody. Molly's pretensions to a higher station are echoed by those of the language, and both pretensions are denied by the actual facts: that Molly is engaged in mud-slinging and bone-throwing, and Fielding in describing it. The mechanism of this kind of parody is very simple. The epic style uses sentences of this type to convey a serious and thoughtful tone. With this established connection of style and content as the ground, the change to slapstick is immediately foregrounded, and the tension induced by the complexity of linguistic structure can be easily released in laughter.

The three example sentences quoted below are all very extended. This length is achieved largely by the use of extended clause-complexes. Depth in sentences is equivalent to internal complexity, the amount of articulation among grammatical units. Depth in these sentences is produced by subdivision of the complexes and by rank-shifting.

```
So great envy had this sack occasioned
    that
        when Mr. Allworthy and the other gentry
        were gone from church,
        the rage,
        which had hitherto been confined,
    burst into an uproar
    and,
        having vented itself at first in opprobrious words,
        laughs, hisses, and gestures,
    betook itself at last to certain missile weapons,
        which,
            though from their plastic nature
            they threatened neither the loss
            of life nor of limb,
        were however sufficiently dreadful to a well-dressed
        lady.
```

The basic structure of this first example is an α clause ("So great . . . occasioned") plus a β member ("that when . . . lady"), but the β is itself composed of two α members ("that when . . . uproar" and "having vented . . . lady"). The first of these α members is subdivided in turn into an interrupted α clause ("that . . . the rage burst into an uproar") and two β clauses ("when Mr. Allworthy . . . church" and "which had . . . confined"). The second α member is also composed of an α clause ("betook itself . . . weapons") and two β members ("having vented . . . gestures" and "which, though . . . lady"). The second of these β members has yet the further structure of an interrupted α clause ("which . . . were however sufficiently dreadful to a well-dressed lady") and a β clause ("though from . . . limb"). The structure $\alpha + \alpha$ within the original β member extends and deepens the sentence while the component clauses within each α member give additional depth. At the end other component clauses within the sentence-ending β also provide additional depth.

> As a vast herd of cows in a rich farmer's yard
>   if
>   while they are milked
>   they hear their calves at a distance,
>   lamenting the robbery
>   which is then committing,
>   roar and bellow,
> so roared forth the Somersetshire mob an hallaloo,
>   made up of almost as many squalls, screams, and
>   other different sounds
>   as there were persons, or indeed passions
>   among them;
> some were inspired by rage,
> others alarmed by fear,
> and others had nothing in their heads but the love
> of fun—
> but chiefly envy, the sister of Satan and his constant
> companion, rushed among the crowd
> and blew up the fury of the women,
> who no sooner came up to Molly
>   than they pelted her with dirt and rubbish.

The second example sentence turns out to be two sentences grammatically, tacked together with the semicolon. The basic structure of the first of these is an α clause ("so roared forth the Somersetshire mob an hallaloo") and two β members ("As a . . . bellow" and "made up . . . them"). The first β then subdivides into an interrupted α clause ("As a vast herd of cows

in a rich farmer's yard . . . roar and bellow") and a β member ("if while . . .
committing"). The β in turn breaks down into an interrupted α clause ("if
. . . they hear their calves at a distance") and two β clauses ("while they are
milked" and "lamenting . . . committing"). The second of these β clauses,
it may be noted, contains a rank-shifted clause ("which . . . committing").
Another rank-shifted clause ("as there . . . among them") occurs in the
sentence-ending β. Here, then, depth is also achieved through rank-
shifting.

The second grammatical sentence of this graphological unit consists of a
clause-complex of two α members ("some were . . . fun" and "chiefly . . .
rubbish"). The first of these consists of three α clauses ("some . . . rage",
"others . . . fear", and "others . . . fun"). The second basic α member
consists of two α clauses and a β clause. The α clauses are: "chiefly envy
. . . crowd" and "blew up . . . women". The β clause with its internal
rank-shift ("than . . . rubbish") takes up the rest of the sentence.

> Molly pursued her victory
> and,
> > catching up a skull which lay on the side
> > of the grave,
> discharged it with such fury
> > that,
> > > having hit a tailor on the head,
> > the two skulls sent equally forth a hollow
> > sound at their meeting,
> > and the tailor took presently measure of
> > his length on the ground,
> > > where the skulls lay side by side,
> and it was doubtful
> > which was the most valuable of the two.

The third example sentence is a *tour de force* of both complexes and
rank-shift. It forms both the climax of the battle and of the fun as it brings
together the two "low" incidents of disrespect for the dead and of women
fighting. The sentence's basic structure is a clause-complex of three α
members ("Molly . . . victory", "catching up . . . side by side", and "it was
. . . two"). The two α clauses at the beginning and end of the sentence are
relatively short and uncomplicated, though the last one contains a rank-
shifted clause. But it is the central α member that carries the burden of both
complexity and action. This α is made up of an interrupted α clause and two
β clauses. The two parts of the α clause are: "discharged it . . . fury that"
and "the two . . . side". The β clauses are "catching up . . . grave" and the
interrupting "having hit . . . head". The second part of the α clause is itself

composed of two α clauses ("the two . . . meeting" and "the tailor . . . ground") and a β clause ("where . . . side"). The sentence is further complicated by the fact that this second part of the α clause "the two . . . side" is itself part of a rank-shifted clause. Indeed, everything in the sentence from "that" to "side" (apart from the interrupting β) is part of the qualifier element of the head element "fury". This makes for enormous and rather untidy depth in the middle of the sentence. The result, linguistically, is something like a heap in which lies buried not only the ancestors of the villagers, the tailor, and Molly's hopes for dignity, but also the wreckage of "heroic" syntax.

Besides clause complexes, other complexes occur in these sentences and contribute to the epic feeling. In the first example sentence the nominal group "opprobrious . . . gestures" contains a word-complex at head element of four α items: "words", "laughs", "hisses" and "gestures". In the second example sentence the Subject element—"envy, the sister of Satan and his constant companion"—is made up of two α members in apposition ("envy" and "the sister . . . companion"). The second of these is in turn made up of two α nominal groups ("the sister of Satan" and "his constant companion"). Similarly, other rank-shiftings occur besides rank-shifted clauses, particularly at the qualifier element of the nominal group where rank-shifted prepositional groups frequently appear, and at completive element in prepositional groups of all sorts, where rank-shifted nominal groups typically appear.

Depth and Style

By manipulating depth, as produced by complexes and rank-shifting, an author can vary his syntax from simple to complex. Depth can be measured exactly. Each downward step in a diagram of the grammatical structure of a sentence is a step in depth. Each subdivision of a complex and each rank-shift is a step in depth. What simplicity or complexity of style suggests, of course, depends on the situation the text is elaborating. If that situation is a serious one, the fact that depth is intellectually demanding, and hence slows the progress of the communication, helps to reinforce the considered and weighty nature of what is being said. Thus depth and a "high" or serious purpose have come to be associated to such an extent that if instead the situation suggested by the text is trivial or comic the effect is one of ludicrous inappropriateness, of the "ridiculous".

If, in addition, as in the passage from Fielding we have been examining here, further markers of the particular variety of language we call "epic" style appear (the epic simile, the reference to another epic writer, the invocation of the Muses), then the feeling of inappropriateness takes shape as a parody or burlesque. At this point not only the style is perceived as

ridiculously inappropriate to the action, but the action itself, now contrasted by association with the action of serious epics, is also seen as
ludicrous. Molly and her grimy opponents become epic heroes comically
shrunken. The linguistic frame in which they appear is vast in lexis and
syntax, but themselves and their actions seem petty and futile, like children
pretending to be adults. Part of Fielding's point, of course, is that Man *is* a
child in the universe. It is this that makes him and his endeavours both
pathetic and charming. The mock heroic style is a warm and effective way
of puncturing his puffed-up sense of himself.

II. FRAMEWORK: Depth in the Unit-complex and in Rank-shift

As YOU remember, the unit-complex is a grouping of units of the same rank. These units usually follow each other in the sentence, but not always. Complexes should not be confused with sequences of different elements realized by units of the same rank. Units of the same rank realizing different elements of structure have different functions. Because these elements are of different grammatical functions, we say they make up "multivariate" structures. Units of the same rank in complexes realize the same single element. Because they thus have the same grammatical function we say they make up "univariate" structures.

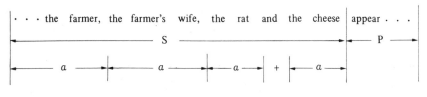

groups in univariate structure

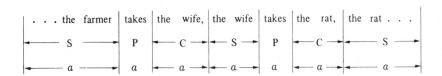

groups in multivariate structure

Previously we have noted that the units clause, group, word and morpheme belong to the rank-scale (Unit 5). Now we should understand that the unit-complexes belong to the rank-scale too. The unit-complex takes its place in the rank-scale between the simple units. The rank-scale is thus a hierarchy of four simple units and four unit-complexes, each unit-complex appearing in the scale between the unit rank of which it is composed and the next highest unit rank. Just as *all* the simple units are considered to be present in every sentence, no matter how brief, so also must we consider *all* the unit-complexes present in every sentence. This explains why we always write an *α* in structure diagrams between elements of single simple units and those of the next largest simple unit. The ranks of unit-complex are present in the sentence even when each is realized only by a single simple unit (just as clause, for example, is present even when realized only by a single group). Rank-shifting is then the use of a unit or unit-complex of one rank as if it were of another rank. Rank-shifting is always downward since we assume that units of one rank always make up one or more elements of the unit of the next highest rank.

You will recall that "depth" is a descriptive measure of the articulation of a unit by its constituent units. Even the least articulated sentence has six "nodes" or diagram points where articulation occurs. The final element in the following diagram, B, refers to the structure of word, in this case, the element "Base":

$$\begin{array}{|c|}
\text{Help!} \\
\text{S} \\
\alpha \\
\text{P} \\
\alpha \\
\text{h} \\
\alpha \\
\text{B}
\end{array}$$

The number of nodes in such a sentence is the measure of its depth, that is, the complexity of its articulation. Starting from the least possible depth of six nodes, the complexity of articulation may be increased by including in the sentence unit-complexes subdivided into more unit-complexes, and by including rank-shifts. The more subdivisions in unit-complexes and the more rank-shifts, the more nodes occur, and the greater is the depth.

Clauses, Groups and Words

Members of a unit-complex can be related in two ways. Independent units are related paratactically: $\alpha\alpha$. Dependent units are related hypotactically: $\alpha\beta$; $\alpha<<\beta>>\alpha$. At the clause rank, independent clauses frequently stand alone as sentence components. But they may occur together as a complex, where subsequent α clauses will often begin with conjunctions: "and", "but", "or", "neither", and so on. As we have seen in the second example sentence from Fielding, semicolons are frequently used to join independent clauses graphologically. Syntactically, these are separate sentences.

Dependent clauses, by contrast, do not typically stand alone as sentence components. These clauses add additional or conditional information. They are often set off by commas, and may precede, succeed, or interrupt an α clause. Dependent clauses fall into four classes: adverbial, relative, nominal and adjectival.

The adverbial clause is named by analogy with the semantic meaning of adverbs, which often convey circumstantial information. These clauses often begin with adverbs or conjunctions: "if", "when", "why", "because", "so", and so on. They are conventionally, but not always, set off from the α clause by commas.

The relative clause is so named because it is explicitly related to some preceding group which forms its "antecedent". These clauses start with a relative pronoun: "who", "whom", "whose", "which", "that". Be careful to distinguish β relative clauses from rank-shifted relative clauses at the qualifier element of the nominal group (such as the long "that" clause of the third example sentence from Fielding). The β relative clauses are usually set off by commas, or may be displaced from directly following their antecedents.

The nominal clause is so named because some of its functions are analogous to those of the nominal group. The most common kind of nominal clause occurs after predicators of saying or thinking, and begins with "that": "He said *that he would go*". Another kind uses a participial form of the predicator ("-ed", "-en", "-ing") with a Subject, and presents some circumstance of the action: "He said no more, *the matter having been settled*".

The adjectival clause is so named because many of its functions are analogous to those of the adjective. It always has a participial predicator ("-ed", "-en", "-ing") but has no Subject. Be careful not to confuse the adjectival clause with the nominal clause. The adjectival clause is set off by commas or displacement from its antecedent nominal group which would otherwise look like the Subject of a nominal clause: "He, *having eaten hurriedly*, left soon after".

As you remember, the paratactic relationship of independent units and the hypotactic relationship of dependent units pertain also to group and word ranks. Independent groups, for example, can occur alone as single units realizing separate elements of clause structure. The clause so constituted is a multivariate structure. But the groups can occur as a paratactic sequence, each successive group lending new information to the univariate structure they constitute. These groups may be in apposition as well.

The butcher	and	the baker
$\longleftarrow a \longrightarrow$	$+$	$\longleftarrow a \longrightarrow$

Tom,	the baker's son
a'	$\longleftarrow a' \longrightarrow$

Dependent groups, by contrast, cannot usually occur alone as single units realizing elements of clause structure. Nominal dependent groups usually begin with an adverb or conjunction as in the adverbial clause: "my brother, when sober", "Tom, if alive".

Independent words can occur alone as single units realizing group elements. But several of them can occur together in the word-complex to designate a single element, sometimes by means of an appositive structure:

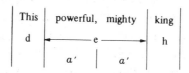

Dependent words, by contrast, cannot stand alone as single units realizing elements of group structure. In nominal groups these dependent words are usually preceded with an adverb or conjunction as the adverbial clause is:

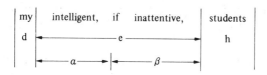

Rank-shifts

When clauses are rank-shifted to group rank, they then realize elements of some clause. These rank-shifts can occur at Subject ("*What you like doesn't matter to me.*") or Complement ("*What you like* I hate."). Clauses rank-shifted to word rank realize elements of some group. The most typical group element realized by a rank-shifted clause is the qualifier element of the nominal group. The most typical clause used for this purpose is the relative clause: "the hat *that he had worn before*". It is also possible to have a rank-shifted clause at the head element of the nominal group: "his *putting on the light* (startled her)". Here the deictic modifier "his" reveals the entire structure to be a nominal group.

You will also recall that groups rank-shifted to word rank thereby realize elements of some group. The most typical case is the use of groups to realize the completive element in prepositional groups:

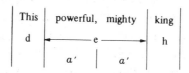

Such prepositional groups frequently occur at the qualifier element of the nominal group: "a worm *in the apple*". You know that groups rank-shifted to word rank typically occur at the determiner and adjectival modifier elements of the nominal group: "the *very first* sign", "*a nearly empty* tank".

Depth-charging

Depth is achievable by recursion of units in unit-complexes and by rank-shifting. Consecutive clauses in a complex merely add length, but if the members of the complex can be subdivided into further complexes, the syntax is deepened by the introduction of the additional nodes:

Note carefully that any member of a clause-complex may be a single clause, or another clause-complex with several members of its own. Consecutive members of clause-complexes are frequently combinations of single clauses and further clause-complexes.

Rank-shifting a clause anywhere on the rank-scale also increases depth by increasing the number of nodes. The degree of depth depends on the degree of the rank-shift and on the number of rank-shift recursions. The following is a typical sentence containing univariate recursion plus rank-shift:

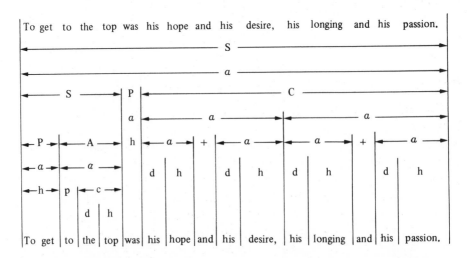

The Subject of this clause is itself a rank-shifted clause with two elements, a Predicator and an Adjunct. The Complement falls into two halves, and each half in turn into two further halves. The rank-shift at Subject adds a depth of one node; the rank-shift in the prepositional group at Adjunct adds a further depth of one node; the subdivision of the complex adds a depth of one node.

Tom Again

Following below is a diagram of the clauses and clause-complexes we distinguished in the first example sentence from Fielding.

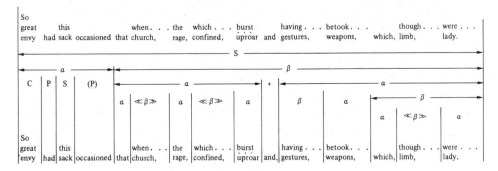

Example sentence #1

As we have indicated, the sentence falls into two parts, an α clause and a β member. The β then falls into two more α members. The first of these is an α clause interrupted by two β clauses. The second α member begins and ends with β members and the second β is realized by an α clause itself interrupted by a β clause! At its deepest point these clause-complex subdivisions add three more nodes to the depth of the sentence.

After this strongly heroic style has set the scene, Fielding introduces overtly the idea of the epic burlesque with the references to Butler's mock epic and the invocation to the Muses. As we noted, the joining of two grammatical sentences by the semicolon to form one graphological "sentence" helps maintain the idea of flowing periods and high style. The first of these grammatical sentences is now diagrammed below:

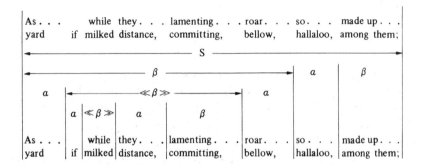

It contains a subdivided complex early in the sentence that adds two additional nodes for depth, thus embellishing the epic simile Fielding has under way.

The second grammatical sentence, given below, is very regularly organized, and its intellectual balance of structure contrasts very oddly with the emotional disorder it describes. The clause-complexes add an extra node and the group-complexes and rank-shifts add more.

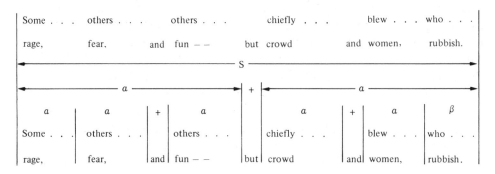

But it is the last example (diagrammed below) that shows both battle and heroic style reaching a ludicrous low point. Molly stoops to slinging graveyard bones and the sentence structure adds a grand total, including clause-complex subdivisions and rank-shifts, including a prepositional group at Adjunct, of six additional nodes of depth. This is Fielding at his deepest. The low point, as we have suggested, is reached in the rank-shifted clause at the qualifier of the nominal group "such fury that . . . the two side by side" that is interrupted by a β clause for even greater intricacy and louder echoes of its Latin originals. It's an interesting circumstance that in English the term "depth" is used in describing the kind of grammar that best conveys the "highest" sentiment. It takes a Fielding to set such things straight by turning, as Molly did the tailor, the language upside down.

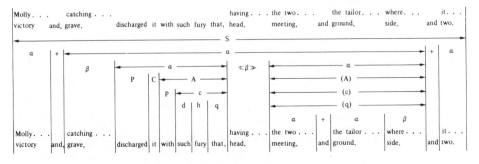

Example sentence #3

III. APPLICATION: the Depth of Feeling

A FICTION writer attempts to create in the reader the feelings of his characters. One way he does this is to create a situation to which a certain feeling is appropriate. Below is a key scene in the novel *The Egoist* written by George Meredith and published in 1879. It is the moment when the heroine (Clara) falls in love with Vernon Whitford, and he with her. The situation is this: Clara is betrothed to the "Egoist", Sir Willoughby Patterne, and has just realized fully her horrible mistake. A previous fiancée of Sir Willoughby had come to the same conclusion and run off with another man. Such a thought is in Clara's mind, and so is the man, Vernon Whitford, who is a relative of Sir Willoughby. Vernon is a scholar, as is Clara's father. Clara is in the company of Crossjay, a young boy who is Vernon's ward, and who is in danger of being spoiled by Sir Willoughby's indulgence. Clara and Willoughby have just parted after a scene in which Willoughby made clear that he cuts people off once and forever if ever they stray from allegiance to him. Vernon has expressed a desire to leave. Three lives, then, hang in the balance in this little scene. A potential family is gathered under the double-blossom wild-cherry. Will what it symbolizes—marriage, beauty, purity, spiritual magnificence, happiness—be sufficient to save them from Sir Willoughby's narrow domination?

Meredith has obviously done his job with regard to situation, but he must also find a language, a style, sufficient to release the feelings potential in that situation. To find fit words for our emotions is what we charge our authors with. The text here manipulates our feelings by contrasting different depths. It builds emotion by a combination of lexis and depth of grammar, then releases the accumulated energy with simpler constructions. The changes in depth parallel the growth and release of feeling in the situation. It is Meredith's willingness to vary his style in this way that is one of the marks of its modernity.

Examine the following passage, analyze the depth of key sentences—both the amount of rank-shifting and of layering in unit-complexes—and relate depth to the themes of the sentences. Take note of the effects of both deep and shallow sentences.

> She asked the boy where Mr. Whitford was. Crossjay pointed very secretly in the direction of the double-blossom wild-cherry. Coming within gaze of the stem, she beheld Vernon stretched at length, reading, she supposed, asleep, she discovered, his finger in the leaves of a book. And what book? She had a curiosity to know the title of the

book he would read beneath these boughs, and grasping Crossjay's hand fast she craned her neck, as one timorous of a fall in peeping over chasms, for a glimpse of the page; but immediately, and still with a bent head, she turned her face to where the load of virginal blossom, whiter than summer-cloud on the sky, showered and drooped and clustered so thick as to claim colour and seem, like higher Alpine snows in noon-sunlight, a flush of white. From deep to deeper heavens of white, her eyes perched and soared. Wonder lived in her. Happiness in the beauty of the tree pressed to supplant it, and was more mortal and narrower. Reflection came, contracting her vision and weighing her to earth. Her reflection was: "He must be good who loves to lie and sleep beneath the branches of this tree!" She would rather have clung to her first impression; wonder so divine, so unbounded, was like soaring into homes of angel-crowded space, sweeping through folded and on to folded white fountain-bow of wings, in innumerable columns. But the thought of it was no recovery of it; she might as well have striven to be a child. The sensation of happiness promised to be less short-lived in memory, and would have been had not her present disease of the longing for happiness ravaged every corner of it for the secret of its existence. The reflection took root. 'He must be good!' That reflection vowed to endure. Poor by comparison with what it displaced, it presented itself to her as conferring something on him, and she would not have had it absent though it robbed her.

She looked down. Vernon was dreamily looking up.

—George Meredith, *The Egoist*

IV. QUESTIONS FOR REVIEW

1. Can you give a meaning to each of these terms?

Hudibras	hypotactic
burlesque	adverbial clause
depth	relative clause
unit-complex	nominal clause
multivariate	adjectival clause
univariate	antecedent
articulation	apposition
node	recursion
paratactic	

2. Create some examples of multivariate and univariate structures (both hypotactic and paratactic) at the rank of clause, of group and of word.

3. Create some examples of adverbial, relative, nominal and adjectival clauses (not rank-shifted). Can you do this in one sentence?

4. Create some examples of rank-shifting, including the following types:
   (a) rank-shifted clauses at group rank,
   (b) rank-shifted clauses at word rank,
   (c) rank-shifted groups at word rank.

5. Authors use sentences of varying depths to produce variety in their style, and for specific effects. Write a paragraph in which you experiment with various sentence depths. What relationship between depth and the particular effect desired can you detect in your paragraph? In the individual sentences?

6. The following poem contains four sentences of different depths. Analyze these sentences and comment on the relationship of sentence depth to the theme of the poem. What is the effect here of the long, deep first sentence? Where have you heard or read similar sentences? In this poem, do unit-complexes or rank-shifts account for most of the depth?

A REFUSAL TO MOURN THE DEATH, BY FIRE, OF A CHILD IN LONDON

Never until the mankind making
Bird beast and flower
Fathering and all humbling darkness
Tells with silence the last light breaking
And the still hour
Is come of the sea tumbling in harness

And I must enter again the round
Zion of the water bead
And the synagogue of the ear of corn
Shall I let pray the shadow of a sound
Or sow my salt seed
In the least valley of sackcloth to mourn

The majesty and burning of the child's death.
I shall not murder
The mankind of her going with a grave truth
Nor blaspheme down the stations of the breath
With any further
Elegy of innocence and youth.

Deep with the first dead lies London's daughter,
Robed in the long friends,
The grains beyond age, the dark veins of her mother,
Secret by the unmourning water
Of the riding Thames.
After the first death, there is no other.

—Dylan Thomas

UNIT 8

Theme and Information

I. ANALYSIS: the Miltonic Clause in *Paradise Lost*

Silence, ye troubl'd waves, and thou Deep, peace,
Said then th' Omnific Word, your discord end:
Nor stay'd, but on the Wings of Cherubim
Uplifted, in Paternal Glory rode
Far into Chaos, and the World unborn;   5
For Chaos heard his voice: him all his Train
Follow'd in bright procession to behold
Creation, and the wonders of his might.
Then stay'd the fervid Wheels, and in his hand
He took the golden Compasses, prepar'd   10
In God's Eternal store, to circumscribe
This Universe, and all created things:
One foot he centred, and the other turn'd
Round through the vast profundity obscure,
And said, thus far extend, thus far thy bounds,   15
This be thy just Circumference, O World.
Thus God the Heav'n created, thus the Earth,
Matter unform'd and void: Darkness profound
Cover'd th' Abyss: but on the wat'ry calm
His brooding wings the Spirit of God outspread,   20
And vital virtue infus'd, and vital warmth
Throughout the fluid Mass, but downward purg'd
The black tartareous cold Infernal dregs
Adverse to life; then founded, then conglob'd
Like things to like, the rest to several place   25
Disparted, and between spun out the Air,
And Earth self-balanc't on her Centre hung.
Let there be Light, said God, and forthwith Light
Ethereal, first of things, quintessence pure
Sprung from the Deep, and from her Native East   30
To journey through the airy gloom began,
Spher'd in a radiant Cloud, for yet the Sun
Was not; shee in a cloudy Tabernacle

Sojourn'd the while. God saw the Light was good;
And light from darkness by the Hemisphere   35
Divided: Light the Day, and Darkness Night
He nam'd. Thus was the first Day Ev'n and Morn:
Nor past uncelebrated, nor unsung
By the Celestial Quires, when Orient Light
Exhaling first from Darkness they beheld: 40
Birth-day of Heav'n and Earth; with joy and shout
The hollow Universal Orb they fill'd,
And touch't thir Golden Harps, and hymning prais'd
God and his works, Creator him they sung,
Both when first Ev'ning was, and when first Morn.   45

—John Milton, *Paradise Lost,* VII, 216–260

How does one speak with the tongues of angels? Epic poets have always had to face the problem of creating a voice "large" enough to speak of their whole race, their whole history. This is the reason for the development of what is known as "epic style". In English, Milton's style in *Paradise Lost* has long been seen as the culminating attempt to achieve grandeur in both theme and voice.

Paradise Lost tells the biblical story of the fall in Eden; and Milton chose the third-person omniscient point of view, traditional to the epic poet, to tell it from. To achieve the impressiveness Milton felt was proper to his theme, he adopted many features of the classical epics: the epic simile, the beginning *in medias res,* the characterization of both gods and men, the elaborate descriptions of battle array, and the latinization of his vocabulary. This gave his poem the weight of centuries of tradition. However, it is Milton's clause structure, in which all of these features are embedded, that in the end gives the poem the majesty of voice required by its mighty subject. That clause structure manipulates the systems of theme (the importance of what comes first in the clause) and information (the item which carries the "sentence stress") to achieve in written English many of the effects obtainable by a great preacher (or bard) through his manipulation of the spoken voice. The thunder and sweet song necessary to tell the fall of angels and the innocence of our first world are both encompassed in the Miltonic clause.

John Milton

Milton had a strong sense of purpose in writing his epic, a purpose that grew out of his own life and his times. Milton's life was involved with that of the Puritan Commonwealth. From 1646 until 1660, regicide and revolution placed all of England under the rule of, first, a middle-class religious oligarchy, and then a dictator, Oliver Cromwell. The Commonwealth and Cromwell represented the political victory of Calvinism in England, and along with it the temporary intellectual victory of Puritan ideas.

Milton himself was a Calvinist, but he was also an intellectual giant, steeped in all the various learning of the seventeenth century, with its roots in heathen classical texts as well as the Bible. His pamphleteering on behalf of the Puritan cause made him famous in Europe, and the ideas of his party respectable. However, his greatest achievement was in poetry as he undertook the reconversion of the whole Christian deposit of beliefs into English verse.

Milton's purpose in this was to place the history of man's salvation on a par with the great classical epic stories of the *Iliad* and *Aeneid*. *Paradise Lost* tells not only the story of the fall but, through the angel's prophetic account to Adam after the fall, the salvation of Christ to come. This history was told from the Puritan perspective but enriched by Milton's great classical learning. Milton had also a particular apologetic intention, as announced at the beginning of his poem: to "justify the ways of God to men," to show God's purpose in human life. Since much of the poem was written after the Puritans' fall from power, Milton may well have had his own compulsion to make sense of the ups and downs of history after the fall.

Paradise Lost

The poem begins in the midst of things just after the great fall of Satan and his legions into Hell after the battle in Heaven. The devils hold a council, as the result of which Satan sets off to the newly made Paradise to tempt Adam and Eve. God meanwhile sends the angel Raphael to warn Adam and Eve to remain obedient, and to describe their enemy to them. Obedience to God's will is the great theme of Calvinism and of *Paradise Lost*. Raphael then, at Adam's request, tells the story of the fall of Satan's angels up to the point where the poem begins. He goes on to tell how God sent His Son to create Paradise, in which he placed Adam and Eve in order to repopulate heaven.

The passage above describes the first day of the seven days of creation. In lines 1–2 the Son of God commands Chaos to end its discord. In lines 9–27, with golden compasses He circumscribes the space of the new world. In lines 28–37 Milton describes the creation of light and its division into day and night, perhaps a doubly significant passage for a blind man. In lines 38–45 the Creator's efforts are praised by the attendant angels. The whole passage stays close to the account in *Genesis* but elaborates and expands it:

> In the beginning God created the heaven and the earth.
> And the earth was without form, and void; and dark-
> ness was upon the face of the deep. And the Spirit of God
> moved upon the face of the waters.
> And God said, Let there be light: and there was light.
> And God saw the light, that it was good: and God
> divided the light from the darkness.
> And God called the light Day, and the darkness he called
> Night. And the evening and the morning were the first day.
>
> —Genesis 1: 1–5

An additional source, for the golden compasses, is Proverbs 8: 27: "When he prepared the heavens, I was there: when he set a compass upon the face of the depth."

Beneath the simple succession of events, however, are underlying philosophical principles. Milton's Judao-Christian universe has a single history with a fixed beginning (the one described) and end (foretold by the angel Michael after the fall). Milton's account of God sending His Son to perform the creation is consistent with Christian theology which interprets the Word of God as God's intelligence of Himself, and hence a separate, creating person. The conception of the physics of creation, the separation of heavier and lighter elements, has its origins in Greek physics. The basic idea of chaos here is non-existence; but it is imaged as noise, discord and water ("waves"), which suggests that non-existence is really formlessness, an appropriate point of view for an artist. Any scholarly text of *Paradise Lost* provides on every page extensive footnotes testifying to Milton's wide-ranging knowledge of classical and Christian philosophy.

The style of *Paradise Lost* is famous in English poetry. Indeed, some have called it a great mountain range that prevented the expansion of English verse for decades afterward since any other style seemed paltry beside it; yet to adopt its techniques was to risk comparison with the great original. The general features of this style have often been cited by critics. It represents a serious attempt to Anglicize the classical epic style and is redolent of its classical origins, including complicated grammar sequences and a Latinate vocabulary. But beyond this, Milton is a poet of sounds and metre. His lines move with a stately rhythm, slow and momentous, and he is capable of the loveliest metrical effects:

> Some natural tears they dropp'd, but wip'd them soon;
> The World was all before them, where to choose
> Thir place of rest, and Providence thir guide:
> They hand in hand with wand'ring steps and slow,
> Through *Eden* took thir solitary way.

The above are the last lines of the poem, which ends on a quiet note, but the earlier passage we are analyzing here also exhibits skilled metrical effects. For example, the perfectly regular metre of line 31:

"Tŏ/jóurněy/thróugh thě/áirў/glóom bě/gán"

reflects the regulation of time, itself a symbol of order, which the Creator is establishing. The lines on either side are metrically contrasted to this regularity. In line 14, "Round through the vast profundity obscure", consonant clusters (–nd thr– –st pr– –nd –bsc–) and the long accented syllables reflect the sense of effort required to turn the compasses. The Latinisms of the passage: *omnific, fervid, circumscribe, profundity, circumference, tartareous, infernal,* etc., are skillfully woven into both sound effects and metre. The poem represents a monument not only to English verse but to the English language.

The Miltonic Clause: Theme

If students claim Milton is hard to read, it is usually because, like his favourite Latin authors, he shifts the elements of his clauses out of their normal locations. This frequently results in some initial confusion as to what exactly the grammar is. For example, in lines 19–20 ("but on . . . outspread") the structure +ACSP obscures the identity of S which is "the Spirit of God". The normal order would be +SPCA ("but the Spirit of God outspread His brooding wings on the wat'ry calm"). The alternating CP, PC orderings that follow (lines 21–27), without any repetition of the S, and combined with verbs of obscure transitivity, make the identification of the C elements difficult. Is "Earth" (line 27) S or C?

Yet it is this very willingness to play with the normative order of clause elements that is the key to Milton's style and his reverberating sound effects. To understand why this is we must understand both what normal order is, and what effects that this order, or deviations from it, provide. Just above we said that +SPCA would be the norm of comparison for lines 19–20. SPCA is the normal order of elements for all modern English clauses, with some qualifications on A. Conjunctions come first, and adverbs often appear in the middle of clauses, next to the Predicator, but all other adjunctival elements usually appear last.

When this order is not followed, the deviating element stands out as a "marked" choice. This "marked" character carries meaning as pointing a contrast; it is potentially symbolic of something; it is a sign of some stylistic import, some modification of the normally presented information. In this passage, and in *Paradise Lost* as a whole, the very great number of marked choices contributes to the majestic stateliness of the lines. They reinforce the sound patterning and the metrical effects by suggesting Latin grammar with all its weight of culture and authority, and by slowing the rate of conceptual movement. One must frequently wait until the end of a Miltonic period before constructing its grammar.

Systemic grammar helps us to describe exactly what is happening with Milton's marked clause elements by elaborating the systems of *theme and rheme*. The theory of *theme* is that there is an important contrast between the first place in clause structure (after the conjunction if present) and the rest of the clause. This first element is called the "theme", and the rest the "rheme". The theme is the "topic" place, stating what the clause is about. The clause and the theme are unmarked in this system when the theme position is filled by the Subject element, but marked when any other element is placed first. This is the basis of the old stylistic dictum to vary your sentence structure by not always beginning with the Subject. Milton has taken this advice, which is a commonplace in Latin versification, very much to heart.

A compact example of marked theme in the passage is provided in lines 3–4, ". . . on the Wings of Cherubim/Uplifted, in Paternal Glory rode . . .", where the A element is twice presented before P. In the first instance the significant or "topic" term is "on the Wings of Cherubim", as the first element of the clause, rather than "Uplifted", which it would be if the clause were unmarked. The effect of "Uplifted", while we still did not know what was doing the uplifting, would be lost. But with the glory of "Wings of Cherubim" all around us, the uplifting becomes a palpable experience with a strong spiritual as well as physical meaning. It is not just that the new topic element achieves significance in marked clauses that is important, but also what happens to the other elements as the result of the shift.

In lines 9–16, "Then stayed . . . World", the density of marked themes makes for a syntactic pattern that runs through the entire passage. Theme-marking occurs in lines 9–10, 13 and 15, beginning each of the three grammatical sentences, and so adding significance to each of God's three actions—His stopping and taking up the compasses, His turning of the circle and His speech. In addition, each instance of theme-marking contributes its own particular meaning. In line 9, "the fervid Wheels" is Subject, but "stay'd" is a marked theme. The braking action preceding the active movement gives an impression of power acting to bring the chariot to a halt. The fact that it is the Wheels themselves which stop, obedient to God's will, but not His causal hand on the brake, has been established earlier in the text: "Celestial Equipage . . . now came forth/ Spontaneous, for within them Spirit liv'd,/ Attendant on thir Lord . . .". Our momentary uncertainty as to what is the subject of "stay'd" is resolved by the little miracle of the self-stopping wheels.

In the same line the theme-marked Adjunct "in his hand" precedes the act of taking up the golden compasses. The effect is of giving us a quick close-up of God's hand moving toward the compasses before they appear. It is the hand of God, not the compasses, which is the real power here. In line 13 the two Complements "One foot" and "the other" precede their Subject and/or Predicator, effectively drawing our attention to the two points of the compasses at work. And in line 15, the Adjunct "thus far" precedes the Predicator "extend" in the first clause of the sentence pronounced by God on His work. The same effect is achieved in the second clause despite the omission of the Predicator. The limit has been firmly set before extension is permitted. God retains control over creation. Indeed, the whole Calvinist doctrine of predestination, of God's absolute control over events, which is the major theme in *Paradise Lost*, is implicit in this theme-marking.

The Miltonic Clause: Information

Milton is such an extraordinary master of auditory effects it would be a shame to miss the intonational aspect of his performance. Moreover, his extensive use of theme-marking helps him to shift to a greater degree than is usually possible in written works the place of his "tonic" syllable. In English five basic "tunes", or patterns of pitch change, have been distinguished. These tunes extend over varying stretches of text but centre mainly on one stressed syllable, called the "tonic", which is the nucleus of the "tone group". The five basic tunes are numbered and distinguished as follows: Tune #1, a fall in pitch; tune #2, a rise; tune #3, slight rise; tune #4, emphatic rise; tune #5, emphatic fall. The type of tune, the frequency of tone groups, and the placement of the tonic syllable are all stylistic factors in a text, adding emphasis and contrasts, and contributing to symbolic and onomatopoeic effects. Since discussing auditory effects requires a spoken text, the following analyses are based on what we consider to be a normal performance of the text.

In lines 1–2, in our reading, there are no less than six tone groups. The density of tone groups establishes the slow, measured tones of the delivery of God's word. The tonic syllables and their tunes are: "*Silence*" (5), "*waves*" (1), "*Deep*" (1), "*peace*" (5), "*Word*" (1), "*end*" (1). The emphatic #5 tunes are employed for "Silence" and "peace", the directives that calm unordered Chaos. Remember that it is pitch change that is important, not loudness. The vocative Z elements, such as "ye troubl'd waves" and "thou Deep", are frequently set off in different tone groups (marked by commas), as are separate clauses. The written form of a text implies the normal reading. The selection of #5 tunes for "*Silence*" and "*peace*" is a performance choice, but seems a reasonable one to make for a dramatic rendition, as is obviously required by the situation presented.

In lines 28–33, "Let there . . . Was not", the tunes are: "*Light*" (5),

"*Ethereal*" (5), "*first*" (5), "*pure*" (5), "*Deep*" (1), "*East*" (1), "*gloom*" (1), "*Cloud*" (5), "*Sun*" (1). Again, the relative density of tunes slows the lines, adding to the majesty of the event described. In addition, the tunes fall into sequences that add further patterns to the sounds of the passage. The four #5 tunes of lines 28–29 emphasize the momentousness of the appearance of light. This contrasts with the more normal #1 tunes that follow in lines 30–31 when light's temporal journey begins. This pattern is repeated in miniature in lines 32–33 with first one #5 tune and then a #1 tune. Such patterning of tunes is very common in both poetry and prose and partly reflects the clause construction. This passage exploits it to the fullest. Note also that the passages here are free of rising tunes, which semantically correlate with indefiniteness or incompleteness. The falling tunes, the #1 and #5, indicate definiteness and finality. The creation as recreated by Milton is firmly under God's control.

The tone group and the location of the tonic syllable within it also give rise to marked and unmarked possibilities described as the "information" systems. In the normal clause there is only one tone group and the tonic syllable appears in the last lexical item. When a clause has more than one tone group, or when the tonic syllable is not in the last lexical item, the clause is said to be marked. Semantically, the tonic syllable identifies lexis as "new information". The last lexical item is the newest so it normally carries the tonic. More than one tonic syllable in a clause indicates an accumulation of new information. Shifting the tonic forward is an effective way of emphasizing a particular bit of lexis as new.

Milton's style, since it supports a high proportion of tone groups, is a highly marked or highly emphatic one. Again, the theme-marking of his clauses is a factor here since it tends to break up clauses into smaller tone groups. In lines 28–30 the tonic on *Light* at the end of the first clause is unmarked. However, the tonics on "E*there*al", "*first*", "*pure*" and "*Deep*" each represent another tone group, making this subsequent clause very marked indeed. Furthermore, one of those tone groups contains a marked tonic, "first", because it is not the last lexical item in the tone group. Note that "Ethereal" and "pure" are the last lexical items in their respective tone groups only because Milton has inverted the usual order of the nominal group, putting the adjective word at q element instead of at e. It is the quality of Light—its ethereal-ness, its first-ness, its purity—that is represented as new information here. Poetry generally is rich in tunes for the same reason that this line is, because a marked tonic suggests discovery or expresses wonder.

II. FRAMEWORK: Systems of Theme and Information

WHEN we use language we are always choosing to say one thing rather than another. If we become aware of this selection process we also become aware that we do not choose in a vacuum. We are selecting within some kind of framework. We choose one noun from among a fixed set of noun lexical items, and within a fixed m h q grammatical structure. Left-to-right frameworks like the latter are fairly easy to visualize. They are called "syntagmatic" frameworks, and one simply fills, or does not fill, the slot in the framework.

"Paradigmatic" frameworks, however, are lists of options, like the list of verb forms. One is not simply filling the slot P in the syntagmatic framework S P C, one is selecting from a list of options at P. Moreover, the selection here may influence other parts of the clause, such as the presence or absence of S or C or A. Our paradigmatic choices, therefore, begin with the assumption of a syntagmatic framework, and influence that framework. Because they influence the framework, they also finish by providing the conditions for further choices.

For example, the apparently simple choice we began with above, the selection of a noun lexical item to fill a slot in m h q, implies a series of choices: the choice of common or proper noun; if common, the choice of countable (cups) or non-countable (jam); if countable, the choice of singular or plural. Choices tend to further choices. It is convenient to show choices and the preconditions of choices (the singular/plural choice does not arise if proper noun is selected) as a "system" in a diagram form which includes both the "entry condition" for a choice, and the number of choices available:

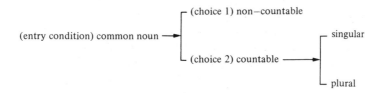

The Systems of Theme

As you remember from Unit 5, the Subject element can perform several different functions in the clause. One function is that of what is talked about. Another is that of an agent, as the actor or instigator of action. The subject also has the attribute of agreeing with the verb form. The first of the potential roles for Subject is called the "theme". The "theme" is the first item in a clause (usually the Subject); the rest of the clause is the "rheme". The second possible role for the Subject is called "participant". The Subject usually participates in the action of the clause as an actor, instigator, or (with a copular verb) equivalent. However, it is the "concord" or agreement aspect of the Subject that is referred to when we speak of the "grammatical" Subject.

These different aspects of the Subject can be abstracted or detached. For example, we can detach the theme function by removing the Subject from its accustomed first place. That is how we can see that this function of Subject is really a property of place. Subject takes on this function only when in first position, as it usually is. When the Subject is elsewhere in the clause, one of P/C/A/Z replaces it as the theme. However, the Subject element still retains other features such as participation or concord. Similarly, in the sentence "It is raining", we think of "It" as Subject although it is not an actor or instigator nor even an equivalent, because it still shows concord and is in first position.

She	sells seashells by the seashore.	
S	P C A	
Sells	she seashells by the seashore.	
P	S C A	
Seashells	she sells by the seashore.	
C	S P A	
By the seashore	she sells seashells.	
A	S P C	
← THEME →	← RHEME →	

The categories of the grammatical elements are thus really bundles of properties, and not all of these properties need be present to classify the element. The phenomenon of the coincidence of several properties in an element is called "mapping". Even partial mapping of the properties onto one another is enough to constitute an element, given the existence of the framework of normal full mapping. Thus demapping some properties from Subject still leaves Subject.

These mapping and unmapping options may be stated as a system of choices defined as "marked" or "unmarked". When Subject is also theme, we have the normal unmarked situation. If any other element is theme, we have an unusual or theme-marked situation. "*These roses* are lovely" is an unmarked clause. "*Lovely* are these roses" is a marked clause.

When we map the theme function onto other elements we set up a further set of choices since we must choose which non-subject element is to be theme. All these choices can be diagrammed systemically:

Combining a system with a previous system, one choice of which is the entry requirement for the second system, creates a systemic network. The systemic network shows the progress of consecutive choices, as well as being a paradigm of all the possibilities. The description of an actual example can be read off from such a network from right to left. The description for our example above, "Lovely are the roses", is "Complement-thematic, marked-theme clause".

Notice that "the roses" remains Subject, since it shows concord with the Predicator; but "Lovely" is now the theme, meaning that we are now talking (unusually) about "Lovely". The point is that we have done more than shuffle the order of the elements in the clause; we have also specifically drawn attention to one of them. The marked clause is semantically different from the unmarked one because of this emphasis.

Information Systems

As well as the theme/rheme distinction in the clause, we find a distinction between "old" and "new" information. Most elements in a clause reflect established context, the information already given. But usually one element is an addition to the discourse. This element is usually the last item, or part of the last item. Consider the following paragraph of technical prose:

How to weatherstrip a door. Close and lock the door so the door and casing are tight together. If you're using a rigid stripping, measure and cut the 3 or 4 pieces you need, mitering them to fit well at the top corners. If your weatherstripping is flexible, you may want to cut it in pieces for convenience or use one continuous piece for the sides and top.

—Energy, Mines and Resources Canada, *100 Ways
to Save Energy & Money in the Home*

In the first sentence (*"How to weatherstrip a door."*) the word which contrasts most strongly with the ideas of the preceding text is *"door"*. This is because the preceding text has already involved the ideas of weatherstripping and procedure for the application of weatherstripping. But the text hasn't yet gotten to doors. Hence the item *"door"* can be labelled "new" information, and the rest "old". In the next clause ("Close and lock the door") the word "door" is now old information, and what is introduced as new information is "Close and lock". In the next clause, even "casing" is relatively old information, by comparison with the new and contrastive "tight". In the subsequent clauses, you will probably pick out as new or newest information the items "rigid", "need", "mitering", "corners", "flexible", "pieces", "continuous" and "sides and top". Note that some of the old information in clauses is presupposed only by implication; that is, it is just less contrastive than the item you selected as really new.

But while theme is signified by position, new information is signified by intonation, the way the clause is pronounced. As you have learned, clauses are usually spoken with characteristic intonation contours, called "tunes". These usually end the clause, although a clause may have more than one tune. The critical part of the tune, where the most distinctive pitch changes occur, falls across a single stressed syllable which is called the "tonic" syllable. It is the tonic which signals the "new" information.

In the above paragraph about weatherstripping, each of the words we selected as "new" information carries the most distinctive variation in tune on its own stressed syllable, which is therefore the tonic syllable. In the case of word-complexes, "close and lock", "sides and top", the tonic syllables are "lock" and "top", the latest or newest new information given. The reason you probably agreed with us that the words we selected *were* the new information was that you heard the tonic quality of the stressed syllables in each of these words. If you think you missed it, read the paragraph to yourself aloud, listening for the change in pitch on these syllables. This signifies to you and to any hearer that the words in which they are placed are contrastive with the context, and that the rest of the information is somehow presupposed.

A single sentence may contain several tunes, several presentations of "new" information. Normally a main clause and a β subordinate clause will each contain new information, signified by separate tunes. However, an embedded clause will less normally have its own tune. Non-normal clauses could contain more than one tune. Even a fragment of a clause may contain a tune. From this we can abstract the concept of a "tone-group" or stretch of combined old/new information signified by just one tune.

It is possible (but not normal), then, for several tone groups to fall across one clause, or even for several clauses to be in a single tone group, depending on how the stretch of language is pronounced. We can abstract a system of *tonality* from these variations. The just-mentioned cases are said to be "marked". In "unmarked" or normal tonality the tone-group boundaries and the clause boundaries coincide. These options make for a system of choices.

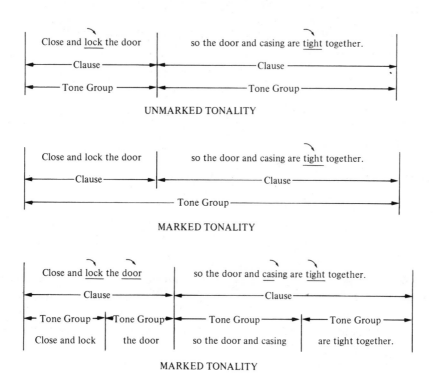

Just as the thematic element can be changed by relocating the clause elements, so the specification of the "new" element can be changed by moving the tonic syllable. The tonic syllable can occupy any stressed syllable location in the syllable string of the tone group. In fact it is possible for the same element to carry both the "theme" and the "new" information: "The *but*ler did it!".

From this phenomenon we can construct a second system of *tonicity*. The unmarked case is that in which the tonic syllable falls in the last lexical item in the tone group. Since both marked and unmarked cases (depending on the clause order) may have the tonic syllable fall on any of the clause elements (S P C A Z), the system of marked–unmarked gives rise in either case to a system network with further options. Here we diagram the further system for the marked-tonicity choice only:

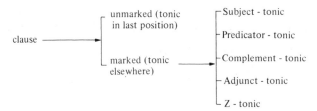

The description for our example just above would be: Subject-tonic, marked-tonicity clause.

The Tone Group

Closer inspection of the tone group becomes necessary in order to understand these ideas clearly. The whole tone group stretches over any pretonic syllables and may go on past the tonic if any syllables follow it. The tonic syllable itself is identifiable as the carrier of the most radical variation in pitch. It must also carry stress. Whether the tonic is rising or falling is easy to determine by reference to the last part of the pretonic segment. The tonic may include all of the pitch change in the contour, or only part of it. Tunes are classified, as you know from Unit 3, according to the shape and direction of the pitch change on the tonic syllable and on syllables beyond it. Each tune type may also have several different pretonic types conveying subtly different semantic contexts. For example, tune #1 has the possible pretonics of *neutral* (with a relatively level-pitch pretonic) meaning no added sense; *bouncing* (pretonic goes up and down slightly) often suggesting ironic patience; *listing* (a series of separated shallow upward curves) meaning "Note this item!". A man who knows it all already would use the second pretonic. A railway station announcer would use the third.

In the following example from our *Paradise Lost* passage we have analyzed the clause structures into elements, divided them into tone-groups (/ . . . /), underlined the tonic syllables, marked the stresses, and, with a subscript at the beginning of each tone group, classified the tunes into types. The analysis, of course, is based on our interpretative reading of the text. Following it, you should be able to realize our reading and, hopefully, call forth Milton's ringing angelic tones once more. You should also be able to appreciate the great amount of marked cases in the passage, according to the systems of theme and information we have outlined. Such an abundance of marked cases itself indicates Milton's desire to raise his language to something extraordinary. His success is attested by the fact that over a century later Wordsworth had to write a preface calling on poets to return to the language of "ordinary" men.

/₅ Lét there be <u>Líght</u>, said Gód, and /₅ fórthwith Líght

   P   A   P   Z   P   S   +   A   (S . . .

Ethéreal, /₅ <u>fírst</u> of thíngs, /₅ quintéssence <u>púre</u>

                                    . . .)

/₁ Sprúng from the <u>Déep</u>,   and from her /₁ Nátive <u>Eást</u>

      P   (A . . . . . .) + (A . . .   . . .)

To /₁ jóurney through the áiry <u>glóom</u> begán,

       P   (A . . .   . . .) P

/₅ Sphér'd in a rádiant <u>Clóud</u>, for /₁ yét the <u>Sún</u>

       P   (A . . .   . . .) A   A   S

Was nót; /₁ shée in a clóudy <u>Tábernacle</u>

   P   S   (A . . .   . . .)

/₁ Sojóurn'd the whíle.

      P   A

III. APPLICATION: Pope's Heroic Couplet

ALEXANDER POPE was an eighteenth-century poet who was widely read and quoted in his own day. Indeed, quotations from the source of the following selection, *Essay on Criticism*, published when he was 23, still occupy three columns of *Bartlett*. Pope was also one of the first English writers to make a good living out of writing and to be widely esteemed as well as widely read. In the course of an *Essay on Criticism*, Pope makes use of some eighteenth-century philosophical ideas familiar to the educated audience of his time. Among these is the conception of Nature as a divine guide or standard provided by God to man. Nature's laws are supposed to be clear to human reason, as well as universal and eternal. If a writer will but follow Nature he will be in accord with God's will; and a critic, of course, can use Nature as his standard in judging the writer's work.

The first verse paragraph below expresses the idea that man's "wit" (his general mental capacity) has several aspects: memory, understanding, imagination. Each of these, if indulged in, is liable to produce an imbalance. In the second verse paragraph the successful management of wit is described. To guide one's wit by the laws of Nature is the only way to proceed successfully. Nature is clear, eternal, universal and divine. Art conforming to Nature is good. Art in which wit is not checked by an understanding of Nature's laws or limits, is not.

The poem is written in "heroic couplets": iambic pentametre lines that rhyme in pairs. Chaucer wrote in the same form, and Pope is its most famous subsequent exponent. He used it for his translations of Homer, and in his day it was still considered the proper form for epic poetry, and serious poetry generally, despite Milton's arguments for blank verse.

Our interest in the form here, as with the blank verse passage from Milton we have already examined, lies in its adaptability to manipulation of the theme and information systems of English. As other poets have demonstrated, both blank verse and heroic couplets can be written in more straightforward ways; but Milton and Pope illustrate the great capacity of these forms for such manipulation. Their works stand stylistically as the extreme examples of this kind of exploitation of these forms; consequently, any poet who dares the same techniques risks the accusation of imitation.

In the following passage, find examples of deviation from the normal order of the clause. Discuss the relationship of the theme-marking of these clauses to their sense. For a given performance of the poem divide one of the verse paragraphs into tone-groups. Designate the clauses in which there is more than one tone-group. Indicate the tonic syllables for these tone-groups. What tunes do they carry? Is there a pattern in the tunes for the passage generally? The placement of the tonic syllable anywhere but in the last lexical item itself constitutes marking. Which clauses or tone groups are so marked? Would you consider Pope an "emphatic" writer? Why?

> Nature to all things fixed the limits fit,
> And wisely curbed proud man's pretending wit.
> As on the land while here the ocean gains,
> In other parts it leaves wide sandy plains;
> Thus in the soul while memory prevails,   5
> The solid power of understanding fails;
> Where beams of warm imagination play,
> The memory's soft figures melt away.
> One science only will one genius fit;
> So vast is art, so narrow human wit: 10
> Not only bounded to peculiar arts,
> But oft in those confined to single parts.
> Like kings we lose the conquests gained before,
> By vain ambition still to make them more;
> Each might his several province well command   15
> Would all but stoop to what they understand.
> First follow Nature, and your judgment frame
> By her just standard, which is still the same:
> Unerring Nature, still divinely bright,
> One clear, unchanged, and universal light,   20
> Life, force, and beauty must to all impart,
> At once the source, and end, and test of art.
> Art from that fund each just supply provides,
> Works without show, and without pomp presides:
> In some fair body thus th' informing soul   25
> With spirits feeds, with vigor fills the whole,
> Each motion guides, and every nerve sustains;
> Itself unseen, but in th'effects, remains.
> Some, to whom Heaven in wit has been profuse,
> Want as much more, to turn it to its use;   30
> For wit and judgment often are at strife,
> Tho' meant each other's aid, like man and wife.
> 'Tis more to guide, than spur the Muse's steed;
> Restrain his fury, than provoke his speed;
> The wingèd courser, like a generous horse,   35
> Shows most true mettle when you check his course.

—Alexander Pope, *Essay on Criticism*, 1711

IV. QUESTIONS FOR REVIEW

1. Can you give a meaning to each of these terms?

epic style	marked tonality
epic simile	marked tonicity
in medias res	syntagmatic framework
latinization	paradigmatic framework
systems of theme	participation
systems of information	concord
Miltonic period	mapping
theme	new information
rheme	Complement-thematic
marked theme	Adjunct-tonic
tonic syllable	tone group

2. Give some examples of paradigmatic frameworks; of syntagmatic frameworks. Given an example of a systemic network.

3. Name and describe some of the different roles of the Subject element in clause structure. To what other elements can the role of theme be shifted? If "Lovely are the roses" may be described as "Complement-thematic, marked-theme clause", how may one describe "With great abandon, he kissed them all"?

4. What is the "new information" in the sentence "He hit the umpire solidly", if the sentence is given a normal reading? What is it if the meaning of the sentence is "He hit the *umpire* [not the ball] solidly", and the reading is changed accordingly? What system is involved in these examples?

5. Divide the first paragraph of the text given in the last question below into tone-groups. Which clauses have marked tonality?

6. Mark the tunes for your reading of the same passage. Can you find a pattern in them? Is there a relationship between this pattern and what the passage seems to be trying to convey?

7. The passage below begins a novel, *Tender is the Night*, by F. Scott Fitzgerald. It is set at the beginning of the "Jazz Age" in Western

culture, when Paris and the Riviera became meccas for wealthy American tourists.

The novel is concerned with the effects of wealth on human beings, and makes a distinction between those who are strong enough to use wealth for their purposes and those who are weak enough to be used by it. The history of the "Jazz Age", Fitzgerald seems to argue, turned on just this distinction. It was a time of sudden, immense wealth, and some survived it and some, like Fitzgerald himself, did not.

The passage below attempts to set a particular mood appropriate in some way to Fitzgerald's theme. Analyze the passage according to the systems of theme and information, and attempt to relate your analysis to the creation of the particular mood you feel intuitively that Fitzgerald is trying to convey.

On the pleasant shore of the French Riviera, about half way between Marseilles and the Italian border, stands a large, proud, rose-colored hotel. Deferential palms cool its flushed façade, and before it stretches a short dazzling beach. Lately it has become a summer resort of notable and fashionable people; a decade ago it was almost deserted after its English clientele went north in April. Now, many bungalows cluster near it, but when this story begins only the cupolas of a dozen old villas rotted like water lilies among the massed pines between Gausse's Hôtel des Étrangers and Cannes, five miles away.

The hotel and its bright tan prayer rug of a beach were one. In the early morning the distant image of Cannes, the pink and cream of old fortifications, the purple Alp that bounded Italy, were cast across the water and lay quavering in the ripples and rings sent up by sea-plants through the clear shallows. Before eight a man came down to the beach in a blue bathrobe and with much preliminary application to his person of the chilly water, and much grunting and loud breathing, floundered a minute in the sea. When he had gone, beach and bay were quiet for an hour. Merchantmen crawled westward on the horizon; bus boys shouted in the hotel court; the dew dried upon the pines. In another hour the horns of motors began to blow down from the winding road along the low range of the Maures, which separates the littoral from true Provençal France.

—F. Scott Fitzgerald, *Tender is the Night*

Chapter Four   **Lexis**

As A method of description, grammar always stops short of telling us what is really going on in a sentence. Grammar can tell us that the sentence is an ordered collection of clauses, groups, words, morphemes, Subjects, Predicators, Complements, deictics, qualifiers and so on. It can tell us that the sentence involves the roles of actor, transitive action, receiver, modifier, modified, auxiliary and the like. But it always stops short of telling us just who did just what to just whom. What is left to describe after grammar has been described is called lexis.

In one sense, another name for lexis is "diction". We are accustomed to thinking of diction as the right words selected to suit a particular text. We are also aware that diction is found in the dictionary. This should help us get at the exact notion of lexis. The individual lexical item is usually a word item in grammar. The same thing then can be both a grammatical item, with grammatical features, e.g. singular noun, and a lexical item, e.g. "carpenter". The appropriate place to find out about the grammatical meaning of "carpenter" is a book on grammar, and the appropriate place to find out about the lexical meaning of "carpenter" is the dictionary or lexicon. All lexis in texts, then, is represented by items which also represent grammar, although the opposite is not true. But grammatical meaning and lexical meaning are very different. Grammatical meaning tells us what a thing is only in a general sense, but how it is used in a text in a very particular sense. Lexical meaning tells us what a thing is in a very particular sense; but lexical meaning, as found in a dictionary, tells us nothing about how the thing will be used in a text. Both kinds of meaning are necessary in order to constitute language. You can think of lexical items as slotted in to fill the blank spaces left by the generalities of grammar.

The aspect of lexis which is most noticeable in literary texts is connotation. Dictionaries tell us very little directly about the connotative potential of lexical items, but you will see that imaginative writers are masters of connotation. In Unit 9 we will scrutinize the lexical basis of literary images. In Unit 10 we will see how to describe the connotative effects of lexis.

UNIT 9

Collocation and the Lexical Item

I. ANALYSIS: the Play of Lexis in Emily Dickinson

THERE'S A CERTAIN SLANT OF LIGHT

There's a certain Slant of light,   1
Winter Afternoons—
That oppresses, like the Heft
Of Cathedral Tunes—

Heavenly Hurt, it gives us—   5
We can find no scar,
But internal difference,
Where the Meanings, are—

None may teach it—Any—
'Tis the Seal Despair—   10
An imperial affliction
Sent us of the Air—

When it comes, the Landscape listens—
Shadows—hold their breath—
When it goes, 'tis like the Distance   15
On the look of Death—

—Emily Dickinson, *c.* 1861

The mystic and the lyric poet share the same problem: how to convey obliquely what cannot be described directly. The necessity for such a "slanting" approach lies in the unusualness of the experience described. We have many words for repeated and shared experiences, few for the extraordinary. The writer's problem, poet or mystic, is not to describe, for one cannot describe something unique, but to trick the reader into having a similar experience, entering a similar intellectual, emotional, intuitional and sensory state. One way to do this is to use words to suggest more than one context. Confused as to which is meant, knowing somehow that all are meant, but also that none are exactly meant, the reader can resolve his problem only by entering the writer's experience. It is out of this play of lexis that the poetry of Emily Dickinson is spun. By comprehending her many suggested contexts, we may enter her visions.

Emily Dickinson

Emily Dickinson was a New England poetess of the nineteenth century who published just seven poems in her lifetime, all anonymously. Her fame began in the 1890s when various editions began to be published of the over 1700 poems discovered in her papers after her death. She is now recognized as one of the finest of American poets, a specialist in the short lyric with a style that blends wit and language play with luminous imagery. She was the daughter of a prominent lawyer and grew up in a tightly ordered society dominated by a Puritan religious ethic. She had some education but little experience of the world outside her father's house in Amherst, Massachusetts, where she was born, lived and died. In later years she became a recluse, though continuing to send her friends small notes, poems and gifts. It seems that she lived so intensely that a very little of human society sufficed her.

Many of her poems centre on religious feelings and questions. There seemed to be a tension in her between her own intermittent experiences of glowing awareness in which the world was illuminated and she felt herself united with all, and the adamant refusal to know an unknowable God that infused her Puritan surroundings. Perhaps this is the same tension that fired Hopkins' genius. Her mystical experiences, however, unlike Hopkins', seemed to produce in her as much negative as positive feeling. The absence of the joyful feeling, afterward, brought despair; and she seemed unable to fit her direct emotional experience of "heaven" into the practical, iron framework of her religious upbringing. This is a problem for all mystics, but one exacerbated for Emily Dickinson by a creed that, because it saw earth as hell, allowed not heaven to enter. An additional problem was that her experiences, taking place in the immediate now, gave her no knowledge of the afterlife; and she did not accept her sect's ideas on that subject. Death, then, becomes for her a cessation of both pain and ecstasy—a blank. Many of her poems touch on this intuition of death.

Reading the Poem

As regards form, the poem presents few difficulties. It is written generally in a trochaic metre, with either three or four feet in a line, in stanzas that rhyme regularly in the pattern a b c b. The a and c lines seem also to employ various kinds of partial rhyme. The general impression is of simplicity and artlessness, since the form is regular but not pedantically so; and it is certainly not complex or difficult. (The art concealed by the form tends to be revealed only when one attempts to emulate it.)

Our first impression on reading the poem for sense is of a negative experience: "Winter Afternoons", "oppresses", "Hurt", "Despair", "affliction", "Death". But this seems paradoxical since the source of this negative experience is "light", which usually has positive connotations. The solution of the mystery would seem to lie in the particular quality of this "certain Slant of light". Some kinds of light, it seems, bring misery as well as, or perhaps instead of, illumination.

Stanza 1 describes a natural phenomenon—the slanting light of winter afternoons—but adds to it the description of a subjective experience: a feeling of oppression. This is described obliquely by comparing it to the "Heft/Of Cathedral Tunes". Buried in this comparison is another subjective experience, that "Cathedral Tunes" are weighty.

In stanza 2 the effects of this light are further described. It hurts, but in a "Heavenly" way, or perhaps the "Hurt" is done by Heaven? In any event no bodily scar is made by this hurt. Rather, it is a severing of the internal sense of significance. In this stanza the poet includes us directly in her experience by using the plural pronoun "us" rather than the singular "me", an effect she had begun in stanza 1 by leaving out the singular pronoun "me", expected after "oppresses" which usually takes an object Complement.

In stanza 3 the hurt becomes, first, an unteachable discipline, then the "Seal Despair", then "an imperial affliction": all things that no one can do anything about, but must simply endure. Here, the hurt is caused by the "Air", rather than heaven or "light".

In stanza 4 the effects of the "light" on the landscape are recorded. The landscape seems to "listen", and shadows seem to "hold their breath". The visual experience has been transformed to an auditory one, as though, alerted by one sense, the landscape is straining other senses for more information. When the light has passed, the experience of its passing is like the sense of distance we get when we see the "distant" expression on a dead person's face.

The whole four-stanza sequence seems to tell the story of an unexpected attack, a hurt inflicted, for which there is no cure, and a final dying. Such a summary of the meaning of the poem, however, is inadequate. We are aware that more than this is going on here. But how do we get at the rest? One way is by taking a closer look at some of the poem's lexis.

Looking at Lexis

The most important element of diction in the poem, that is, the most important "lexical item", is "light". Its denotation or central meaning is that of a natural phenomenon in a landscape. Its connotations, or associated meanings, include intellectual insight, which is picked up by "Meanings" later in the poem, and religious illumination, which is confirmed by "Cathedral Tunes" and "Heavenly". The item "light" is part of a nominal group which includes two other lexical items: "Slant" and "certain". The denotation of "Slant" here is of obliqueness in angle, like that of the winter light, but the connotation of intellectual insight also applies, as in "getting a slant on things", an angle, a point-of-view. The item "certain" denotes here "one of several possibilities". Its connotations include both intellectual insight, in the sense of conviction or certainty, and religious illumination, since the experience of "certainty" is one that religion seeks to provide.

These denotations and connotations, of course, can be carried through the poem, since the poem is about this "certain Slant of light" and its effects. The "certain Slant of light" is thus an intellectual way of looking at things that causes intellectual trauma, differences in "Meanings". It is also a kind of religious illumination ("Heavenly"), but one that produces "Despair" rather than ecstasy. And it is a natural phenomenon, "Sent us of the air", that affects the "Landscape" and reminds us of the look on a dead face. In the interplay of the three contexts—natural, intellectual, religious—throughout the poem, we may be able to recreate the state of Emily Dickinson's visionary experience: the perception of extra significance in the ordinary. Lexical items which seem odd or mysterious when viewed in the light of the single context of nature make sense when further contexts are provided for them.

Lexical Analysis of the Poem

A proper lexical analysis of the poem would include a discussion of all the lexical items in it. Let us see, at least, how separate lexical items work to produce images. The image of the natural landscape lit by the "Slant of light" is created by "Winter", "Afternoons", "Air", "Landscape", "Shadows" and "Distance". This is the most prominent image of the poem so we can say that the notion of light as a natural phenomenon is "foregrounded".

Intellectual insight is mid-grounded in an image of sudden comprehension, of seeing the "light", getting a new "Slant" on things. Lexical items that support this image are "internal", "difference", "Meanings", "teach", and "Sent".

Religious illumination is backgrounded in an image of sudden mystical inspiration, the shaft of light that reaches suddenly from Heaven to transfix the seer. Supporting this image are the items "Cathedral", "Heavenly", "internal", "Meanings", "teach", "Despair" (in its theological connotation as the worst sin), and "Death" (both physical, and, in its theological connotation, spiritual death).

Once an image has been established in a poem, *all* lexical items in the poem may possibly be applied to it by extending their meanings metaphorically. Thus "Winter", which supports the nature image, can also support the spiritual or intellectual images if we see it as a state of the mind or soul as well as one of Nature's seasons. "Afternoons", similarly, may indicate the sense of a waning insight, a fading religious certainty. The presence of items which already support more than one image (like "certain", "Slant", "light") invites such extended interpretations.

Other lexical items in the poem, as yet undealt with, create more images that make yet more complex the experience of the poem. Chief of these is the image of emotional/physical trauma created by the items "oppresses", "Heft", "Hurt", "scar", "Despair", "affliction", "Shadows" and "Death". It is this image that makes the usually positive experience of "light", a negative one. Related to it is a series of lexical items that suggest a political source for this oppression: "oppresses", "Cathedral", "Seal", "imperial". The notion of weight or pressure is added to this expanded image by the item "Heft".

We can see now that the poem, by means of the opening nominal group, "a certain Slant of light", and strings of related lexis, creates and co-ordinates three levels of imagery to convey the sense of a mystical experience, an experience that begins with a phenomenon of the natural world but touches the poet also in her intellectual and religious being. It is the negative quality of this experience, conveyed by other lexical strings, that makes the "light" ironic, and the mystical experience paradoxical. For this is no glowing intuition of God's presence and love, such as illuminates the poems of Hopkins, but rather the fading of light and hope that occurs when experience of God is denied.

Who or what denies that experience for Emily Dickinson? We can only speculate. A too inflexible religious authority? The loss of a loved one? The frustration of those human desires for understanding or sympathy or love that we all hold dear? We cannot know. But perhaps it is enough to accept the community Emily Dickinson offers us, in her inclusive plural pronouns, and share with her that sensation of utter deprivation. Perhaps then, when we find ourselves once more *there*, we shall discover we are not quite so alone.

II. FRAMEWORK: a Modern Theory of Lexis

LEXIS suggests context, and many distinct lexical items suggest several contexts each. "Block", for example, can suggest the context of urban streets, rugby football, sailing, construction, mental effort, or selling stocks. We determine which context is the appropriate one by looking at nearby items in the passage we are reading: "football" or "uniform" clarifies "block", but "tackle" is not sufficient. The more tightly clustered the words pointing to a single context are, the more highly defined is the field of meaning. Technical writing of any kind shows this high density of field. Poetry tends to suggest or refer to many fields, often simultaneously.

What is Lexis?

Grammar and lexis are two different approaches to variables in language structure. Grammatical items are chosen to fill certain places in structure from a small number of possible items: the set of personal pronouns, for example. Lexical items are chosen from many, many possibilities: all the plural nouns, for example. The constraints on the choice of a lexical item are largely semantic. In the following grammatical structure, many different lexical items may occur:

S	P	A	A	
Mayors	contribute	generously	to charitable	organizations.
Workers	labour	continuously	for monetary	rewards.
Writers	fail	perpetually	in homely	tasks.

and so forth.

The other side of lexical items is that they can appear in different places in grammatical structure. For example, the lexical item "labour" can appear in different places in the structure given above:

Labourers	work	continuously	for monetary	rewards.
Workers	labour	continuously	for monetary	rewards.
Workers	toil	laboriously	for monetary	rewards.
Workers	toil	continuously	at remunerative	labours.

A dictionary, which is a collection of lexical items, must therefore not only show all the possible meanings of a lexical item according to all its possible contexts, it must also show all the possible places in grammatical structure that it may occupy. A dictionary is thus truly a "lexicon".

We have used the term "lexical item" rather than "word" in our discussion up to now because a lexical item is something different from a word. The words change as they occupy different positions in the grammatical structure above: "labourers", "labour", "laboriously", "labours". The lexical item remains the same. It is the word that does the grammatical job; it is the lexical item that alternates with other lexical items, or takes different positions in structure. Sometimes word and lexical item do not even coincide. This happens when more than one word makes up a lexical item, as in "brown study" which appears in the dictionary as an item separate from either "brown" or "study". Verbs plus different prepositions often form different lexical items. This is not a grammatical change, but a lexical one: "*look* (it) *up* (in the dictionary)", "don't *look down* (on him)", "*look out* (for number one)", etc.

Lexical Meaning

For reasons of space, a dictionary gives relatively few meanings of a lexical item. *Webster's*, for example, gives 23 for the noun form of "block", 12 for the transitive verb, 1 for the intransitive, and 5 for the adjective. This sounds like a lot until we think of the infinite number of possible particular situations in which this lexical item might be used, each with a different shade of meaning. To distinguish the general dictionary meanings from the subtler possibilities we use the term "denotative" for the former and "connotative" for the latter. Connotative meaning may range from the fairly obvious to the quite faint. "Egg", for example, denotes an obvious and humble phenomenon: a pre-embryonic vehicle for reproduction. But it also connotes "food" because of the many contexts in which it is eaten. It connotes fragility because in some contexts it gets broken; and it even connotes, in a few contexts, the universe because of its shape and suggestions of remote origins. A writer, like Alice Munro, may choose to exploit even fainter connotations of "egg" in a phrase like "children coming home from Sunday School, their faces innocent as *eggs*". A dictionary could hardly include this kind of complex, subtle and highly specialized meaning.

As we have said, and as you can see from these examples, what limits lexical meaning is context. The meaning of a single lexical item depends on the other lexical items in its immediate context. This context will permit some of the possible denotations and connotations, but rule out others, or make them less probable. A scientist will seek, through his style, to rule out all meanings but the one denotation he wants. A poet will seek to include many connotations, perhaps as many as possible.

Collocation

When we seek to define the meaning of a lexical item, we turn to its neighbours in the linguistic structure. These nearby lexical items are called "collocates" of the original item. To define the meaning of our item we look at the meaning of items on either side. How far we look each way has, of course, practical limits. In careful analysis, we will decide on a set "span" of so many items to either side of our target item. The meaning of the item *in context* will depend on its collocates in the span. The meaning of the item *in general* will depend on its collocates in all spans. The following text is an example of lexical analysis with "style" as the target word, and using a span of ten.

> Up to this <u>point</u>, the <u>book</u> has been <u>concerned</u> with what is <u>correct</u>, or <u>acceptable</u> in the <u>use</u> of <u>English</u>. In this <u>final</u> <u>chapter</u>, we <u>approach</u> <u>style</u> in its <u>broader</u> <u>meaning</u>: <u>style</u> in the <u>sense</u> of what is <u>distinguished</u> and <u>distinguishing</u>. Here we <u>leave</u> <u>solid</u> <u>ground</u>. Who can <u>confidently</u> say what ignites a certain combination of words, causing them to explode in the mind?

Any one lexical item will, over many spans, have a core of recurring collocates. In the example above we would expect to find items like "correct", "meaning", "English" and "chapter" as collocates for "style". An item like "ground" is less expected. Items that repeat define the denotative meaning of the lexical item. The denotative meaning represented above would seem to be a conflation of definition 3—"manner or mode of expression in language"—and 4—"excellence . . . in . . . literary expression" from *Webster's*. (This confusion of style as manner or mode with style as excellence is, alas, too common.) The less expected items produce the connotative meaning. We call the distributional pattern of the collocates in *all* occurrences of the lexical item, the "collocational range" of the item.

The Lexical Set

Some lexical items will have similar collocational ranges. Items like "juice", "water", and "beer" will share many collocates like "thirst", "drink", "refresh", "spill", etc. Their collocational ranges will overlap. Lexical items that overlap in ranges in this way are called a "lexical set". Items like "garbage", "perfection" and "polar bear", on the other hand, do *not* form a lexical set. They do not share very many collocates. The sorting of lexical items into sets is at the heart of the kind of analysis we did with Emily Dickinson's poem.

This analysis can be done mathematically, using very large collections of texts, and the collocates tabulated in terms of probability of occurrence. These results in turn can be sorted into sets. But in practical terms, even in dictionary-making, the sorting is done intuitively, according to our own learned expectation of occurrence. We know from experience that there is a higher probability of an item like "Cathedral" occurring near an item like "Heavenly", than there is of its occurring near an item like "Heft". The following example shows an intuitive sorting into sets of the lexical items from the passage on style given above.

language	*meaning*	*excellence*	*movement*	*certainty*
English	use	correct	point	certain
book	meaning	acceptable	final	confidently
Chapter	sense	distinguished	approach	solid
words	mind	distinguishing	leave	
style	causing	concerned	combination	*explosion*
say	distinguished			explode
	distinguishing			ignites

Besides the items in the groups above there remain "broader" and "ground". Note that some of the choices are obvious, some less so, and that one might produce slightly different sets by choosing slightly different categories. As in all linguistic analysis there is an element of probability. But, as Northrop Frye remarked, although we may never be able to say the exact truth, some statements are truer than others. So it is with analysis. Some sortings are more revealing than others.

The themes of our example passage are now laid before us: the movement of an argument towards a conception of linguistic excellence. One interesting point about this text is that the increasing lack of certainty in this conception as one leaves the black and white idea of correctness is conveyed in the text not just by lexis alone but also by an image—"leave solid ground"—and by using the interrogative mood. The author's style also becomes lexically more subtle. "Correct" and "acceptable" are obvious members of some set of quality; but "distinguished" and "distinguishing", which are lexically the same item, denote rather different things in different sets. Notice how unexpected the *explosion* set is, suddenly introduced in the last sentence. Perhaps this is intended as a warning to stylisticians not to push analysis too far, lest meaning blow up in our faces. The passage, we might add, was written by a more conventional critic for a much more prescriptive book on style, Strunk and White's *The Elements of Style*.

Diction, Metaphor, Image

We are accustomed to think of *diction* as a special vocabulary linked to a person or situation, for example, the vocabulary of dentistry or fishing. We can see now that a particular diction in a text consists of lexical items which share a range of collocates, thus forming lexical sets. These items share this range because they are usually present in the linguistic contexts associated with the said person or situation. Returning to Emily Dickinson's poem, we find the diction of the philosopher briefly represented in "certain", "Slant", "light", "find", "difference", "Meanings", "teach", "listens".

Similarly, our accustomed notion of *metaphor* may be reformulated. We can define metaphor as certain colligations (syntactical unions) of items of different meaning, for example, "wine" and "sea" in Homer's phrase, "The wine-dark sea". The pleasant surprise of metaphor, the sudden sense of rightness in a colligation of unexpected items, occurs because we suddenly recognize these items as being members of the same sets (*liquidity* or *fellowship*). While they remain *denotatively* different, they become *connotatively* related. To understand a metaphor is to find the set to which both halves of the metaphor belong. This requires reformulating one's intuitions of language, and hence one's intuitions of the world. It is in this way that poetry infuses originality and freshness into our tired perceptions. In Emily Dickinson's poem the metaphor "oppresses, like the Heft/Of Cathedral Tunes" links together the apparently different items "oppresses", "Heft", "Cathedral", and "Tunes". Both "oppresses" and "Heft" belong to the set of *weightiness* and "Tune" belongs to the set of *hymns* which links with "Cathedral" in a *church* set. The sense of rightness occurs when we perceive that some members of both the *weightiness* and *church* sets also share membership in a *serious* set.

The literary term *image* also can be redefined according to this theory of lexis. Instead of calling image an elaboration of metaphor in visual terms, we can now describe it as a lexical set, in which various items, however dispersed in grammatical structure, share a range and thus suggest a context, which in turn suggests the visualization of a situation. The *trauma* set in the poem above is an example. Beginning with the injury itself by means of "Hurt", "scar", and "affliction", it then draws in the inflictor through items like "oppresses", "gives", "Sent" and "imperial". It paints the result with "Despair" and "Death". Even items like "Heft" (via the *weightiness* set—"oppresses", "Heft") and "Seal" (via the *government* set—"imperial", "Seal") are drawn into the growing image.

The collocational range of a single lexical item spans many contexts. Some of these are core contexts, and some, more remote. Any whole set of items will select from all these possible contexts. Items in the set reinforce each other, thus bringing some possible contexts forward, making others more remote. This creates a play of connotative reference. In poetry, this play is particularly subtle and lively. In Emily Dickinson's poem each selected general context of "light" is initially suggested by only another item or two, one following the other very rapidly: "Winter", "Afternoons"; "Cathedral", "Heavenly"; "Meanings". But within these broader areas of nature, religion and understanding, each individual item suggests more particular, subtly different contexts as well: "Winter" light and "Afternoon" light are somewhat different; "Cathedral" light and "Heavenly" light are certainly different.

We consider Emily Dickinson one of the forerunners of "modern" poetry because of her skill in the rapid creation of contexts. Each context suggested by the lexis is a momentary experience for the reader of the poem, contrasting or combining with other contexts. Her poems, therefore, are patterns of experiences as well as of thought. These lexical effects are created above and beyond grammatical relationships, and in this sense operate suggestively, independent of surface meaning. We have previously seen that sound patterns and grammatical structures reinforce meanings set in motion by the lexis. Lexical patterns—rapid shifts, surprises, fulfilled expectations—can carry similar reinforcements. We in the twentieth century are coming closer and closer to an aesthetic view of poetry that sees it as an abstract experience of language. We are already used to this idea from music that is without content, and from abstract painting. Read Emily Dickinson's poem again and see if the rapid shifts of context, helped by the movement of sound and grammar, do not give you an impression, a series of experiences, apart from the mere statements of fact that the poem would otherwise reduce itself to.

III. APPLICATION: Lexis in "Fern Hill"

LIKE Emily Dickinson, Dylan Thomas found in nature both a source of life and an ultimate sadness. In the following poem we can see, by studying the lexical patterns, just how Thomas' mind moves in attempting to fashion a religion out of life itself. The two largest sets in the poem are those of *farm* and *nature*, which establish the setting and action of the poem: the experiences of a boy's growing up on a farm in Wales. But these are interwoven with a *religion* set, with items like "mercy", "sabbath", "holy", "blessed", "Adam", "spellbound", "praise", "grace", "lamb". To this is linked a set of *nobility*: "hail", "honoured", "prince", "lordly", "famous", "honoured". The effect is to install the juvenile hero of the poem as the "Christ" of natural existence. But "God" here is the personification "Time", and so this heathen Christ's life leads also to a crucifixion: "Time held me green and dying/Though I sang in my chains like the sea".

Many lexical items are repeated in the poem, like "green" and "golden", to the extent they almost become refrains, and we look for them in each stanza. "Time", "happy" and "sun" are some others. Thus a context is established against which the substitution of an unexpected item for the expected stands out. After seeing "green" associated with "golden" four previous times, it comes as a shock to read "green and *dying*".

Tracing the lexical patterns through the stanzas provides more keys to the arresting power of the last lines of the poem. The item "sang" in the last line has been well prepared for with items like "lilting", "singing", "sang", "horn", "rang", "tunes", "tuneful", "songs". These have previously been associated with a *happiness* set, so again the new association of "sang" with "dying" and "chains" in the last stanza is a shock.

The poem may be viewed, then, as a series of lexical sets skillfully woven through the stanzas, many of them sustained right through the poem. Trace the set of *flight*, for example. Notice how the sets of *farm* (with items like "horses" and "ricks") and *nature* (with items like "pheasants" and "foxes") unite in a set of *country*. To the young hero of the poem the farm was all one: nature's and man's handiwork not distinguished. He was "huntsman and herdsman". Tracing the *colour* set and the *water* set will also contribute to your understanding of the power of the last stanza. Aside from the striking individual images of the poem—"the spellbound horses walking warm/Out of the whinnying green stable/On to the fields of praise"—it is Thomas' skill in weaving a lexical tapestry through all the stanzas that makes this poem one of the most beautiful, and sad, expressions of the existentialist twentieth century.

FERN HILL

Now as I was young and easy under the apple boughs
About the lilting house and happy as the grass was green,
 The night above the dingle starry,
  Time let me hail and climb
 Golden in the heydays of his eyes,   5
And honoured among wagons I was prince of the apple towns
And once below a time I lordly had the trees and leaves
 Trail with daisies and barley
 Down the rivers of the windfall light.

And as I was green and carefree, famous among the barns 10
About the happy yard and singing as the farm was home,
 In the sun that is young once only,
  Time let me play and be
 Golden in the mercy of his means,
And green and golden I was huntsman and herdsman, the calves 15
Sang to my horn, the foxes on the hills barked clear and cold,
 And the sabbath rang slowly
 In the pebbles of the holy streams.

All the sun long it was running, it was lovely, the hay
Fields high as the house, the tunes from the chimneys, it was air 20
 And playing, lovely and watery
  And fire green as grass.
 And nightly under the simple stars
As I rode to sleep the owls were bearing the farm away,
All the moon long I heard, blessed among stables, the nightjars 25
 Flying with the ricks, and the horses
  Flashing into the dark.

And then to awake, and the farm, like a wanderer white
With the dew, come back, the cock on his shoulder: it was all
 Shining, it was Adam and maiden,   30
  The sky gathered again
 And the sun grew round that very day.
So it must have been after the birth of the simple light
In the first, spinning place, the spellbound horses walking warm
 Out of the whinnying green stable   35
  On to the fields of praise.

And honoured among foxes and pheasants by the gay house
Under the new made clouds and happy as the heart was long
   In the sun born over and over,
      I ran my heedless ways,   40
   My wishes raced through the house high hay
And nothing I cared, at my sky blue trades, that time allows
In all his tuneful turning so few and such morning songs
   Before the children green and golden
      Follow him out of grace,   45

Nothing I cared, in the lamb white days, that time would take me
Up to the swallow thronged loft by the shadow of my hand,
   In the moon that is always rising,
      Nor that riding to sleep
I should hear him fly with the high fields   50
And wake to the farm forever fled from the childless land.
Oh as I was young and easy in the mercy of his means,
   Time held me green and dying
  Though I sang in my chains like the sea.

                     —Dylan Thomas

IV. QUESTIONS FOR REVIEW

1. Can you give a meaning to each of these terms?

lexis	grammatical item	collocational range
context	lexical item	lexical set
Puritan	lexicon	stylistician
trochaic	denotative	diction
foregrounded	connotative	metaphor
mid-grounded	collocates	image
backgrounded	span	collocation
field	distribution	colligation
		existentialist

2. In a good dictionary, look up some word (like "block") that seems to you to have several contexts. Count the number of denotative meanings given. How many grammatical forms can this lexical item take? Use the same denotative meaning in three different sentences. What are the connotative differences?

3. Analyze the lexis of a piece of technical writing and compare its "density of field" to a sports column in your local newspaper. What does this tell you about sports writing?

4. Change the following lexical items into different grammatical forms: subdivide, conquer, existential.

5. How does a dictionary deal with the fact that, in English, the addition of a preposition to a word may create a new lexical item? (Look up the item "catch", for example.)

6. In our discussion in the *Framework* of this Unit, under the heading *Collocation*, we demonstrated lexical analysis using a "target item" and a set "span". Do a similar lexical analysis on a text of your choice. What happens when you vary the span?

7. Formulate concepts of diction, metaphor and image according to the principles of "collocation" and "set".

8. William Blake lived at the end of the eighteenth century, a period of political turmoil involving the American and French revolutions when many traditional ideas about church and state were challenged. Mary Wollstonecraft at this time wrote a book upholding the "rights of

women". There was an outcry against child labour, and, in France, the very existence of God was questioned. Blake himself wrote several poems upholding free love and calling sexual jealousy the real source of sin. Blake's rebellion was against the rule of law which he saw as suppressing man's individuality and natural instincts, and which was itself only a symptom of a deeper rigidity of imagination, of "mind-forg'd manacles". All the cruelties of man's civilization, according to him, were the products of the human brain. All could be solved by the proper use of imagination.

The following poem is built of several strong lexical sets: *misery*, *proscription*, *mankind*. Search out the members of each set, and note any divisions into subsets. Is there another important set in the poem? What function does it have? Describe how the various sets come together to form a powerfully effective last stanza. "Church", "Palace" and "Marriage" here are associated by Blake with the sets of *misery* and *proscription*. What sets do you more normally associate with them? Remembering that this kind of lexical analysis is based on an intuitive understanding of lexical sets, attempt to reorganize the lexis of the poem into sets different from those we have supplied. Is your analysis more effective? Less effective? Does working with lexis in this way deepen your understanding of the poem?

LONDON

I wander thro' each charter'd street,   1
Near where the charter'd Thames does flow,
And mark in every face I meet
Marks of weakness, marks of woe.

In every cry of every Man,   5
In every Infant's cry of fear,
In every voice, in every ban,
The mind-forg'd manacles I hear.

How the Chimney-sweeper's cry
Every black'ning Church appalls;   10
And the hapless Soldier's sigh
Runs in blood down Palace walls.

But most thro' midnight streets I hear
How the youthful Harlot's curse
Blasts the new-born Infant's tear,   15
And blights with plagues the Marriage hearse.

—William Blake

UNIT 10

The Lexical Set

I. ANALYSIS: Multi-dimensional Reference in Lawrence Durrell

Walking about the streets of the summer capital once more, walking by spring sunlight, and a cloudless skirmishing blue sea—half-asleep and half-awake—I felt like the Adam of the mediaeval legends: the world-compounded body of a man whose flesh was soil, whose bones were stones, whose blood water, whose hair was grass, whose eyesight sunlight, whose breath was wind, and whose thoughts were clouds. And weightless now, as if after some long wasting illness, I found myself turned adrift again to float upon the shallows of Mareotis with its old tide-marks of appetites and desires refunded into the history of the place: an ancient city with all its cruelties intact, pitched upon a desert and a lake. Walking down with remembered grooves of streets which extended on every side, radiating out like the arms of a starfish from the axis of its founder's tomb. Footfalls echoing in the memory, forgotten scenes and conversations springing up at me from the walls, the café tables, the shuttered rooms with cracked and peeling ceilings. Alexandria, princess and whore. The royal city and the *anus mundi*. She would never change so long as the races continued to seethe here like must in a vat; so long as the streets and squares still gushed and spouted with the fermentation of these diverse passions and spites, rages and sudden calms. A fecund desert of human loves littered with the whitening bones of its exiles. Tall palms and minarets marrying in the sky. A hive of white mansions flanking those narrow and abandoned streets of mud which were racked all night by Arab music and the cries of girls who so easily disposed of their body's wearisome baggage (which galled them) and offered to the night the passionate kisses which money could not disflavour. The sadness and beatitude of this human conjunction which perpetuated itself to eternity, an endless cycle of rebirth and annihilation which alone could teach and reform by its destructive power. ("One makes love only to confirm one's loneliness" said Pursewarden, and at another time Justine added like a coda "A woman's best love letters are always written to the man she is betraying" as she turned an immemorial head on a high balcony,

188

hanging above a lighted city where the leaves of the trees seemed painted by the electric signs, where the pigeons tumbled as if from shelves. . . .) A great honeycomb of faces and gestures.

—Lawrence Durrell, *Clea*

Durrell's avowed aim in his famous tetralogy, *The Alexandria Quartet*, was to create a "word-continuum", a structure of language so resonant and self-contained that within it all meanings are relative. Moreover, such a continuum would be infinitely extensible; any number of volumes could be added to it. Reading this work is like watching an abstract mobile turning in the wind. The meanings of events shift with each volume, until eventually the reader ceases reaching after any kind of objective truth. He is left with the "names" of characters, the "name" of a city, and the musical impression of many woven and rewoven themes. But this is not to say the work is without meaning: rather, it is infinitely meaningful.

What is happening on a large scale in *The Alexandria Quartet* is also happening in miniature, in the lexis of many extended descriptive paragraphs. The passage above is an example. Here, words are placed in the context of other words to create meaning, a meaning soon dissolved and reshaped into yet another context and another meaning. Our analysis attempts to make clear only the technique of multi-dimensional reference employed by Durrell in this paragraph. The final "meaning" of Alexandria, the "unreal" city mused on above, and the subject of all four novels, is indeed a continuum.

Durrell and The Alexandria Quartet

Durrell comes from a family of individualists. Gerald Durrell, the author of a famous series of books relating his adventures with animals, is one of them, and perhaps one model for Narouz in *The Alexandria Quartet*. The family lived in Corfu, and Durrell has spent most of his life in one part or another of the Mediterranean. He has also worked in an administrative capacity for the British there. Thus he himself forms one model for Darley in *The Alexandria Quartet*.

The series of novels when they first appeared instantly placed Durrell in the forefront of twentieth-century novelists. That reputation has faded somewhat since, but the work can still evoke an intoxicating sense of the exotic in both landscape and the human mind. It also is of great interest formally, since it does not behave like other novels. Through the apparently loose patterns of shifting talk and incident, however, there does emerge a predictability of process, a point of philosophical view. One could say the novels are Hellenistic in a contemporary way, blending an eastern fatalism with a keen and sensual interest in the particular forms of unfolding life. Durrell includes critiques of English society and literature that seem to have been arrived at because of his immersion in another culture. His characters have a similar experience: their views of life are "changed" by living in Alexandria.

The Alexandria Quartet

The four novels of *The Alexandria Quartet* are: *Justine*, *Balthazar*, *Mountolive* and *Clea*. They are set in Alexandria before and during the Second World War. Each novel is named after a character, one of the lovers or friends or acquaintances of Darley, a would-be writer who is attempting to make sense out of them and out of his own experiences. The first three novels are three versions of the same time period. The fourth advances in time. The first two novels and the fourth are subjective, and from Darley's point of view; the third is objective and written in the third person. *The Alexandria Quartet* is thus experimental in form, with no two novels telling quite the same story in quite the same way, though all focus on the same characters and—largely—on the same events.

The form of *Clea*, the fourth novel, is motivated by the experience of recollection. New events occur but these are perceived in the light of past ones, and past ones are re-perceived in the light of the new. Darley, who has just returned to Alexandria after several years' absence, provides a continuing meditation on the significance of these past and present events.

In this passage Darley renews his acquaintanceship with the city, while Durrell offers us in a paragraph a miniature of both the themes and the techniques of the whole of *The Alexandria Quartet*. The city of Alexandria is not only the setting, but also the chief character of the novels, in that the city is described many times as though it had a human personality and attributes: "Alexandria, princess and whore". The city, as the matrix of the lives of its characters, is metaphorically both mother and lover. All the characters of the novel react with Alexandria as a symbol of their interrelation. This sense of Alexandria as a world-creating centre is here supported by the image of Adam who, in medieval times, was a symbol for the unity of all being. Darley, as Adam, walks through the world which is Alexandria, feeling himself a part of all, identified with all. Mareotis, the lake upon whose shores Alexandria is situated, is made part of the city here. Darley pictures himself as floating in both city and lake, as in the novel he floats in both present and past.

The simple meaning of the paragraph is not difficult. Darley again walks the streets of Alexandria, meditating on his memories. He passes many remembered shops and restaurants. He considers the demography of the city and its riot of illicit loves. He observes the city, the desert adjacent, and the lake, and remembers old friends and snatches of old conversations. Pursewarden is another writer, now dead by suicide. Justine is the woman Darley was in love with before his self-imposed exile.

But along with these matters of experience and fact exists the whole associative, subjective experience of the city for Darley: the notion of the city as a prostitute, the fancy of the lake covering the city, and much more suggested not only by explicit metaphor, but by the woven web of the words themselves. To get at all these meanings we must analyze the lexical items themselves, and see what sorts of patterns they make.

Some Lexical Sets

The prominent lexical sets in the passage are those of town, body and nature. These constitute the underlying metaphors for Alexandria as a social community, and for Darley's relationship to it. Alexandria is obviously a town, but much less obviously a body; since "town" and "country" are contrasts, it seems strange that it is also "nature". Let's look more closely at these prominent sets.

The *town* set is used to evoke the basic scene of the walking tour. The items "streets", which appears four times, and "city" (three times) are the core of the set. To these we may add items like: "mansions", "minarets", "capital", "founder's", "Alexandria", "squares", "walks", "café", "shuttered", "rooms" and so on.

The *body* set is used initially to evoke Darley moving through the town and landscape, and then to evoke the inhabitants of the city. This set includes items like: "walking", "asleep", "awake", "body" (twice), "flesh", "bones" (twice), "blood", "hair", "eyesight", "breath", "appetites", "arms", "footfalls", "whore", "*anus*", "flanking", "galled", "disflavour", "faces" and so on.

The third prominent set is that of *nature*. It is used to evoke an Alexandria surrounded by nature, but also to suggest that Alexandria is part of nature, as the metaphor of the lake and Alexandria being one suggests: ". . . I found myself turned adrift again to float upon the shallows of Mareotis with its old tide-marks of appetites and desires refunded into the history of the place: an ancient city with all its cruelties intact, pitched upon a desert and a lake." Members of the *nature* set are: "summer", "spring", "sunlight", "cloudless", "sea", "shallows", "Mareotis", "tide-marks", "starfish". The sustained metaphor of Darley as Adam adds many nature items to this list: "soil", "stones", "water", "grass", "sunlight" and so on. The effect of these nature items is to produce a scene that is less city-bound than we might perhaps expect—an effect found in Mediterranean cities where the climate allows a kind of mingling of men and weather, of rooms and patios, that is different from northern urban places.

If we go more particularly into these major sets we find subsets that cohere to produce contexts of their own. The *town* set breaks down into a *building* set and a *city* set. In the *building* set are items like "walls", "café", "shuttered", "rooms", "ceilings", "minarets", "mansions", "balconies". This turns Alexandria into a place of human habitation, a place for bodies. The other subset of the *town* set, the *city* set, has items which suggest Alexandria as a *public* place, a place for buildings as opposed to a place for bodies. This distinction will eventually emerge as an important one.

The *nature* set also breaks down into subsets. Here we may distinguish a subset of three of the old "four elements" which in ancient Greek philosophy were supposed to form the world. Of these elements—water, earth, air—the *water* set is the most prominent. It contains items like: "sea", "water", "adrift", "float", "shallows", "Mareotis", "tide-marks", "lake", "starfish", "vat", "gush", "spout", "calms". This liquidity is around Alexandria, is part of Alexandria, is even suggested as a metaphor for the inhabitants of Alexandria: "the races continued to seethe here like must in a vat". The *earth* set contains items like: "world", "soil", "stones", "grass", "*mundi*" ("of the world") and "mud". This is a strongly established set, but much less prominent than the *water* set which is pervasive through the passage. Members of the *air* set are: "cloudless", "wind", "clouds", "weightless", "up", "sky", "high", "pigeons", "above" and so on. Some of these items are associated with Darley himself, as are members of the *earth* set.

There is one more important general set to isolate before we attempt to see the significance behind this lexical patterning. That is the *centre* set. This set contains items like: "extended", "side", "radiating", "out", "axis", "*anus mundi*". The radiating hierarchy—*centre, body, building, city, nature*—is an important one in many mythologies. We will see how suggestive it is here in Durrell's multi-levelled "word-continuum", as we try next to explore the possible meanings of these many lexical contexts.

The Unity of Being

Ancient man, typified here by Adam, first of his race, and suggested by the Latin "*anus mundi*", felt that all being radiated from, and was an expression of, a cosmic Centre. The Centre or *axis mundi* was surrounded by every body, building and city just as it was surrounded by the whole cosmos. In ancient man's mythological thinking this Centre is not a fixed geographical point, but an intellectual conception. Everything is conceived of as outside of this Centre and created by this Centre. This means that all containing structures, like bodies, buildings and cities, are organized by their own localization of the Centre. If one enters a church one approaches the Centre. If one goes inward from the outside of one's body, one approaches the Centre. The paradox is that there is only *one* Centre and *every* body, building and city contains it. Furthermore, every body, building and city are at one with each other and with nature because they are all found around the *same* Centre. So Darley, entering Alexandria once more, approaches the Centre, as he does also by entering the body of Adam which is equated with nature.

The surface meaning of the text is a pattern of statements, the statements Darley makes about his walk and his thoughts. Underlying the statements, however, is another pattern, the pattern of lexical sets. The lexis has sorted itself into these groupings: *centre* set, *body* set, *building* set, *city* set, *nature* set. This string of concepts is precisely that hierarchy of organization which appears as a principle in so many mythologies and cultures, and very notably in the mythologies of ancient Mediterranean civilizations. The effect of this lexical patterning is to elevate Darley's actions and thoughts to the plane of mythology. Darley now becomes Adam, Darley now becomes at one with the Centre and all its various radiations.

The four elements, which we have mentioned above, are also a hierarchy with an ancient significance: the ancients thought earth was at the bottom of the cosmos, with water, air and fire above it. (Fire is represented in this text only by "sunlight".) In their various combinations these four constituents were supposed to make up all the materials and qualities of the world as we know it—even the emotions. The distribution of lexis into sets which represent the elements in this text reinforces the suggestion of "ancient thought" and lays bare the constitution of "nature" as combinations of earth, water, air and fire. Similarly, Alexandria, for Darley, contains all the possible combinations of human emotions: ". . . these diverse passions and spites, rages and sudden calms . . . A great honeycomb of faces and gestures."

The distribution of the items in all the sets suggests that Darley, the Alexandrians, and Alexandria itself, are one thing, and also one with everything, centred on the *axis mundi*. Through colligations and the overlapping items of the lexical sets, Darley has been equated with body, with nature and with the city. The citizens have been equated with nature and the city. The city has been equated with nature. Even the simple existence in the passage of lexical items pertaining to all levels of the hierarchy, plus the existence of the *centre* set, is enough to suggest that all these equations pertain.

The passage yields other interesting sets as well, adding to the richness and intricacy of the experience described. The sense of age and repetition is realized through lexical items pertaining to memory and history: "legends", "history", "remembered", "echoing" and so on. One of the themes of the novels is political power, which items like "princess", "royal", "exile" and "power" call forth. Related to this is the question of wealth, for Alexandria is a city of great extremes in wealth, which the passage reflects: "A hive of white mansions flanking those narrow and abandoned streets of mud. . .". Items from the *money* set include "mansion", "refunded", "offered", "money". History, memory, politics, power, are all aspects of the life of Alexandria because they are the counters in the great games of emotion the Alexandrians play. Words like "desire", "passion", "rage", "seethe", "spites", "kisses", "sadness", "love", "loneliness", "betraying", "appetites", counterpoint the paragraph. The city is a well of human feeling, just like Darley as he walks its streets, seeing and remembering.

Just as all the disparate lexical sets of the paragraph can be seen as one unity, a hierarchy of being revolving around one centre, so the different novels of the quartet revolve around an aesthetic core. We approach the centre anew with our entrance into each novel, with our rediscovery of each old character, with the next revelation of the meaning of old events.

Can we, finally, make any statement as to the meaning of *The Alexandria Quartet*? Perhaps we are only extending its meaning once more; but is there not in the shifting patterns of significance, both in individual paragraphs, and in the events of the story, an echo of the consciousness of the drunk or the drugged? This would be comparable to the effects of Malcolm Lowry's *Under the Volcano*, that other multi-dimensional portrait of a consciousness. Only here the consciousness portrayed is not that of Darley, the supposed narrator, but of Alexandria herself, of the city's collective state of being with which Darley has so successfully identified.

Cities are natural paradigms for the consciousness of man, and are, of course, infinitely extensible in both meaning and time. The older the city, the more cosmopolitan, the more effective it is as an image of the mind or the state of mind of a race. Durrell said his theme was "modern love". Alexandria is a city of lovers. But Alexandria is also a city of drunkards drunk on love, and the story turns on the times in men and women's lives when they are drunk on love. Like all drunkards the characters are charming—to a point. But like all drunkards, in the end they are lost. The central problem of the novel is that there is—in the Alexandrian state—no other possible kind of existence. It is only at the end of *The Alexandria Quartet*, when the leading characters leave the city at least temporarily, that a change in their state of mind occurs; and this change is refreshing: all are awakened, changed, renewed. But that is not part of Durrell's continuum, nor could that fresh experience be conveyed by Durrell's style here. To represent Alexandria as a state of drunkenness—half-myth, half-reality— requires the careful patterning of lexis, the juxtaposition of universal and particular contexts, revealed in our analysis.

II. FRAMEWORK: Generation and Definition of Lexical Sets in Texts

FIRST, let's review some basic concepts about lexis. Most basic is the notion that the formal meaning of a lexical item is a function of its collocates, that is, the distribution of collocates in the language. Contrast this with the formal meaning of a grammatical item which is a function of its colligations, of the places it can occupy in grammatical structures. In other words we can as readily spot an unusual lexical item in a text as we can an unusual grammatical usage: "Her look spoke libraries".

To ascertain this distribution of collocates, one selects a nodal item in a body of text and locates all instances of it. Next, one assigns a span (of so many words either side of the nodal item) and enumerates all the collocates in this span. The distribution of collocates in the span is the collocational range of the nodal item, giving us a distribution of the item's collocates from the most common to the least.

Since lexical meaning is formally equivalent to a specific collocational range, synonyms will have nearly identical collocational ranges. Related lexical items will have proportionately related ranges. Items with similar ranges are said to be members of a lexical set.

The semantic meaning, as opposed to the formal meaning, of a lexical item is the product of associating particular situations with particular collocational ranges. The most common situations are suggested by the core collocates of the range. This is the denotative meaning of the lexical item. Less common situations are suggested by the less frequent collocates. This is the connotative meaning of the lexical item.

The Behaviour of Sets in Literary Texts

As we have said, the phenomenon of lexical sets is the basis of metaphor. Putting lexical items from different lexical sets together in a colligation can produce the paradox of equating things that are not the same. This forces us to find ways to relate the two sets. The simile "She loves men like whiskey" is effective in that we can perceive some shared collocates of the whiskey and men sets: "desire", "pleasure", "warmth", "compulsion". But it is also effective in that we can perceive some collocates that are *not* shared: "drinking", "glass", "bottle" for the *whiskey* set; "mind", "feeling", "humanity" for the *men* set. The mental problem of sorting out appropriate and inappropriate collocates and the insights resulting from it are part of the metaphor's effect.

But metaphors may also be "submerged" in a text, a phenomenon that is very important in literature. For example, the *water* items in the *Clea* text are distributed widely through the passage, not linked directly to each other. They combine as an image of Darley "floating" through Alexandria, "floating" through his memories; Alexandria becomes an inexhaustible "sea" of life. These metaphors are not so much explicit in the text as implicit in the occurrence of the *water* set.

Discerning such sets is a matter of good literary intuition in the first place, plus the seeking out and tabulating of supporting items. We become aware of a general "water" presence in the *Clea* text, then set about listing related items that seem to have similar collocational ranges, like "lake". The boundaries of such sets are established by contrast with adjacent sets. For example, both *water* items and *earth* items might be included in a *nature* set, but are obviously contrastive with each other as well.

In the single sentence near the middle of the passage beginning "She would never change" and ending "sudden calms", there are many items suggesting tumultuous existence: "change", "seethe", "must", "gushed", "spouted", "fermentation", "diverse", "passions", "spites", "rages", "sudden". Yet inside this set we can distinguish two sets that contrast enough to make a boundary, a set of *passion* and a set of *fermentation*. Items in the *passion* set include "seethe", "gushed", "spites", "rages"; in the *fermentation* set are "seethe", "must", "gushed", "spouted". Sets thus form hierarchies, not unlike the hierarchy of body, town, nature, cosmos. In the widest sense a set would be all the items in a text, so the sorting out of sets is really a sorting out of subsets.

What is crucial is the placing of the boundaries between sets, which depends on intuited contrasts, organized around the sense of different contexts—wine-making, love-making—which we possess as the result of our linguistic experience. Thus, when we intuit a subset boundary we are really intuiting the contexts which give these sets meaning.

The Concept of Self-generation

How does a useful set in a literary text emerge into our consciousness? It does so by our perception of the contrast between the contexts it suggests and the contexts suggested by other sets. This contrast creates a perception of the boundary between the sets. The more clearly we perceive these contexts the more clearly we can define and limit the sets. In this sense the sets mutually generate themselves, since they are defined and distinguished in relation to each other.

This phenomenon of self-generation can be most clearly perceived in a short lyric poem, like Emily Dickinson's in the previous Unit. The number of lexical items in such a text is sharply limited by its short length, and the text itself is sharply severed from context by the isolation created by a unified poetic structure. A lyric poem by definition takes place in a timeless moment of perception—the "lyric" moment. The only context it possesses is that suggested by itself through its own lexis. Mutual self-generation of sets works here in relative isolation, giving the poetic matrix control over its own meaning. Next time you attend a poetry reading, note the difference between your perception of a poem alone, and your perception of it when it comes accompanied by the author's account of its making, that is, when it is not isolated. It is this isolation from context that makes poetry the formal "art" of language.

Prose texts, however, are usually embedded in a larger prose text, as our paragraph is embedded in *Clea*, and beyond that, in *The Alexandria Quartet*. Moreover, prose texts tend to belong to strongly marked genres and varieties: newspaper language, scientific writing, mystery novels. Both these circumstances make for the provision of context outside the resources of the text itself. Thus prose tends to be less a matter of abstract patterning, less a pure game of lexis, than poetry is. Long poems, of course, tend to behave like prose in this respect.

"Textuality" is the property which texts have that marks them as texts, that makes us perceive them as cohesive wholes. The single set of lexis supplied by the whole text provides a self-generated context, contrasting with the rest of the language. This set of the whole text may break into subsets which are mutually self-generated, as we have seen; but there still remains something that makes these sets hang together in one whole. Sometimes critics speak vaguely of this as the "theme" or "subject" of the text, but linguists discuss its "textuality".

There are two senses in which a set has a context. First there is the referential context of the set, those other texts in the language with similar lexical sets. Second, the set has a context provided by its own surrounding text, and the other sets in it which define the set by contrast. In this second sense a text, lexically, is a composite of sets and their contexts which mutually define one another. This is the inner activity of a text revealed through lexical analysis. And it is the fact that this inner activity is played on for its own sake, as well as to make a point, that makes literary texts different from other texts. We see this most clearly in poetry. This is also why, very largely, a literary work is unique. Since it comes into being by a process of mutual self-definition of sets, there cannot be another poem or story or play quite like it, while there might easily be a number of very similar works—in terms of lexical sets—about a certain historical incident, or a chemical process.

The notion of mutual self-definition, and so self-generation, might well be applied to artifacts in general. Artifacts, especially works of art, achieve definition by locking together elements that are distinguished by mutual contrast. When it comes to literature, particularly poetry, it is lexis that serves as the basic element in this process.

Practicum

Using the theory of sets we have outlined in this Unit for literary and stylistic purposes takes both discipline and inspiration. The beginning of this critical process is, as we have stressed throughout this book, a literary intuition. This is nothing more than an intelligent, informed response to the text, the sort of response the author expects from the general reader of his works.

Reflecting on this intuition, this sense of what the text is about, brings forth an apprehension of some lexical sets as operative features of the text. For example, in our analysis of the *Clea* text, the references to Adam, to the *anus mundi*, to the eternal and repetitive nature of Alexandrian life brought forth the intuition that the text was attempting to make of Alexandria an archetypal, unifying symbol. This realization helped us to isolate the sets of the four elements, of the hierarchy of body, building, city, nature and of the Centre, since these are old, unifying concepts, originating also in the Mediterranean.

This connection of particular sets to an intuited meaning clarifies the lexical structure. With the lines laid down we can now move to closer distinctions, and discern contrasts between lexical items in previously recognized sets, thus producing subsets. Gradually a structure of unifying and mutually defining sets emerges. Very important to this emerging structure are those lexical items that can be members of more than one set. We saw an example of the importance of this in our analysis of Emily Dickinson's poem in Unit 9, when we discovered the various possibilities of set membership for the item "light": *nature, intellectual knowledge, spiritual experience*. These "cross sets" are especially important in the imagery of poetry.

The original perception of sets is thus modified, as the process of analysis goes on, by the later refinement of subsets and cross sets. It may be necessary to re-do one's structuring of the lexical pattern several times to achieve a result that seems to fit best with both the lexical items of the passage and your intuition of the sense. What this means, of course, is that you are simultaneously improving your original literary insight, as it is modified in turn by the lexical patterns discovered.

In fact the use of set theory in this way is an empty exercise unless it forms the basis for an intelligent critical description of one's literary intuition, as it has been refined and confirmed by the process of analysis. Your restatement of the lexical patterns must go from their structure back to your literary intuition, asking and answering the questions: Why this particular structure? Why this particular substructure?

As a final example let's ask and answer the question: Why the use of the *fermentation* set in Durrell's paragraph? To suggest a state of intoxication? Certainly Darley is "floating" earlier in the passage; certainly he is "high" on Alexandria, intoxicated by her image as both "princess and whore". Justine, later in the paragraph, is described in language that might well describe the famous portrait head of Nefertiti, Queen of Egypt: ". . . as she turned an *immemorial head* on a high balcony . . .". We might note again that Darley is "high" on Justine as well as on Alexandria. He is "half-asleep and half-awake", feeling himself a part of the landscape he walks on, hallucinating forgotten scenes and conversations. Thus the sets of *weight-lessness* and *fermentation* assume importance in retrospect as a unified set of *intoxication*. For Darley, and the reader, the whole experience of *The Alexandria Quartet* is like a dream. Darley, walking the streets of Alexandria, has planted his body in the landscape, while his freed consciousness ranges widely into past and present, high over Alexandria.

III. APPLICATION: the Crab and the Cosmos in Archibald MacLeish

VICISSITUDES OF THE CREATOR

Fish has laid her succulent eggs   1
Safe in Saragossa weed
So wound and bound that crabbed legs
Nor clattering claws can find and feed.

Thus fish commits unto the sea   5
Her infinite future and the Trade
Blows westward toward eternity
The universe her love has made.

But when, upon this leeward beach,
The measureless sea journey ends   10
And ball breaks open, from the breach
A deft, gold, glossy crab extends

In ring-side ritual of self-applause
The small ironic silence of his claws.   14

—Archibald MacLeish

MacLeish, in his poetry and in his life, seems to be obsessed by the idea of an imminent darkness threatening the world, and thus rendering its activities, especially those of love, meaningless. He served, first as an ambulance driver, then as a soldier, in the First World War, and prior to the Second wrote extensively to alert Americans to the dangers of fascism. He is the author of a famous poem called "The End of the World" which ends with the line (and the perception) "Of nothing, nothing, nothing—nothing at all."

In this poem the fight against death and meaninglessness again ends in defeat for love and life. "Fish" can lay her eggs with love and forethought in the tangled and drifting seaweed of the Sargasso Sea in order to protect them from crabs; but all the while the northeast tradewind is blowing the weed south to the beaches of the West Indies the little pincers are at work within. At the end of the voyage, like a boxer, the little crab raises his claw in victory. The fish eggs have served only to extend the life and range of fish's mortal enemy.

Language is used throughout MacLeish's poem with great skill, but the most striking feature of the lexical patterning is the concentrated set of *idealized love* that extends from line 5 to line 12: "commits", "infinite", "future", "eternity", "universe", "love", "measureless", "gold". This kind of diction seems wildly inappropriate for talk of fish and eggs. And its ridiculous impracticality, of course, is revealed by the crab's victory at the end. Just as the bubble of "ideal" language is burst by the mundanity of "fish", "eggs", and "claws", so man's spiritual pretensions are laid waste by his physical reality.

The ironic reversal that is the intention of the whole poem is reinforced by other ironic shifts in lexis. The last item of the *idealized love* set—"gold" (with its connotations of value and purity)—is ironically associated with the crab, not the fish or her eggs. Similarly, the small set of *intricacy*— "wound", "bound", "ball", "deft"—ends with an item that modifies "crab".

There are other small interesting sets in the poem. Pick out some and explain their function in emphasizing the theme. What is the large establishing set in this poem? List its members. Does it break into subsets? Can you find any lexical items in the poem that are members of more than one set? What effect does this have on the lexical patterning of the poem? How do the two lexical items of the title relate to the lexical patterning of the poem? Is the word "Vicissitudes" ironic?

IV. QUESTIONS FOR REVIEW

1. Can you give a meaning to each of these terms?

anus mundi	semantic meaning	textuality
must (in a vat)	formal meaning	referential context
continuum	core collocates	literary intuition
matrix	set boundary	archetypal
axis mundi	self-generation	the four elements
synonym	lyric poem	cross sets

2. Describe the process of ascertaining the *formal* meaning of a lexical item in a given text. Define "synonym" according to this formal meaning. How is the semantic meaning of a lexical item obtained?

3. What does it mean to say "metaphors may . . . be 'submerged' in a text . . ."? In the text given in the last question below, find such a "submerged" metaphor.

4. From the Durrell passage give an example of a lexical set, and of its breakdown into subsets. Do not use a set referred to in the Analysis or the Framework.

5. Discuss the concept of "boundary" between sets, and exemplify. Discuss the concept of "mutual self-generation". Describe the process of intuition and analysis by which a set is isolated in a text.

6. What elements make up a lyric poem's "unified poetic structure"? Illustrate using MacLeish's poem from the Application section of this Unit.

7. In the fall when the days became crisp and gray, and the long Minnesota winter shut down like the white lid of a box, Dexter's skis moved over the snow that hid the fairways of the golf course. At these times the country gave him a feeling of profound melancholy—it offended him that the links should lie in enforced fallowness, haunted by ragged sparrows for the long season. It was dreary, too, that on the tees where the gay colours fluttered in summer there were now only the desolate sand-boxes knee-deep in crusted ice. When he crossed the hills the wind blew cold as

misery, and if the Sun was out he tramped with his eyes squinted up
against the hard dimensionless glare.

—F. Scott Fitzgerald, "Winter Dreams"

This passage occurs near the beginning of a short story with the usual
Fitzgerald themes of wealth and its effects on people, and of idealized
romantic love. Dexter is a caddy who later becomes a wealthy man. He
caddies for a rich man's little girl with whom later he falls in love. His
tragedy is not that he loses the girl, but that he loses the dream of having
her. The winter experience described above is his foretaste of that spiritual
grief at the end of the story. His weapons against it are the memories of the
gaiety of summer with its golf (the rich man's game, in 1922), and his
"winter dreams" of success. As in his famous novel, *Gatsby*, Fitzgerald is
intent on showing the fatality of chasing the pot at the end of the rainbow.
The rainbow fades, whether you attain pot or not.

Analyze the lexis of this passage, and show how its patterns establish the
setting and mood of the incident described, and also reinforce the themes of
the story.

Chapter Five **Context**

WE HAVE actually been talking about context all along throughout this book. That was unavoidable because no item of language in a text operates without a context. Context is related to the surroundings of a language event. These may be the real-life surroundings of a whole text; or they may be the text itself, as the environment of some small portion of that text. Context is a source of meaning for every language event. Consider what happens to items in the formal level of language when context changes. The imperative "Shoot!" means one thing in the context of a hockey game, quite another in the context of a firing squad—a principle that many comedy routines testify to.

Context is also a level of language, the highest level of abstraction on which language exists. This is because it is context that attaches meaning to the formal items of grammar or lexis. Grammar books and dictionaries are catalogues of the normal contexts in which formal items and formal structures occur. Since we have been talking about context all along, you should have realized by now that literary artists are also masters of context. In literature, context can be found attaching meaning even to phonological and graphological effects. On the formal level the literary artist searches for the right word in the right context—which is very frequently an extraordinary word in an extraordinary context. In Unit 11 we will not only examine the use of context in literary language, but also see how literary language works on all levels in conjunction with contextual categories. In this final Unit you will see all stylistic analysis brought to a focus by the consideration of context.

LOL-I

UNIT 11

Context and Varieties

I. ANALYSIS: the Inner World of Sylvia Plath

TULIPS

The tulips are too excitable, it is winter here.   1
Look how white everything is, how quiet, how snowed-in.
I am learning peacefulness, lying by myself quietly
As the light lies on these white walls, this bed, these hands.
I am nobody; I have nothing to do with explosions.   5
I have given my name and my day-clothes up to the nurses
And my history to the anaesthetist and my body to surgeons.

They have propped my head between the pillow and the sheet-cuff
Like an eye between two white lids that will not shut.
Stupid pupil, it has to take everything in.   10
The nurses pass and pass, they are no trouble,
They pass the way gulls pass inland in their white caps,
Doing things with their hands, one just the same as another,
So it is impossible to tell how many there are.

My body is a pebble to them, they tend it as water   15
Tends to the pebbles it must run over, smoothing them gently.
They bring me numbness in their bright needles, they bring me sleep.
Now I have lost myself I am sick of baggage—
My patent leather overnight case like a black pillbox,
My husband and child smiling out of the family photo;   20
Their smiles catch onto my skin, little smiling hooks.

I have let things slip, a thirty-year-old cargo boat
Stubbornly hanging on to my name and address.
They have swabbed me clear of my loving associations.
Scared and bare on the green plastic-pillowed trolley   25
I watched my teaset, my bureaus of linen, my books
Sink out of sight, and the water went over my head.
I am a nun now, I have never been so pure.

I didn't want any flowers, I only wanted
To lie with my hands turned up and be utterly empty.   30
How free it is, you have no idea how free—
The peacefulness is so big it dazes you,
And it asks nothing, a name tag, a few trinkets.
It is what the dead close on, finally; I imagine them
Shutting their mouths on it, like a Communion tablet.   35

The tulips are too red in the first place, they hurt me.
Even through the gift paper I could hear them breathe
Lightly, through their white swaddlings, like an awful baby.
Their redness talks to my wound, it corresponds.
They are subtle: they seem to float, though they weigh me down,   40
Upsetting me with their sudden tongues and their colour,
A dozen red lead sinkers round my neck.

Nobody watched me before, now I am watched.
The tulips turn to me, and the window behind me
Where once a day the light slowly widens and slowly thins,   45
And I see myself, flat, ridiculous, a cut-paper shadow
Between the eye of the sun and the eyes of the tulips,
And I have no face, I have wanted to efface myself.
The vivid tulips eat my oxygen.

Before they came the air was calm enough,   50
Coming and going, breath by breath, without any fuss,
Then the tulips filled it up like a loud noise.
Now the air snags and eddies round them the way a river
Snags and eddies round a sunken rust-red engine.
They concentrate my attention, that was happy   55
Playing and resting without committing itself.

The walls, also, seem to be warming themselves.
The tulips should be behind bars like dangerous animals;
They are opening like the mouth of some great African cat,
And I am aware of my heart: it opens and closes   60
Its bowl of red blooms out of sheer love of me.
The water I taste is warm and salt, like the sea,
And comes from a country far away as health.   63

—Sylvia Plath

The poems that affect us are those that catch completely experiences of
life that we all know. But what are we to say of poems that take familiar

experiences and transmute them into something extraordinary? In "Tulips", Sylvia Plath takes the fairly commonplace experience of hospitalization after surgery and makes of it a major exploration of the most powerful and dangerous possibilities of the human psyche.

At first, the poem seems innocuous enough. In form it is an interior monologue. The setting is a hospital room, the "speaker" a woman recovering from the trauma of surgery. Through her commentary we become aware of certain facts about her. These facts emerge gradually in the course of the first half of the poem, as one might become aware of oneself and one's surroundings slowly after being unconscious. She is thirty years old, married, a housewife with a small child. We do not discover the exact nature of her "wound" (39) but she does make clear that whatever has happened to her has been serious enough for her to want to let go of life and her concerns in it. At the end of the poem she seems preparing, however painfully, to re-enter the world.

Most of her monologue, however, does not consist of the objective details of either herself or her hospital room. Rather, it is a confession of her most intimate feelings about life. These feelings are organized as a tension between satisfaction and irritation, longing and immediacy. Her satisfaction is found in her experience of "winter" (1), in the peace of being nobody, of having no attachments, of being laid out like one who is dead. Her irritation comes from the little nagging reminders of life, of her family, of her possessions, but especially from the presence of the tulips which, as living things and a token of her human attachments, disturb her repose. This tension between the longing for peace and the intruding demands of life increases through the poem, sparked by the presence of the tulips, and betrayed by the increasing violence of the speaker's language. This is a conflict that we can recognize, but so uniquely and vividly is it presented here that we cannot help wondering what lies behind this apparently straightforward situation. What has led this woman to perceive in such unusual terms, with such extraordinary intensity of language, such unsettling extremes of feeling?

Sylvia Plath

The unique intensity of Plath's creation may be partly explained by reference to her life. For many of us the conflicts in our personalities and in the demands made on us by experience may sometimes appear overwhelming. For her this was tragically so. Compelled to stage a series of ritual suicide attempts, she died at last when she was not rescued as she apparently intended to be. This poem is one of a number written during a great outburst of creativity just prior to her death, and published posthumously. The persona of the poem is thus a projection of herself, and the ordinariness of this kind of hospital-recovery experience is intensified by the extraordinary personality and experience of the poet projecting it.

She herself had a husband and child. But her husband had left her at the time of the writing of the poem and she and her child were alone. Depressed, morbid, blaming herself, a potential suicide, she was yet in a curiously heightened state of creativity, writing two or three poems a day, seemingly excited by the approach of her ritual suicide attempt. This extreme, disturbed condition of mind manifests itself in fantastic imagery and paranoid fantasies, particularly in the latter half of the poem when the tulips seem like "dangerous animals" (58) and "eat my oxygen" (49). Yet what the poem speaks of directly is simply a heightened version of a common experience—the desire to be free of conflict—and in the structure and firm control and easy flow of the poem there is no hint of derangement, only a luminous, vivid clarity.

The Structure of "Tulips"

This control is demonstrated by the poem's clear organization. The poem is symmetrical in the distribution of its subject matter and formal in its stanza patterning. It is composed of nine stanzas, each of seven lines. The first four stanzas make one statement, the last four a counter-statement. Stanza 5 is pivotal. In the first part the persona expresses her satisfaction with her state of passive repose, but her irritation at having to experience sensations is also beginning to surface: "The tulips are too excitable" (1), "Stupid pupil" (10)—her eye, that persists in seeing—"little smiling hooks" (21)—her family. In the last part she expresses directly her growing dislike and fear of the tulips with their demand that she return to the conflicting feelings of life. The first part begins with the sentence "The tulips are too excitable" (1), the last with "the tulips are too red" (36). The pivotal stanza 5 begins "I didn't want any flowers" (29). The change to the past tense here parallels a change in her mood: peacefulness is passing; life is beginning to reassert itself.

The Poem of Contexts

The careful structure of "Tulips" is a means of confining and setting off that intensity of feeling we have referred to. We can see how this intensity itself is conveyed if we recognize that "Tulips" is a poem of contexts. The persona of the poem in her eventful monologue is the victim of conflicting impulses, impulses which lead her to abstract from her situation only certain features, and to refer these features suggestively to imagined contexts which reflect the deep desires and fears of her emotional state.

The process works like this. The persona, emerging into consciousness, finds herself involved in two main situations. There is the immediate and obvious situation of the hospital room with its bed, white walls and nurses passing in and out. Beyond this is the wider world which slowly comes back to memory: the world of her husband and child, her house and belongings. This second situation is represented in the room by the tulips, the patent leather overnight case, the family photo.

But this wider situation is disturbing to the persona. She seeks to escape it by seizing on different aspects of the hospital environment and relating them to more soothing contexts, contexts that will allay the frightening and painful feelings aroused by thoughts of her family, of her wider situation. And so she creates the context of a snowscape: "it is winter here./ Look how white everything is, how quiet, how snowed-in." (1–2); of a school-room: "I am learning peacefulness" (3); of a funeral parlour: "They have propped my head between the pillow and the sheet-cuff/ Like an eye between two white lids that will not shut." (8-9); of a seashore: "The nurses pass and pass, they are no trouble,/ They pass the way gulls pass inland in their white caps" (11–12); of a running brook: "My body is a pebble to them, they tend it as water/ Tends to the pebbles it must run over, smoothing them gently." (15–16); of a convent: "I am a nun now, I have never been so pure." (28).

Despite her efforts, thoughts of her family and the painful feelings her wider life arouses in her intrude again. Features of this second situation are taken up and referred to other contexts; but this time the contexts are active and violent, such as those of war: "My patent leather overnight case like a black pillbox" (19); of fishing: "My husband and child smiling out of the family photo;/ Their smiles catch onto my skin, little smiling hooks." (20–21); of a sinking cargo boat: "I watched my teaset, my bureaus of linen, my books/ Sink out of sight, and the water went over my head." (26–27). It is consideration of features of the tulips themselves that gives rise to the most sinister of these contexts in the last half of the poem, contexts of misshapen births: "an awful baby" (38); of forcible drowning: "A dozen red lead sinkers around my neck" (42); of asphyxiation: "The vivid tulips eat my oxygen." (49); of carnivores in the jungle: "The tulips should be behind bars like dangerous animals;/ They are opening like the mouth of some great African cat" (58–59).

At this point the persona has lost her fight to make safe her environment. She has come face to face with the demands of her family duties, signified by the tulips in their most dangerous manifestation: a great mouth opening to swallow her. But just at this moment, when reality has reached an extremity of distortion through the creation of this last impossible context, the persona is saved by a return to her actual situation, to an awareness of her body, of her own human sensations: "And I am aware of my heart" (60); "The water I taste is warm and salt" (62). Now the abstraction of features from situation to form new contexts is working to reconcile and heal the persona's conflict. The heart is related to the tulips in a positive way: "it opens and closes/ Its bowl of red blooms out of sheer love of me." (60–61). The water is "like the sea,/ And comes from a country far away as health." (62–63). With the word "health" a final context is reached which resolves the persona's dilemma, and both hallucinations and poetry cease.

Among the larger contexts sustained throughout the poem which unify more particular contexts created by the persona are those of an underwater experience, of children and animals, and of eating. The water context starts as an aspect of oblivion, one of the many attempts to reinforce the safety of the hospital environment (often morbidly, with images of death). It transforms itself into the context of a hooked fish as the family situation strengthens. It ends with the sea as a symbol of health: "The nurses pass . . . the way gulls pass inland in their white caps" (11–12); "My body is a pebble to them, they tend it as water/ Tends to the pebbles it must run over, smoothing them gently." (15–16); "Their smiles catch onto my skin, little smiling hooks." (21); "I have let things slip, a thirty-year-old cargo boat" (22); "I watched my teaset, my bureaus of linens, my books/ Sink out of sight, and the water went over my head." (26–27); "A dozen red lead sinkers round my neck." (42); "the air snags and eddies round them the way a river/ Snags and eddies round a sunken rust-red engine" (53–54); "The water I taste is warm and salt, like the sea" (62).

The contexts of children and dangerous animals are unified in that both are partly abstracted from features of the tulips themselves. It is as though the sequence begins with human children but as feelings grow more intense the children turn into African carnivores. Initially, the tulips are seen in the image of demanding children: "The tulips are too excitable" (1); "I could hear them breathe/ Lightly, through their white swaddlings, like an awful baby." (37–38); "Upsetting me" (41); "The tulips turn to me" (44); "Before they came, the air was calm enough/ Coming and going, breath by breath, without any fuss." (50–51); "like a loud noise" (52); "They concentrate my attention" (55). But near the end of the poem the tulips are also imaged as dangerous animals: "they hurt me" (36); "their sudden tongues" (41); "I am watched" (43); "the eyes of the tulips" (47); "warming themselves" (57); "The tulips should be behind bars like dangerous animals;/ They are opening like the mouth of some great African cat" (58–59).

The context of eating also helps to relate the children and animals contexts, because both children and animals are seen as consuming the persona. Like the water context, the sequence undergoes modifications through the poem. First it is part of the Communion of oblivion; then it turns menacing, the eating of oxygen; and lastly, with the taste of salt, it becomes an image of restoration. Remember that eating is important in hospitals, part of the process of healing: "It is what the dead close on, finally; I imagine them/ Shutting their mouths on it, like a Communion tablet." (34–35); "Upsetting me with their sudden tongues" (41); "The vivid tulips eat my oxygen" (49); "They are opening like the mouth of some great African cat" (59); "The water I taste is warm and salt, like the sea,/ And comes from a country far away as health." (62–63).

The Poem at All Levels

We have seen how Sylvia Plath's poem is built on the creation of many imaginary contexts, derived by abstracting features of the persona's actual situation and relating them to features abstracted from other circumstances. In this section we will examine how these contexts are suggested on the formal and substance-related levels of language. But first, let us distinguish between "situation" and "context" as we have used the terms so far. We have used "situation" to describe the real-life circumstances of someone or something. In the case of the persona these are her environment (the hospital room); her family situation; and her mental and emotional state. We have used "context" to mean a conceptual abstraction from situations, therefore a *type* of situation, which determines the meaning of features in situations.

When we turn to the language by which these situations and contexts are conveyed, we find useful a distinction between the *co-text* and the *context* of a lexical item. Any lexical item exists in a particular co-text, i.e. the actual surrounding text; but it also has associations derived from its general context—the *type* of text in which we are accustomed to find it. For example, in "I am learning Latin", the co-text confirms the expected linguistic context of "learning". But in "I am learning peacefulness" (3), the expected linguistic context of "learning" is contrasted with the unexpected co-textual item "peacefulness". Such confirmations and contrasts of expected linguistic contexts form the "play of lexis" which makes up much of contemporary poetry, and which "Tulips" itself is built on. The point here, however, is not simply that such "play" is a feature of literary texts, but that it is made possible by the existence of generalized linguistic contexts for particular lexical items. It is this fact that enables Sylvia Plath to create so easily one after another of those fleeting experiences.

Besides this precise use of lexis (supported by appropriate grammatical constructions) there is also in the poem a more generalized lexical phenomenon familiar to us from Unit 10: extended lexical sets. The general contexts of hospital and family are maintained by clusters of items drawn from these contexts; for hospital we get "white", "quiet", "bed", "nurses", "anaesthetists", "surgeons" in the first stanza; for family "husband", "child", "family", "teaset", "bureaus", "linen" in the third and fourth stanzas.

Similarly, the major conflict of the poem—the desire for peace versus the demands of life—can be perceived in terms of two large contrasting lexical sets: death/nirvana and violence/pain. The first contains items like: "winter", "white", "quiet", "snowed-in", "peacefulness", "lying", "quietly", "light", "lies", "bed", "nobody", "nothing", "given . . . up", "nurses", "anaesthetist" (all from the first stanza). The second has items like: "excitable", "explosions", "surgeons", "trouble", "impossible", "run over", "bright", "needles", "lost", "sick", "pillbox", "hooks" (from the first three stanzas). The balance shifts away from peacefulness, of course, in the later stanzas. Note that these sets are very general and contain within them many subsets, each tending to realize different and more particular contexts, for example, the subsets of winter, lying down, and non-entity in the death/nirvana set. But the unifying power of highly generalized sets is just as important a factor in poetry as the concreteness of subsets.

Let us look now at particular grammatical effects. The grammar of the first verse, for example, is marked by repeated clause elements: the repeated A C structure of "how white . . . how quiet, how snowed-in"; the repeated elements in the S P structures of "*I am* learning peacefulness", "*I am* nobody", "*I have* nothing", "*I have* given my name"; the C C structures following "I have given", viz. "my name and my day-clothes up to the nurses", "my history to the anaesthetist", "my body to surgeons". Inside the latter structure is a further structure of repeated elements at group: "my name", "my day-clothes", "my history", "my body". The effect of such repeated structures is monotonous, hypnotic, incantatory, ritualistic. It fortifies the general situation of the early part of the poem where the persona is trying to maintain a state of emptiness, non-involvement, abstraction from life, unfocused concentration. She is trying to remain in the trancelike state of anaesthesia. Such grammatical repetitions are aided by lexical ones: "white", "white"; "quiet", "quietly"; "lying", "lies".

Similar repetitive lexical and grammatical effects are employed throughout the poem, confirming the obsessive quality of the narrator's consciousness: her attempts to hang on to a slipping peacefulness. Examples include: "The nurses pass and pass", "They pass the way gulls pass" (11–12); "they tend it as water/ Tends to the pebbles" (15–16); "They bring me numbness", "they bring me sleep" (17); "I didn't want any flowers, I only wanted" (29); "How free it is, you have no idea how free" (31); "the air snags and eddies round them the way a river/ Snags and eddies round a sunken rust-red engine." (53–54).

A more subtle form of repetition is the tendency to join sentences by commas, semicolons, dashes and colons: "The tulips are too excitable, it is winter here." (1); "I am nobody, I have nothing to do with explosions." (5);

"The nurses pass and pass, they are no trouble,/ They pass . . ." (11–12);
"My body is a pebble to them, they tend it . . ." (15); "I am a nun now, I
have never been so pure." (28); "I didn't want any flowers, I only wanted
. . ." (29); "How free it is, you have no idea how free—/ The peacefulness
is so big . . ." (31–32); "It is what the dead close on, finally; I imagine them
. . ." (34); "The tulips are too red in the first place, they hurt me." (36);
"Their redness talks to my wound, it corresponds." (39); "They are subtle:
they seem to float . . ." (40); "Nobody watched me before, now I am
watched." (43); "And I have no face, I have wanted to efface myself." (48);
"The tulips should be behind bars like dangerous animals;/ They are
opening . . ." (58–59); "And I am aware of my heart: it opens and closes
. . ." (60). This may be seen more generally as a unifying element in the
form of the poem—a feature of the persona's voice—but also as a
consequence of her lying-down position, and possibly of her weakness. The
phonological effect of such graphological cues is a change in the tune at the
end of the first sentence. The sentence is not laid to rest in the usual way,
but caught and continued in a rather breathless manner, such as would
happen if the narrator was anxious, but without much strength.

Grammar here, of course, is influencing phonology, the next level of
language we wish to discuss. Other supra-segmental effects, besides the
repetitions and tonal effects we have already mentioned in connection with
grammar, include the examples marked below in stanza 8. The unvarying
#1 tunes found in this verse are typical of the poem as a whole, and
contribute to the sense of a rhythmic, monotonous monologue.

$//_1$ (X) Be/fore they /came the /air was /<u>calm</u> e/nough// 50
$//_1$ Coming and /going $//_1$ breath by /<u>breath</u> with/$/_1$out any /fuss//
$//_1$ (X) Then the /tulips /filled it /up like a /loud /<u>noise</u>//
$//_1$ Now the /air /snags and /eddies /round them the /way a /river//
$//_1$ Snags and /eddies /round a /sunken /rust-red /<u>engine</u>//
$//_1$ (X) They /concentrate my at/<u>tention</u> $//_1$ (X) that was /happy// 55
$//_1$ Playing and /resting with/out com/<u>mitting</u> itself//

However, if we look more closely at this stanza, we also hear, beneath
the pervasive impression of monotony set up by the #1 tunes, variations
reflecting particular perturbations in the persona's tranquility. For example, the contrast in the distribution of tonics between line 51 (three tonics)
and line 52 (one tonic) reflects the sense of these two lines. Line 51 sets up a
regular, repeated rhythm akin to the "breath by breath" quiet desired. Line
52 is "filled" with a "loud noise", and carries only a single tonic.

Another factor in supra-segmental phonology is stress. Variations in
stress pattern in this "free verse" poem can reinforce particular aspects of
meaning. In line 52 the sense of the "loud noise" is reinforced by the

contrast in the distribution of syllables between feet 1 to 4 (2, 2, 2, 3) and feet 5 and 6 (1, 1) when the /loud/noise/ arrives. Another example of this same use of varied stress patterns to reinforce the context of specific lines is the contrast between line 53 when "snags and eddies" is first mentioned, and line 54 when the phrase is repeated. The first mention is embedded in an irregular line. The distribution of syllables in feet runs: 2, 1, 2, 2, 3, 2, 2. The second mention occurs in a completely regular line: 2, 2, 2, 2, 2, 2. It is as though the first abrupt contact with this foreign object (part of the previously mentioned sunken cargo boat?) causes a flutter in the flow of the stream; but this is quickly smoothed away as the current adjusts to its new channel. In a similar way, the persona is constantly attempting to incorporate disturbing features of her environment (the tulips) into the smooth state of her trance like repose.

Turning to segmental phonology, and using the first stanza as an example, we may note the great amount of repeated sounds of one kind or another, above and beyond the straight repetitions of "how", "quiet", "white", "my" already noted elsewhere. These include the alliterations of "learning" and "lying"; "light" and "lies", "white" and "walls", "nobody" and "nothing", "name" and "nurses"; the rhyming of "light" and "white"; and the general prevalence of the /aɪ/ diphthong. This use of repeated sounds occurs throughout the poem. Alliteration, for example, occurs in stanza 2 as "propped", "pillow", "white", "will"; in stanza 3 as "bring", "bright", "family", "photo"; in stanza 4 as "plastic", "pillow", "bureaus", "books", "sink", "sight", "water", "went", "nun", "never"; in stanza 5 as "nothing", "name"; in stanza 7 as "nobody", "now", "tulips", "turn"; in stanza 8 as "came", "calm", "Coming", "like", "loud", "round", "river", "round", "rust-", "red"; in stanza 9 as "walls", "warming", "be", "bars", "bowl", "blooms", "salt", "sea", "comes", "country". These repeated sounds generally function to reinforce the sense of repetitiveness, free association, and monotony of the poem.

Other segmental effects contribute to homonymy and puns. The poem begins with an example of homonymous repetition: "The *tu*lips are *too* excitable", which is repeated in line 36 to open the second half of the poem: "The *tu*lips are *too* red". Note that "tulips" (two lips) is also a pun, one that is realized later in the poem when the petals are described as "tongues" (41) and the flowers as a "mouth" (59). Other puns are "eye" (I) in line 9, and "Stupid pupil" in line 10; "close on" (end on, close mouth on) in line 34; "face", "efface" in line 48. These puns tend to be bizarre, the sorts of jumps in association, mediated by sound, that occur in special states of consciousness. These puns are further examples of the way the persona's basic conflict leads her to distort reality in a surreal way.

In summary, all of the grammatical effects noted, and most of the segmental phonological effects, lead to an experience of dense repetition, supported by a similar effect in lexis. This corresponds to a context of monotony and featurelessness, against which the persona hallucinates. This context is part of the general situation of hospital, with its bland environment, and of the persona's attempt to seek oblivion as a way of escape from the demands of family.

In general language, such contexts, representing aspects of situations, are realized by items from the formal (lexical and grammatical) levels of language. In literary language, such contexts may also be supported by phonology or graphology directly. What is important to remember is that in both kinds of language the meaning of items at the formal or substance-related levels is derived from the contextual presentation of situations. That this presentation, in the hands of a master of language, can take us deeply and immediately into a bewilderingly rich experience, is Sylvia Plath's final poetic message to us.

II. FRAMEWORK: a Different Situation for Every English

WE HEAR the word "context" used generally to refer to the surroundings or neighbourhood of a text, as in "He quoted me out of context", or "What was he doing when he said that? What was the context? Was he mad?". More precisely, we can separate the *textual* neighbourhood of a text from the general context and call it the *co-text*. The *non-linguistic* environment of the text is its *situation*. "He was really mad. His fists were clenched. That was the situation when I came in."

Context and Meaning

And yet a word or text may have also a more abstract existence, apart from either co-text or situation. This vaguer "context" is really a stock abstraction from all possible situations. The general "context" of "Run for your life!" is crisis. To use this text in a non-critical situation (for example, when a child is imitating a monster) is to be ironic.

Similarly, just as words or longer texts may carry a "context" abstracted from all the *situations* that give them meaning, so they may carry a "context" abstracted from all the possible *co-texts* they have. The co-text of "Romeo", for example, includes "Juliet". The co-text of "bread" includes "butter". Puns and other linguistic jokes depend on a text carrying a "context". This may be either situational, or co-textual as in "once *below* a time" or "people who live in grass houses shouldn't stow thrones", where the joke depends on the audience knowing the original text from which the given is derived.

So far we've been talking generally about "words" or "texts", but we can see that each of the aspects of language is associated with meaning derived from context. A lexical item has an obvious context: its collocational range. It is precisely this context that gives an item its lexical identity, its "meaning". If we put a lexical item into a clashing co-text we create an effect frequently used in poetry ("*pungent* words", "the gabbled *toil* of broadcasters", "the short-haired, *mad* executive". The expectedness or unexpectedness of an item's co-text is one of the main stylistic effects of all kinds of literature.

A grammatical item also has a "context": its colligational range. For example, we expect Subjects to go with Predicators, and articles to go with nouns. These expected structural possibilities give the formal item its grammatical value. Again, clashing co-texts make for poetry: "love is more thicker than forget".

Even if we change levels we can see how phonology or graphology can relate directly to "context" to affect meaning. Phonology and graphology represent the formal organization of noises and marks into symbols for grammar and lexis, but they can also relate directly to context by skipping over this intermediate level. "New Yawk" tells us something more than that "New York" has been misspelled. We don't have to ask a Glaswegian what country she comes from.

Thus stylistic analysis is ultimately a study of context and situation. The ordinary context of phonology/graphology, or of grammar/lexis provides a norm. Stylistically marked texts clash with that norm, thus producing the phenomenon of linguistic play that seems to be part of literary texts. Stylistic analysis isolates particular phonological/graphological and grammatical/lexical items, evaluates their normal contextual relations, evaluates their actual co-textual relations, and thus evaluates their particular stylistic effect by relating deviancies and norms to meaning. This process feeds back on itself since evaluation of an item in relation to its co-text also makes for evaluating its function as co-text itself to another item. Items in literary texts thus mutually define their meanings.

The notion of an abstracted "context" for all the items of a language, composed partly of the probable co-text, partly of the probable situation of each item, establishes the meaningfulness of formal items in English. But as we have already noted individual items, like "block", have also well-established meanings inside various well-established contexts: stock-buying, urban development, football, sailing. From this, we can see that English, as far as its meaningfulness is concerned, is really composed of various sub-varieties. There are different "Englishes" to fit different situations. These different varieties of English have their own norms, their own set of expectations, and consequently their own kind of stylistic effects. A regional English, or dialect, may have its own grammar forms, peculiar lexical items, and unique phonology. Similarly, the language of one particular time may show formal features, like "thee" and "thou", or pronunciation different from the formal features or pronunciation of another time. Even different social classes may be distinguished by their dialects.

Regional, temporal, or social differences in a language endure through various situations, and so are called "dialectal" varieties. But there are also differences linked to changes in the specific situation in which language is being used. For example, "polite" language is different from "crude" language. The language of speech is different from writing. The language you use when you want something is different from the language you use when you describe something. Differences that result from differences in particular situations like this are summed up as "diatypic" varieties of language. Another name for them is "registers".

These differences, both dialectal and diatypic, are of great interest to stylisticians. Poets often use such varietal differences to suggest contexts in their poems, like the language of "Anglo-Saxons" we noted in "Anglo-saxon Street" way back in Unit 1. A system of "varieties categories" has been worked out to help isolate these consistent relationships between particular features of language, and the particular situations in which they occur.

The Dialectal Varieties of English

The dialectal varieties are based on the categorization of language *users*, grouping those speakers together who share a certain situation in time and space, giving rise to shared linguistic features. We are used to the concept of geographical varieties of language. We know English English differs from American English; but there are also social dialects, historical dialects and institutional dialects. The grand impetus behind all these differences in the formal features of language is difference in situation, in environment and culture. A Robert Burns poem is an example of geographical dialect. If we look at such texts we can formulate cultural, political and geographical situations for them which are specific to each text. Then we can distinguish formal items which identify each variety.

A Burns poem, of course, is also an example of a historical dialect. English has changed over time, and so a description of the language at any given point will give rise to a historical variety. The following statements are all roughly equivalent, but each uses different formal items and structures to render it: "Hēo lufode hlāford" (Old English, *c.* 700–*c.* 1100), "Sche luved þe louerd" (Middle English, *c.* 1100–*c.* 1500), "She loved the lord" (modern English *c.* 1500–present).

Social situations are also structured so that certain groups of people are separated from others, and develop a language suitable to their own situation. We can abstract upper-class, middle-class, working-class Englishes—probably more easily in historical dialects than in contemporary ones. English English, however, retains a distinctive pronunciation (called RP, for "Received Pronunciation") for its upper classes, despite the best satirical efforts, from Shaw to *That Was The Week That Was*, to eradicate it.

People may also be grouped by the institutions they participate in. Subcultures of all kinds may constitute institutions in this sense. Drug users, for example, have traditionally developed an exotic and rapidly changing lexis, one of whose purposes is to distinguish the "with-it" user from an imposter. Cockney rhyming slang from a few years ago is another example. In it a friend or "mate" was called a "china", because "*mate*" rhymes with china "*plate*". How's that for an odd structural principle for choosing lexis? Increasing bureaucratization has created a variety of language distinguished by word-formations like the second word of this sentence. Lately, there's been a rash of punning advertising texts: "egg-conomy" ("get cracking"); "how soft in the head can you get?" (for pillows); "anyone who pays more than 20 cents for a TV magazine is misguided"; "we're for women's rights—and lefts" (pantyhose). These examples aren't, of course, full-fledged dialects, but they do proceed from very particularized situations, and are (apparently) understood by those using them.

The Diatypic Varieties of English

Another name for the diatypic varieties is "registers". Registers do not have quite the sort of permanent features that dialects have. They are sorted out not just by the situation of the speaker, but by the situation of *both* speaker and auditor. They account for variations in language that occur because of different relationships between speaker and auditor, the different situations that might lead them to communicate in specific ways. These different kinds of language will be found, of course, within each of the previous dialects. Each historical or regional dialect will probably contain the diatypic varieties.

The major diatypic varieties are those sub-languages that reflect the situations of "formality"—the personal relationship between speaker and auditor (or reader and writer)—of "medium"—whether one is writing or speaking—and of "function"—why one is communicating: to convince, to explain, to beseech, to curry favour, etc.

People speak or write more or less formally, or intimately, depending on how they feel about their auditor/reader. Letters to bank managers differ from letters to best friends. Some teachers call students "John" or "Mary". Students call teachers "Mr. Jones" or "Miss Smith". But students alone refer to each other as "Johnny" or "Mar", and to teachers as "Old Jones" or "Smitty". These language usages reflect in formal structure the degrees of formality in different situations. Woe to him who gets language and situation mixed. Advertising often attempts to exploit this feature of language by turning it back on itself: using intimate language to create the impression of friendship and trust. Salesmen like to be on a first-name basis; they tell you jokes, talk about themselves. The condition of intimacy or informality may be suggested by language to such an extent you forget you're in the formal environment of a new car showroom, and start to trust the salesman as a friend. At the other extreme, banks and schools in an earlier age strove to foster formality in relationships through elaborately printed "cheques" and "correct grammar". In armies, the distinctions in formality are clear, rank by rank, to the point of having to ask permission to speak at all. In our own text we have produced informality through jokes and the use of the first and second persons in an attempt to offset the forbidding formality of linguistic technical language. Teachers are salesmen too.

A major distinction in registers is that between written and spoken English, as anyone who has seen a transcript of a taped conversation knows. Spoken English is full of false starts, interruptions, repetitions, grunts, shrieks and "er's" which do not appear in written texts. Yet these odd noises do often carry meaning, and may even be codified by the speakers and auditors to carry such signals as "I'm not finished yet—don't interrupt me", "I've run down—please rescue me", or "That's so fantastic I can't speak—I have to shriek!". Written language, of course, has meaningful features that do not occur in speech. Punctuation often directs attention to grammar; it may show by a semicolon that a sentence is composed of two independent clauses. But written and spoken language also differ from each other in the proportion of Z elements, theme-marking, hypotactic constructions, etc., that each may have. These differences reflect the very different situations that writing and speaking take place in. We might also note that while writing generally might be perceived as a more "formal" method of communication, in both media the full scale of formality/informality occurs.

Further distinctions beyond the basic written/spoken one are possible. Spoken English can be subdivided into dialogue and monologue, for example. Monologue is apt to be somewhat more like written English in its tendency to complete sentences and somewhat greater field-restriction in lexis. However, we might note the breathless non-stop monologue style purveyed by social butterflies, whose sole purpose, it seems, is to keep going and prevent interruption. Here, changes in topic and interrupted sentence structures signal the speaker's dialogue with self. Written English can be "written as if spoken", as in novels; but this written dialogue is itself distinct from actual spoken English, with repetitions and incomplete structures serving the function of pretence, and therefore not as prevalent as in reality. Plays are "written to be spoken before an audience"—yet another variety. We might also have "written to be read as if overheard" and "written to be read as if thought"—both prominent varieties in modern literature.

The third major influence on diatypic variety is the purpose of the discourse. Action narrative has more active-voice Predicators than the technical language of science, which has more relational Predicators. Didactic works use imperative forms. (So, oddly, do prayers, though the power roles are reversed.) We can make long lists of possible functions for language texts; and as with our further distinctions in written/spoken English these can be subdivided in turn. The object is to come up with a descriptive category that most economically, yet completely, describes the purpose of the text. Our own text, for example, has several purposes: to communicate information, to demonstrate stylistic possibilities, to impress the reader, to make him laugh, etc. The differing functions of the "Analysis" (demonstration) and "Framework" (instructional) sections can be inferred from their differing languages.

Varieties and Literature

Literary works often imitate varieties of a language for particular effects. In Unit 1 we talked about the variety of Old English heroic and poetic language in connection with Earle Birney's "Anglosaxon Street". In Unit 4 we saw Emmett Williams playing with the language of a popular augury in "she loves me"; in the same Unit we found a William Carlos Williams poem written in imitation of notes on refrigerator doors. The passage from Jack Kerouac's *Doctor Sax* in Unit 6 is meant to suggest the breathless recitations of small boys. The rhythms and lexis of the Bible and of solemn sermons are suggested by Dylan Thomas' "A Refusal to Mourn" in Unit 7. The free associations of Sylvia Plath's imagery in "Tulips", bizarre and at the same time disturbingly insightful, suggest the speaking and writing style of schizophrenics.

All the different varieties of language are differentiated by different patterns in phonology/graphology and grammar/lexis. They have different "grammars" in the largest sense. Indeed, we might say that when it comes to literature, because of the amazing cohesiveness of literary texts and their capability of self-defining themselves, that each has its own grammar, has become a separate variety of the language, in the same way that the idiosyncracies of an author's style also define his language as his own. And this particular language of each literary text corresponds also to a particular function that text has in a particular situation. It is the business of criticism to get at that function; it is the ability of linguistics to describe that language that enables stylistics to perform its critical function. Happy reading.

III. APPLICATION: the Game of Contexts in Dickens

IN CHANCERY

LONDON. Michaelmas Term lately over, and the Lord Chancellor sitting in Lincoln's Inn Hall. Implacable November weather. As much mud in the streets, as if the waters had but newly retired from the face of the earth, and it would not be wonderful to meet a Megalosaurus, forty feet long or so, waddling like an elephantine lizard up Holborn Hill. Smoke lowering down from chimney-pots, making a soft black drizzle, with flakes of soot in it as big as full-grown snowflakes—gone into mourning, one might imagine, for the death of the sun. Dogs, undistinguishable in mire. Horses, scarcely better; splashed to their very blinkers. Foot passengers, jostling one another's umbrellas, in a general infection of ill-temper, and losing their foothold at street-corners, where tens of thousands of other foot passengers have been slipping and sliding since the day broke (if this day ever broke), adding new deposits to the crust upon crust of mud, sticking at those points tenaciously to the pavement, and accumulating at compound interest.

Fog everywhere. Fog up the river, where it flows among green aits and meadows; fog down the river, where it rolls defiled among the tiers of shipping, and the waterside pollutions of a great (and dirty) city. Fog on the Essex marshes, fog on the Kentish heights. Fog creeping into the cabooses of collier-brigs; fog lying out on the yards, and hovering in the rigging of great ships; fog drooping on the gunwales of barges and small boats. Fog in the eyes and throats of ancient Greenwich pensioners, wheezing by the firesides of their wards; fog in the stem and bowl of the afternoon pipe of the wrathful skipper, down in his close cabin; fog cruelly pinching the toes and fingers of his shivering little 'prentice boy on deck. Chance people on the bridges peeping over the parapets into a nether sky of fog, with fog all round them, as if they were up in a balloon, and hanging in the misty clouds.

Gas looming through the fog in divers places in the streets, much as the sun may, from the spongy fields, be seen to loom by husbandman and ploughboy. Most of the shops lighted two hours before their time—as the gas seems to know, for it has a haggard and unwilling look.

—Charles Dickens, Bleak House

Dickens is an artist in beginning novels, and in painting pictures. Unlike a painter, however, he is not limited to a single visual representation. He can dart all over London, if he likes, and weave a hundred particular details into one large, impressionistic mosaic. And yet he needs a device, a form, a way to hold and frame these many details. What better way than to use a variety of language already well adapted for such a purpose? This is the notebook style of a professional writer: really a list of data to be later turned into polished sentences. Only Dickens can see beyond data to the possibilities of the form itself. The technique is simple: sentences made up exclusively of nominal groups, all other grammatical forms consigned to appear rank-shifted at the Qualifier element. Sentences like this one.

But there's more to this text than the notetaker's form. Lexis like "Lord Chancellor", "sitting", "implacable", is mixed with "mud", "megalo-saurus", "lizard" and with "black", "mourning", "death" and so on. The text is not just a feast of detail, it is a feast of lexis reflecting a bewildering variety of contexts, with London, mighty London, containing them all. "Chancery" is a law court, a place where all the human passions pass, the place of a peculiar institutional dialect whose function seems to be as much to obscure as to make clear. Mud and fog are good images of that. In the second paragraph Dickens even manages a neat reversal of the effects of law-court English when he uses the fog as a device for *revealing* detail after detail of the life of the great city.

Can you verify, discredit, or add to these suggestions? You should now be able to describe, on all three levels of language, the features of this text and show how they relate to Dickens' themes of teeming humanity, obscurity of purpose, magic of language, and impending winter of the soul.

IV. QUESTIONS FOR REVIEW

1. Can you give a meaning to each of these terms?

context	homonym	registers
situation	pun	formal varieties
interior monologue	dialectal varieties	media varieties
imagery	geographical dialects	written English
persona	social dialects	spoken English
co-text	historical dialects	functional dialects
collocational range	institutional dialects	stylistics
colligational range	diatypic varieties	homonymy

2. There are several kinds of "context". Distinguish "co-text" from "situa-tion", and exemplify both with reference to a specific text.

3. What is the co-text of the joke which ends "carp-to-carp walleting"? Can you think of a pun that relies on a situational context?

4. What are the contexts that clash in: "pungent words", "the gabbled toil of broadcasters", "the short-haired, mad executives"?

5. What grammatical contexts clash in "What if a much of a which of a wind" (E. E. Cummings)?

6. What does the following sentence tell you about its context by its graphology? "Lishen, man—If you don' like it—you c'n lumpsh it."

7. How do we know the following text comes from a poem? "Listen. Put on morning." (W. S. Graham).

8. Name the dialectal varieties; name and quote from an example of each. What features of graphology, lexis and grammar mark your texts?

9. Write a paragraph of formal English, a paragraph of informal.

10. Tape record examples of spontaneous dialogue and monologue. What differences do you detect in phonology, in lexis and in grammar?

11. In three short paragraphs, present the plot of *Romeo and Juliet* in the forms of a narrative, an instructional manual, and an argument.

12. Can you detect any function of "entertainment" in the text of these "Questions for Review"?

13. The different varieties of language used by Henry Reed in the following poem are obvious, as is the use he makes of them through the first four stanzas. What is more interesting is the "fugue" he constructs of these different varieties in the last stanza, where the two different contexts are mixed and blended until the language of each takes on additional meaning from the other. The poem, of course, relies on the disparity of situations created by having rifle drill in a neighbourhood of gardens, a disparity that leads, in the mind of the narrator recruit, to a buzzing insanity reflective of war itself. See if you can sort out which bits of texts go with which context in the last stanza, and show how some bits of text (like "Spring") form bridges.

NAMING OF PARTS

Today we have naming of parts. Yesterday,
We had daily cleaning. And tomorrow morning,
We shall have what to do after firing. But today,
Today we have naming of parts. Japonica
Glistens like coral in all of the neighboring gardens,   5
     And today we have naming of parts.

This is the lower sling swivel. And this
Is the upper sling swivel, whose use you will see,
When you are given your slings. And this is the piling swivel,
Which in your case you have not got. The branches   10
Hold in the gardens their silent, eloquent gestures,
     Which in our case we have not got.

This is the safety-catch, which is always released
With an easy flick of the thumb. And please do not let me
See anyone using his finger. You can do it quite easy   15
If you have any strength in your thumb. The blossoms
Are fragile and motionless, never letting anyone see
     Any of them using their finger.

And this you can see is the bolt. The purpose of this
Is to open the breech, as you see. We can slide it   20
Rapidly backwards and forwards: we call this
Easing the spring. And rapidly backwards and forwards
The early bees are assaulting and fumbling the flowers:
      They call it easing the Spring.

They call it easing the Spring: it is perfectly easy   25
If you have any strength in your thumb: like the bolt,
And the breech, and the cocking-piece, and the point of balance,
Which in our case we have not got, and the almond-blossom
Silent in all of the gardens, the bees going backwards and forwards,
      For today we have naming of parts.   30

                           —Henry Reed

Suggestions for Further Reading

The following bibliographical list is intended to introduce the student to a few specialized works in the areas touched on in this book.

Abercrombie, David. *Studies in Phonetics and Linguistics*. London: Oxford University Press, 1965.

Benson, James D. and William S. Greaves. *The Language People Really Use*. Agincourt, Ontario: Book Society of Canada, 1973.

Berry, Margaret. *An Introduction to Systemic Linguistics*. 2 vols. London: B. T. Batsford, 1975–1977.

Chapman, Raymond. *Linguistics and Literature: An Introduction to Literary Stylistics*. London: Edward Arnold, 1973.

Cluysenaar, Anne. *Introduction to Literary Stylistics: A Discussion of Dominant Structures in Verse and Prose*. London: B. T. Batsford, 1976.

Crystal, David and Derek Davy. *Investigating English Style*. London: Longmans, 1977.

Enkvist, Nils Erik. *Linguistic Stylistics*. Janua linguarum ser. critica, 5. The Hague: Mouton, 1973.

Fowler, Roger. *Linguistics and the Novel*. London: Methuen, 1977.

Freeman, Donald C., ed. *Linguistics and Literary Style*. New York: Holt Rinehart and Winston, 1970.

Gregory, Michael and Susanne Carroll. *Language and Situation: Language Varieties and their Social Contexts*. London: Routledge & Kegan Paul, 1978.

Gutwinski, Waldemar. *Cohesion in Literary Texts: A Study of Some Grammatical and Lexical Features of English Discourse*. Janua linguarum ser. minor, 204. The Hague: Mouton, 1976.

Halliday, M. A. K. *A Course in Spoken English: Intonation*. London: Oxford University Press, 1970.

Halliday, M. A. K. *Explorations in the Functions of Language*. London: Edward Arnold, 1973.

Halliday, M. A. K. *Intonation and Grammar in British English*. Janua linguarum ser. practica, 48. The Hague: Mouton, 1967.

Halliday, M. A. K. *Language as Social Semiotic: The Social Interpretation of Language and Meaning*. London: Edward Arnold, 1978.

Kress, Gunther, ed. *Halliday: System and Function in Language*. London: Oxford University Press, 1976.

Leech, Geoffrey N. *A Linguistic Guide to English Poetry*. London: Longmans, 1969.

Scott, F. S., C. C. Bowley, C. S. Brockett, J. G. Brown and P. R. Goddard. *English Grammar: A Linguistic Study of its Classes and Structures*. London: Heinemann Educational Books, 1968.

Sinclair, J. McH. *A Course in Spoken English: Grammar*. London: Oxford University Press, 1972.

Traugott, Elizabeth Closs and Mary Louise Pratt. *Linguistics for Students of Literature*. New York: Harcourt Brace Jovanovich, 1980.

Turner, G. W. *Stylistics*. Harmondsworth: Penguin Books, 1973.

Index